MAN UP!

THE QUEST FOR MASCULINITY

JEFFREY HEMMER

Published by Concordia Publishing House
3558 S. Jefferson Ave., St. Louis, MO 63118–3968
1-800-325-3040 • www.cph.org

Manufactured in the United States of America

Library of Congress Cataloging-in-Publication Data

Names: Hemmer, Jeffrey, author.
Title: Man up! : the quest for masculinity / Jeffrey Hemmer.

Description: St. Louis : Concordia Publishing House, 2017. | Includes bibliographical references and index.

Identifiers: LCCN 2016041637 (print) | LCCN 2016044642 (ebook) | ISBN 9780758654809 (alk. paper) | ISBN 9780758654816

Subjects: LCSH: Men (Christian theology) | Christian men—Religious life.

Classification: LCC BT703.5 .H46 2016 (print) | LCC BT703.5 (ebook) | DDC 248.8/42--dc23

LC record available at https://lccn.loc.gov/2016041637

---

5 6 7 8 9 10 11 12 13 14 28 27 26 25 24 23 22 21 20 19

To my sons: may you have courage
to aspire to the goodness of Jesus;

to my daughters: may you
be loved by good men;

and to my wife: may your reward in
heaven be great for your patience
and forgiveness when the man you
have cannot measure up to the Ideal.

CONTENTS

Foreword vii

Preface: What Are We Doing Here? xi

Part 1: Nuts and Bolts: The Basics 1

Chapter 1: What Is Man? 3

Chapter 2: Not So from the Beginning 17

Chapter 3: Man Down 47

Chapter 4: The Descent of Man 69

Chapter 5: *Ecce Homo*: Behold, the Man! 103

Chapter 6: God Down. Man Up. 125

Part 2: MANifesto: Reclaiming a Biblical Portrait of a Man 163

Chapter 7: A Portrait of Man: Adam 165

Chapter 8: A Portrait of Man: Christ 187

Chapter 9: The Portrait of Fatherhood: God the Father 223

Chapter 10: A Paradoxical Portrait 239

Chapter 11: What Does a Man Do? 251

Chapter 12: Grow as a Man 281

Epilogue: The Perfect Man 313

FOREWORD

When a father says of his son, "I just want him to be happy," it means he has given up hope that his boy will be a man. There may be times in this broken world when the most a father can hope for is his son's happiness, but they are the saddest of times: when a son is in a coma or suffers a closed head injury that renders him unable to work, support a family, and be a father himself; or even when a son is incarcerated and separated from his family. For the most part, we don't want our sons just to be happy; we want them to be virtuous, which is to say, we want them to be men.

Peter Kreeft, a professor of philosophy at Boston College, offers the following thought experiment to demonstrate this. Imagine that your son is a prisoner in Auschwitz concentration camp where Josef Mengele, a German SS officer and physician, is conducting his horrible experiments. Mengele offers your son the opportunity to be spared, but in exchange, your son must become his assistant and help him torture others. You have the chance to advise him on what he should do. What do you tell him?[1]

---

1 Peter Kreeft uses this illustration in chapter 18 of *The Modern Scholar: Ethics: A History of Moral Thought* (Prince Frederick, MD: Recorded Books, 2008. Audiobook.).

You tell him to suffer the torture, to not be Mengele's assistant. This seems counterintuitive to us, because while we would obviously want to make that choice for ourselves, we have the sense that we should want to spare our son's physical pain and death. Nonetheless, we would all give our sons the same advice: don't be Mengele's assistant under any circumstance. Being Mengele's assistant would do more damage to our son than would his suffering torture and even being killed. Some things are more evil than pain and death.

Kreeft's thought experiment helps us see two things: it is more destructive to a man to cause evil than to suffer evil; and we don't really want our sons to be happy, we want them to be virtuous.

Pastor Hemmer has written a book to help us see that reality more clearly, and for that reason, I am eager to give this book to my sons and son-in-law. I am also eager to give it to my acolytes and those men who desire to be married in our church. As soon as I began reading it, I began talking about it and recommending it to my elders and friends and nearly every man I know.

This book is not only for our sons or those men who are about to be husbands or fathers, it is also for those of us who already have those roles, because a man is always a son, whether or not he is a husband and a father. If fathers want their sons to be virtuous, what sons want is for their fathers to respect them. And the way sons get respect from their fathers, and indeed also from their peers and from their wife and from their children, is not by avoiding pain or work, not by taking the easy way, but by being virtuous, that is, by being a man.

That is the essence of what Pastor Hemmer means by "Man up!" Thus he states his thesis succinctly: "The essence of masculinity is not rugged independence. It is sacrificial giving." And again: "Unless [a man's] courage, wisdom, discipline, patience, chastity, and any other virtues serve the good of others, they're not truly virtues, and he's not fully masculine."

This is a preaching of the Law that our age desperately needs. It certainly accuses every one of us. Pastor Hemmer is clear about that. He is not Jesus telling us to be like Him. He is a sinner just like us, and he stands equally accused. Besides being a sinner, a son, a father, and a husband, he is a preacher. He does not point to himself; he points to Jesus. He preaches the Law to accuse us of our sins and to clear away the clutter that sin creates in our minds, seeking to excuse our sins so that we keep on sinning. We need to know that we are sinners. We have not lived up to the standard of masculinity in the self-giving of Christ throughout His life, and indeed throughout history and creation, which culminated in His death on the cross. We have not loved others as ourselves, and the worst of our transgressions have been against the ones we have been called to love first and most: our wife, our children, and our parents. We need to know that and repent.

But we also need to know how we have failed and how our thinking regarding these things has been polluted and confused by our own fallen flesh and by the mixed and demonic messages of our culture. This book provides both those things. It is catechesis in the Ten Commandments according to our stations in life as males.

It is primarily for that catechesis that this book was written. It is almost certainly the reason you are reading it. Good for you. But Pastor Hemmer is a preacher. He weaves in the Gospel as well. This is a book as much about the struggle to be a man as it is about Jesus, about Christology, and about God's forgiving love for us. Throughout this book rings the central reality that "before a man can truly be a man, Christ had to be Man." Christ is our Brother. His Father is our Father by grace. So also He is our Bridegroom. He protects and provides for us, and He makes us His children.

Only in that security can we proceed to struggle to be what He has called us to be, but in that security there is more than freedom to act, there is also power and promise and ongoing forgiveness. With that as the anchor, with Christ as a Man for us, it is quite possible that you are holding the very best book to ever be written on masculinity. Read up, men! You will be blessed and so will those you are called to serve.

Rev. David H. Petersen

PREFACE

WHAT ARE WE DOING HERE?

"Our whole life should be manly; we should fear God and put our trust in him."

—Martin Luther, The Familiar Discourses of Dr. Martin Luther

I don't know what it says about you that you either bought a book on how to be a man or were given a book on how to be a man. Such a tome really should not exist. And yet, you bought it. Or it was given to you. And you started reading it. Such is evidence that as a society, we have simply lost—or forgotten—the collective knowledge of what it means to be a man. That we need to read books to learn what used to be taught by fathers and grandfathers is an indictment of us. Somehow, we've lost this basic human knowledge of what a man is and does.

I tried to talk the publisher into packaging this book with a dust cover you could use to conceal the real contents, like reading a comic book inside your civics textbook—a cover with a more macho title that you could wrap around the book. Perhaps *Perfecting Your Kill Shot, Surviving the Zombie Apocalypse*, *The Ultimate Guide to Self-Defense*, or *Chiseled Pecs and Abs for the Everyday Clergymen*. But you got stuck with this, a book whose title is an exhortation men give to other men who are acting more like boys or women than men. *Man Up!* Sorry about that.

I won't judge you for reading this book if you won't judge me for having had to write it.

Before we begin our journey together, I have a couple admissions.

First, just because I wrote a book on masculinity doesn't mean I am an expert. On this quest, I'm not your example for masculinity; I'm just your guide. Many modern treatments of masculinity amount to little more than "Here are some cool things I do; you should do them too." This book is not that. The advice you find in these pages is not based on what I have found to work in the quest to make me a better man; rather, it is based on the things that I have found to challenge me in this quest.

And this quest is indeed challenging, which leads to my second admission: I hate this book.

Some of it, at least.

I want to disabuse you of the idea that you might thoroughly enjoy this book. I genuinely hope you do not. If this book is easy and enjoyable for you to read, I will have failed in my endeavor. I don't want these pages to lull you into a sense of sedentary complacency in which you pat yourself on the back for a job well done and wonder why all these other dudes can't figure out what you and I obviously know. I want this book to challenge you, to confront you, to encourage you to do something more—something higher, nobler, harder, and holier, than you're presently doing.

So this book is going to tick you off. Probably more than once. No guy likes to be corrected, told how to do a better job, or called out for something that he really likes doing. In these pages, I will inevitably say something you find so preposterous, so outdated, so ridiculous that you'll want to throw the book down and immediately post a half-star review on Amazon. (But even though you'll want to, thankfully you can't give less than one star. Ha!) I know it's going to irritate you, because the call to higher and holier manliness irritates me. I would much rather indulge my selfish nature and join in whatever hedonism *du jour* there is to be found. I hate the call in these pages to something higher, something outside myself.

If I'm being honest with you, I'm not very good at anything I tell you to do in this book—not all the time, anyway. If there are any lessons in here gained from personal experience, they're probably learned from mistakes. Whatever you find profitable or challenging probably came from someone else, from some mentor I've had, or, more likely, from the example of Jesus' manliness.

The third admission I need to make before we embark together on this quest is that this is a book about Jesus. That's going to frustrate you too. If you were hoping for a book to teach you how to shoot big guns, drive big trucks, and get your woman to submit to you, you should see if you can get a refund. Also, if you thought Jesus came to show you how to be a better person, you'll again be sorely disappointed. Yes, He is the standard for masculinity throughout this book, but it's not a standard that you can meet. It's a standard that will mock you and make you feel inferior. You can never be as manly as Jesus. (If you thought Jesus was milksop and nice, we'll put that false notion to bed in just a bit.) But you also don't need to be.

While we're at it, here's another thing you should know: there's nothing new in these pages. I haven't made any profound discoveries. I've simply found something timeless tucked away in the farthest corner of the storage locker of popular Christianity, dusted it off, polished it just a bit, and presented it to you here: the perfect manliness of Jesus. I have found it to be helpful in my own struggle to be a good man. The perfect manliness of Jesus challenges me. It calls me to something outside myself. And it gives me encouragement for the struggles that lie before me.

This isn't a new struggle, to be sure. And it's not unique to any one of us. Nearly as long as men have been leaving footprints in the dirt, we've been unsure how to take the next step as men. Adam—the icon of God in the world, the first man, created in perfection to be the lord of creation—became the source of our modern confusion about masculinity. Since Adam's rebellion, every one of his sons, grandsons, great-grandsons, indeed, every man and boy until today has been thrown into chaos. Before the twenty-four-hour news channels ever started reporting on the disgrace of men we trusted to show us the way of masculinity, the Bible was already chock-full of stories of men failing to live as men, failing to use their courage and strength for the good of others, failing to discipline their natural desires and use them for good in the world. Our unmanly confusion is not new.

This loss of an understanding of masculinity infects us all: from the pubescent boy with a quickly changing body who is faced with the struggle to identify himself as a man; to the young man whose head is filled with hopes and ambitions, trying to carve out his role in the world; to the middle-aged man who looks around at the empire he's built and wonders if what he's accomplished is really worth anything; to the elderly man, who sees the weathering effects of age and his diminishing virility, needs to rely on others for more and more, and questions what it really means to be a man.

I hope to point you to the one Man whose example is exemplary—a Man among men who embodies perfect masculinity and enables you to be the man He intends you to be. "Man up" is not a call to assert your rights in a feminized culture. It's a call, first of all, to fix your eyes and your hope on the Man up on the cross, and second, to find in His selfless sacrifice the perfect example for manliness in a self-indulgent, self-centered society.

So, come along on the journey. It'll be nice to have the company.

PART 1

NUTS AND BOLTS: THE BASICS

WHAT IS MAN?

> *"It is not what he has, or even what he does which expresses the worth of a man, but what he is."*
>
> *—Henri-Frédéric Amiel (1821–81)*

Our confused culture is not the first to ask, "What is man?" The psalmist wonders,

> When I look at Your heavens, the work of Your fingers,
> the moon and the stars, which You have set in place,
> what is man that You are mindful of him,
> and the son of man that You care for him?
>
> Yet You have made him a little lower than the heavenly beings
> and crowned him with glory and honor.
> You have given him dominion over the works of Your hands;
> You have put all things under his feet.
> (Psalm 8:3–6)

So, what *is* man? What is man that God, his Creator, would be mindful of him? This is not man specifically, as in the guy with Y chromosomes and external genitalia, man in contrast to woman, but man broadly speaking, as in mankind. What is man? What is humankind? From these beautiful verses David penned, this much is known: man is not the Creator, not exalted to the highest pinnacle of existence. Instead, he takes a lower role. He is limited. Man is a creature, dependent on his Creator.

The first lesson in masculinity is not how powerful and mighty man is, how much he deserves to be exalted, but how humble he is, how small and inferior he is in comparison to his Creator. Consider this: there are stars, planets, suns, moons, galaxies, nebula, matter and dark matter, power and authority above man. Man is not the ultimate boss. He must submit to a higher Authority.

And yet, there is something in mankind that God is mindful of *him*. This is the nature of man. When God created mankind, He made him in His own image. Among all creation, nothing else is made in God's image and likeness. Only man. So mankind is unique among the rest of creation. And mankind alone, men and women together, has been entrusted with exercising dominion over creation.

Theologians have wrangled for millennia about what this image of God entails. As with other things of God, it's easy to overspiritualize it and make the image of God something purely spiritual. There is a spiritual dimension, to be sure, in the original righteousness man possessed before his fall into sin. He was created with perfect righteousness, just as God has perfect goodness, perfect obedience, perfect health, perfect wisdom and knowledge, perfect intellect, and more.[1] But what of this "likeness" business? Does man look like God? Despite the Sunday School answers that taught you otherwise—that God is exclusively spirit and has no physical likeness—I disagree.

1 Apology of the Augsburg Confession, Article II (I), paragraphs 16–22.

God has human likeness. Or more precisely, mankind has divine likeness. We *look alike*. Certainly, to God the Father and God the Holy Spirit, who are purely spirit, we have no resemblance. But to God the Son, who answered the question "What is man?" in His incarnation—His enfleshment, or becoming man—we bear a striking resemblance. Adam, the man, looks like Jesus, the Man. The shadow of Christ's incarnation casts its form all the way back onto the Garden of Eden. The man God formed in Genesis 1 and 2 is shaped by the Man God became in Matthew 1, Luke 2, and John 1.

HOW DO YOU DEFINE MAN?

So, mankind is distinct among all creatures, unique in the breadth of God's handiwork. But what about *man*? How do you define a man? What makes a human being a man?

Many people today believe gender is a fluid category. You can identify yourself as whatever gender you like. Gone is the simple, binary "male" or "female." On Facebook, for instance, there are dozens of different categories one could use to define himself (or herself, itself, etc.). How many boys were inspired by then-Bruce Jenner's record-setting finish in the 1976 Olympic decathlon, sprinting the last lap of the 1500 meter finale? What do those now-grown men do forty years later when Bruce believes he's Caitlyn? Is the difference between a man and a woman something so arbitrary that it can be changed (or corrected?) by surgeries? Does the man with chiseled arms and a flat chest on the Wheaties cereal box become a buxom woman on the cover of *Vanity Fair* with simply a series of hormone treatments and body-reconstruction surgeries, a wave of medicine's magic wand?

Is manhood hardware or software? Or something else? What makes a man a man? Is the only difference boy parts as opposed to girl parts?

Remember fifth-grade health class when the girls had to leave the room and the boys learned, punctuated by immature jokes and giggles, about the difference between male and female anatomy? The difference was simple. Boys had penises and testicles. Eventually, they'd grow beards and chest hair. Girls had their genitalia on the inside and would eventually grow breasts and wider hips. Boys would grow into men, and girls would grow into women.

Then, in freshman biology, those external differences were explained by internal programming. There was software—chromosomes—that determined male and female characteristics. All male mammals have Y chromosomes. The sex-linked genes on the Y chromosome are what cause men to grow testicles, speak with a deeper voice, develop an Adam's apple, and grow stronger muscles than their female counterparts. There were genetic anomalies, like men with XXY, XYY, or occasionally XX chromosomes, women with Y chromosomes, XXX, or single X chromosomes. But these genetic oddities were the exceptions that confirmed the fundamental biological distinction between men and women. Male genes made men; female genes made women. Again, the difference was simple.

Modern questions of gender identity push the question beyond hardware or software. Neither the chromosomes nor the penis made Bruce Jenner feel very much like a man. How many others suffer from what used to be called Gender Identity Disorder, but now is called merely Gender Dysphoria—a confusion of sorts, but no longer a disorder—wondering whether they have a male mind in a female body or a female mind in a male body? Our culture is confused. We're asked to believe that what

God created in the womb and called by name in Holy Baptism is a mistake. How confused we've become!

So, there's a biological difference between men and women. But simply having boy genitalia and Y chromosomes does not automatically make a person very manly. Women across America are decrying the immature male, the boy-man, who, well into his fourth decade of life, still remains fundamentally an immature boy. Young men refuse to marry for fear of losing their playboy status. Thirty-plus-year-old men are still enamored with Candy Crush Saga and Pokémon Go. Little League dads yell and berate their sons' coaches or umpires from the sidelines. What happened? Remember when boys couldn't wait to grow up?

WHAT IS MASCULINITY?

To shape you into a man, a mature man, is one of the primary functions of the Church, says St. Paul.

> And [Christ] gave the apostles, the prophets, the evangelists, the shepherds and teachers, to equip the saints for the work of ministry, for building up the body of Christ, until we all attain to the unity of the faith and of the knowledge of the Son of God, to mature manhood, to the measure of the stature of the fullness of Christ, so that we may no longer be children, tossed to and fro by the waves and carried about by every wind of doctrine, by human cunning, by craftiness in deceitful schemes. (Ephesians 4:11–14)

"Until we all attain to the unity of the faith . . . to mature manhood . . . that we may no longer be children." That's a tall order.

What is mature manhood? What is real masculinity? How can you know when you've become a man? Here's the problem.

Masculinity is not a single trait. It's a lifestyle, a discipline, a habit cultivated by practice. Simply having anatomy and genes that allow you to stand and pee does not make you manly. Real masculinity is not found in any individual characteristic or trait but in the intersection of male characteristics with the exercise of manly virtue. Masculinity means harnessing the natural power a man possesses and using it for the good of others around him. The essence of masculinity is not rugged independence. It is sacrificial giving.

What exactly is manly virtue? There are numerous sources of virtue. Although not specifically listed as a tidy list of seven in Scripture, the seven cardinal virtues are a fine example of a catalog of habits to hone. Each of the seven virtues is the photographic negative of one of the seven cardinal sins. To exercise one of these virtues is to oppose one of the vices. The virtue chastity is the opposite of the vice lust; temperance is the opposite of gluttony; charity of greed; diligence of sloth; patience of wrath; kindness of envy; and humility is the opposite of pride. Still, these are not virtues expected exclusively of men, and simply practicing them does not yet make you manly.

Brett McKay, a renowned expert in the burgeoning field of the renaissance of manliness, identifies seven classic, manly virtues: manliness, courage, industry, resolution, self-reliance, discipline, and honor.[2] While these are beneficial for any man to cultivate, they still don't make you a man if you possess them. If they aren't practiced for the good of those placed in a man's life for him to protect and provide for, they don't yield genuine manliness. Virtue by itself isn't any good. A man needs someone else to be the recipient of his practice of these (or any) virtues.

2 Find out more about McKay's work at artofmanliness.com.

In the middle of the sixth day of creation, having ended each of the previous five days with the observation that all He had made was "good," God interrupted the cadence of "it was good . . . it was good . . . it was good . . . it was good . . ." with the arresting declaration that something was "not good" (Genesis 2:18). "It is not good that the man should be alone." It may be possible to do the right thing when no one else is there to see or to be served by you. But to be a virtuous man by yourself is impossible. It is not good for man to be alone. Alone, man cannot be good. Alone, man cannot fully be a man. He has no one to love, no one to serve, no one to protect, no one for whom to provide. Alone, man may be courageous, wise, disciplined, patient, chaste, or otherwise virtuous; but unless his courage, wisdom, discipline, patience, chastity, and any other virtues serve the good of others, they're not truly manly virtues, and he's not fully masculine.

THE OPPOSITE OF MASCULINITY

This isn't simply the stuff of being able to look at the reflection of yourself in a mirror and know that you're a manly man. There's more at stake here than that. In 1 Corinthians 6, the apostle Paul lists the opposite of masculinity in a catalog of deliberate sins from which Christians have been set free:

> Do you not know that the unrighteous will not inherit the kingdom of God? Do not be deceived: neither the sexually immoral, nor idolaters, nor adulterers, nor men who practice homosexuality, nor thieves, nor the greedy, nor drunkards, nor revilers, nor swindlers will inherit the kingdom of God. And such were some of you. But you were washed,

> you were sanctified, you were justified in the name of the Lord Jesus Christ and by the Spirit of our God. (vv. 9–11)

But in the original Greek of verse 9, between what the English Standard Version translates as the "adulterers" and the "men who practice homosexuality," is this other class of deliberate sinners: *malakoi*. The ESV simply lumps this peculiar word with the one following it, reducing the list from ten to nine types of people excluded from inheriting the kingdom of God. However, most English translations that do include it render this word as "effeminate men." It's the opposite of masculinity. And it's almost universally decried as a vice. From Aristotle to Aquinas, *malakia* is a kind of softness that men are looked down on for possessing.

This softness is the opposite of perseverance in virtue. It's the pursuit of easy pleasure over duty and responsibility. Many people equate effeminacy with homosexuality, and this seems to be the preference of translators who lump the words together. But not all homosexual men are effeminate. Nor are all heterosexual men masculine. *Malakia* is the moral softness of self-indulgence, self-centeredness, self-preservation. Hundreds of years before the Holy Spirit would lead St. Paul to include the effeminate in the list of sinners excluded from the kingdom of God, Aristotle described this softness in his *Nicomachean Ethics*:

> The deliberate avoidance of pain is rather a kind of Softness [*malakia*]. . . . One who is deficient in resistance to pains that most men withstand with success, is soft [*malakos*] or luxurious (for luxury is a kind of softness [*malakia*]):

> such a man lets his cloak trail on the ground to escape the fatigue and trouble of lifting it.[3]

Following Aristotle's line of thought, one of the Peripatetic philosophers writing closer to the time of St. Paul attributed this softness to the realm of cowardice: "Cowardice is accompanied by softness [*malakia*], unmanliness [*anandria*], faint-heartedness, fondness of life; and it also has an element of cautiousness and submissiveness of character."[4] This represents the world of thought surrounding St. Paul when he warned the Corinthian Christians of their past lives of *malakia*, among other sins.

Why is softness in a man—unmanliness—sinful? It's obviously different from homosexuality (as different as adultery or theft), since Paul lists that separately. If simply understood as referring to some external characteristics, "effeminacy" doesn't capture the full reality of *malakia*. A man could appear outwardly masculine—possess all the external trappings of masculinity—and be labeled soft and unmanly for shirking his duty, for protecting himself instead of others. The word was often used this way to describe cowardly soldiers, afraid of carrying out the duties given to them. This softness, then, is more than we understand with the word *effeminacy*. It's internal effeminacy. It's moral softness. It's loving oneself above others. It's seeking easy pleasure over the pain of doing what's good and right for others according to your calling in life.

Notice that effeminacy is not the same as femininity. Women are to be feminine. Men are to be masculine. Femininity is as desirable and praiseworthy for a woman as masculinity is for a man. And, in as much as it is included in a list of sins, *malakia*

3 Aristotle, *Nicomachean Ethics VII*, translated by H. Rackham (Cambridge, MA: Harvard University Press, 1934), 415.

4 Aristotle, *Nicomachean Ethics VII*, 497, 499.

is just as sinful for a woman as it is for a man. *Malakia* is selfish abdication of a higher calling to serve others. Although both men and women can possess such a selfish character defect, properly speaking, *malakia* is the opposite of masculinity.

From this softness, this unmanly selfishness, you have been set free. After the litany of people who exclude themselves from the reign of God's kingdom by their willful, persistent sin—among which he includes the softness of *malakia*—Paul concludes, "And such were some of you. But you were washed, you were sanctified, you were justified in the name of the Lord Jesus Christ and by the Spirit of our God."

Many of you used to be unmanly, declares the apostle, but now you've been washed, sanctified, and justified. Where do washing, sanctifying (making holy), and justifying (making right before God) happen? In Baptism. Being washed in the name of the triune God is no mere symbol. It's rebirth (John 3:3, 5; Titus 3:5–7). It's death and resurrection (Romans 6:3–6). It forgives sins (Acts 2:38). It saves (1 Peter 3:21). It covers you with the righteousness of Jesus (Galatians 3:27). Baptism is rebirth into the new life of a Christian. As such, as St. Paul says, Baptism is the beginning of the quest for genuine masculinity. You used to be soft, effeminate, selfish; then you were washed, baptized, saved, made new. Made a man.

From the watery womb of the baptismal font, we all are reborn sons of God. The Christian life and the quest for masculinity bear remarkable similarity in their trajectories. And the Church exists to help you develop the mature manhood both of a son of God and of a modern man. Unfortunately, the odds are stacked against you in both regards. Not only have we largely forgotten what it means to be a man, but we have also allowed masculinity to be maligned as a vice in contemporary American society.

The work is hard, but you were washed. Baptism has set you on this quest. Keep going.

BOOT CAMP

WHAT IS MAN?

1. "The first lesson in masculinity is not how powerful and mighty man is, how much he deserves to be exalted, but how humble he is, how small and inferior he is in comparison to his Creator." What does this mean for a man's daily life and work?

2. "Real masculinity is not found in any individual characteristic or trait but in the intersection of male characteristics with the exercise of manly virtue. Masculinity means harnessing the natural power a man possesses and using it for the good of others around him. The essence of masculinity is not rugged independence. It is sacrificial giving." How does this definition of masculinity differ from modern descriptions of what it means to be a man?

3. When men question the masculinity of other men, what characteristics or traits cause them to determine that someone is less of a man? What does St. Paul's use of *malakia* in his catalog of former sinful lifestyles say about what real masculinity is?

4. In your quest to be a better man, what can you do each day to remind yourself what God accomplished for you in Holy Baptism? How can you remember your Baptism daily?

NOT SO FROM THE BEGINNING

> *"In the beginning, therefore, did God form Adam, not as if He stood in need of man, but that He might have someone upon whom to confer His benefits."*
>
> —*St. Irenaeus, Against Heresies*

Jesus seems at times to have a serious case of wistful nostalgia. Life, He suggests, was far better in the "good ol' days," back in the Garden of Eden. This appeal to the beginning, hearkening back to better, bygone days, is how Jesus outfoxed the wily Pharisees with their weaselly question about marriage and divorce. "Is it lawful," they posited, "to divorce one's wife for any cause?" (Matthew 19:3).

Matthew's account makes clear that this was no innocent question. It was a query with an agenda. It was, as the text records, designed to test Jesus. Knowing their malice, of course, Jesus nevertheless answered, "Have you not read that He who created them from the beginning made them male and female, and said, 'Therefore a man shall leave his father and his mother and hold fast to his wife, and the two shall become one flesh'? So they are no longer two but one flesh. What therefore God has joined together, let not man separate" (vv. 4–6). There's Jesus' hearkening for the halcyon days of the past. "Have you not read . . . from the beginning." Back in the good ol' days of Eden, marriage was perfect. People were perfect. Divorce was unnecessary.

The Pharisees replied, "Why then did Moses command one to give a certificate of divorce and to send her away?" Jesus answered, "Because of your hardness of heart Moses allowed you to divorce your wives, but from the beginning it was not so" (vv. 7–8). Sin corrupted this good creation of God. But from the beginning, it was not so.

MALE AND FEMALE HE MADE THEM

So, what was it like in the woefully short-lived good ol' days? Five and a half days after the creation of time itself, God made man. For three days, He created by separating. In the first day, God created light and separated the light from the dark. On the second day, He separated waters from waters and waters from sky. On the third day, He created dry land and plants and separated land from water. The following three days were days of filling up the separated spaces He made in the first three days. On the fourth day, God filled the realms of light and dark with sun, moon, and stars. On the fifth day, He filled the waters with the swimming creatures and the skies with the flying ones. Now on the sixth day of creation, as soon as He had filled the land with monster-sized creatures, livestock-sized creatures, and creepy-crawling-sized creatures, God brought His work of creation to its apex: the creation of mankind.

> Then God said, "Let Us make man in Our image, after Our likeness. And let them have dominion over the fish of the sea and over the birds of the heavens and over the live-stock and over all the earth and over every creeping thing

> that creeps on the earth. So God created man in His own image, in the image of God He created him; male and female He created them. And God blessed them. And God said to them, "Be fruitful and multiply and fill the earth and subdue it, and have dominion over the fish of the sea and over the birds of the heavens and over every living thing that moves on the earth." (Genesis 1:26–28)

IMAGE OF GOD. FRUITFUL AND MULTIPLY.
SUBDUE AND HAVE DOMINION.

We scratched the surface of these themes briefly in chapter 1. The image of God is unique to mankind, and it's given to man and woman alike. Together, this complementary pair shares the Creator's image and likeness. Gregory of Nyssa compares the creation of mankind to the way a painter depicts a person with an assortment of colors, hues, textures, and so on. Thus mankind is like a painting, an image, an icon of the Creator:

> Painters transfer human forms to their pictures by the means of certain colours, laying on their copy the proper and corresponding tints, so that the beauty of the original may be accurately transferred to the likeness, so I would have you understand that our Maker also, painting the portrait to resemble His own beauty, by the addition of virtues, as it were with colours shows in us His own sovereignty: and manifold and varied are the tints, so to say, by which His true form is portrayed: not red, or white, or the blending of these, whatever it may be called, nor a touch of black that paints the eyebrow and the eye, . . . but instead of these, purity, freedom from passion, blessedness, alienation from all evil, and all those attributes

> of the like kind which help to form in men the likeness of God: with such hues as these did the Maker of His own image mark our nature.[5]

The Creator painted mankind with His divine virtues. Man is a depiction of the Creator in the way that a painted portrait is a depiction of a person. He is the *image* of God.

As such, the Creator tasks the man and woman with being His representatives to His creation. He gives them work to do that is distinctly His work: Be fruitful and multiply. Fill the earth and subdue it. Have dominion over the rest of the creatures. It's not that God is, as some have suggested, like a watchmaker, who, having finished his work of creation, winds it up and lets it run on its own. He is still actively engaged in His creation, and His work of creating is ongoing. But here at the very beginning, we get a glimpse into how God still interacts with His creation. He works through *means*.

Whereas in the beginning, He created *ex nihilo*—out of nothing—now He creates out of something else. Life from life. Offspring from parents. The world is filled through the co-creative work of the creatures God has made. His ongoing work of creation now happens, in part, through the *pro*creation of His creatures.

Procreation is normal, natural. Sex is good. Within the very first book of the Bible, God gives what may be His best First Article gifts: sex, marriage, and children. Procreation is the closest man can get to the kind of *ex nihilo*—out of nothing—creating that God does. God created simply by speaking. Man needs intercourse

5 Gregory of Nyssa, *On the Making of Man* 6, in *A Select Library of the Christian Church: Nicene and Post-Nicene Fathers: Second Series*, ed. Philip Schaff and Henry Wace (New York, 1890–1900; repr., Peabody, MA: Hendrickson, 1994), 5:390.

and ejaculation. Yet with these tiny gametes—sperm and egg—a man is given the ability to create new life.

This should spark just a bit of holy fear in us. In fact, it does, even when we don't acknowledge the fear. This is proven by the fact that we frequently try to have these gifts by themselves apart from God's plan and will. Another misuse happens when we pit these gifts against one another. But joined together—sex with marriage, marriage with children, children with sex—the act of intercourse allows us to participate in God's work of creating. That's a frightening role to have, a grandiose thing to do. So we get scared. And we try to back out of this sacred space. We try to avoid considering that we may be participating in God's work by separating these gifts from one another, having sex without marriage, marriage without children, even children without sex. To do so, though, is to miss this calling to be fruitful, multiply, fill the earth, and subdue it. To pit the gifts of God against one another—as if one is good but another is not—is to stubbornly and foolishly refuse to participate in this work as intended. Out of fear, we refuse to join our hands—and the rest of our bodies—to the Creator's in His creative endeavor. It's not just unmanly, it's subhuman. It's neither how we were made to function nor how we were called to participate in creation.

This is part of what it means to have dominion, but only just a part. The root of *dominion* is the Latin word *dominus*, or *Lord*. Dominion is lordship. It is to be in the place of God, to do His work in His stead. This is mankind's calling.

To know what dominion means, then, we must know how the Lord cares for His creation. To have dominion is to serve, give, and love. The Lord exercises authority for the good of His creation, not for His own good. His care is loving, not exploitative; selfless, not self-serving; giving, not taking. Dominion, then, is more for the good of creation than for the good of mankind. This needn't devolve into some kind of overly sensitive concern for creation that would equate the lives of trees, for instance, with human lives. Creation does exist for the good, the support, and the enjoyment of mankind. But man's call to exercise dominion involves more than just the responsibility to "be the boss."

That mankind would be fruitful and multiply, fill the earth and subdue it, and have dominion over it—all this and more is packaged in God's intention to create mankind in His image.

Everything happens on a big scale in Genesis 1. It's creation from the perspective of God. It's the top-down depiction. God creates by speaking and accomplishes universe-size feats with terse two- and three-word phrases in Hebrew. Everything is finished in six miraculous, mind-blowing days. The scale is intended to be grand, to render you wide-eyed and slack-jawed, feeling just a little bit small. After reading the first chapter of the first book of the Bible, you need a whole day to rest.

NOT GOOD

Genesis 2 is a different perspective. It's the view from below—creation as it looks from the perspective of those created. It's much slower. Instead of focusing on big-picture things like light, water, sky, dry ground, stars, and all creatures in six grand swoops, in the second chapter, the focus narrows down to one place: Eden.

> The LORD God took the man and put him in the garden of Eden to work it and keep it. And the LORD God commanded the man, saying, "You may surely eat of every tree of the garden, but of the tree of the knowledge of good and evil you shall not eat, for in the day that you eat of it you shall surely die."

> Then the LORD God said, "It is not good that the man should be alone; I will make him a helper fit for him." Now out of the ground the LORD God had formed every beast of the field and every bird of the heavens and brought them to the man to see what he would call them. And whatever the man called every living creature, that was its name. The man gave names to all livestock and to the birds of the heavens and to every beast of the field. But for Adam there was not found a helper fit for him. So the LORD God caused a deep sleep to fall upon the man, and while he slept took one of his ribs and closed up its place with flesh. And the rib that the LORD God had taken from the man He made into a woman and brought her to the man. Then the man said,
>
> "This at last is bone of my bones
> and flesh of my flesh;
> she shall be called Woman,
> because she was taken out of Man."
>
> Therefore a man shall leave his father and his mother and hold fast to his wife, and they shall become one flesh. And the man and his wife were both naked and were not ashamed. (vv. 15–25)

The sixth day of creation had been chugging along smoothly. It was poised to end as the previous five days had ended, with the Creator's declaration that it was "good," until there is an awkward interruption in the middle of the day. Suddenly, arrestingly, something is "not good." It is not good that the man should be alone.

So God knocks Adam out cold and chops him in half. Well, not half, precisely, but the Hebrew word *tsela* means more than just a "rib." It's a piece of Adam's side, a significant part of him, likely causing him to wake up with the refrain from Stone Temple Pilots' "Creep" in his head. He is less than he was before he went to sleep, but when he wakes up, he suddenly has the potential to be a man, a real man. Alone was not good.

Upon waking, Adam pronounces the first recorded words of any human being. "At last!" "Finally!" "About danged time!" "She shall be called *'ishah* because she was taken out of *'ish*" (Genesis 2:23). *'Ish* is one of the Hebrew words for "man." The one created from man, therefore, is named something that confesses her source: *'ishah,* even as the man was named for his source. *'Adam* is taken from the word for the dirt out of which he was created: *'adamah*. The English still preserves this unique nomenclature. The one with the Y chromosome and the external genitalia is man; his suitable helper is *wo*man.

PROTECT, PROVIDE, PROCREATE

Twenty-five years ago, cultural anthropologist Dr. David Gilmore published the results of his study of masculinity across cultures. Gilmore found that in every culture he studied, there were three things that marked a boy's transition to mature manhood.

Three functions drive every man: protect, provide, and procreate. To the astute reader of the Book of Genesis, it should be no surprise that Gilmore's study of diverse cultures found these three functions of masculinity to be nearly universal. They come directly from the description of mankind in Genesis 1 and 2. The nature of a man can never be fully expressed *alone*. These three innate desires (as old as the garden) man cannot accomplish by himself. They all require someone else for whom to provide, whom to protect, or with whom to procreate. Manhood is the opposite of isolation. This is nearly universal. Gilmore notes, "Manhood ideologies always include a criterion of selfless generosity, even to the point of sacrifice."[6]

NOT GOOD: A MAN NEEDS OTHERS

A MAN NEEDS A HELPER

In the deficit of the sixth day of creation, the Lord's solution is to make a helper for Adam. What God makes is something similar to Adam, yet not the same. Although she is made from Adam's flesh, she isn't another Adam. She's his complement, not his clone. (That's complement with an *e*, not the kinds of compliments your wife needs from you, fellas.) That is, she completes him in a way that neither he himself nor another Adam could.

You doubtless learned that boys and girls are, in fact, different before that day in fifth-grade health class when they talked about the birds and the bees. You knew when you unwrapped your first five-piece wooden puzzle that not all pieces are the same. So the boy bits fit into the girl bits. This biological truth still holds sway in the jargon of plumbers and electricians. Male pieces fit into female fittings. There's no same-sex marriage in the pipefitters' union.

Moreover, boys and girls are genetically complementary in such a way that, in order to come up with any new human beings, you've got to have half the DNA from a man and half

6 David D. Gilmore, *Manhood in the Making: Cultural, Concepts of Masculinity* (New Haven, CT: Yale University Press, 1990), 229.

from a woman. Two sperm cannot yield a baby without an egg. Nor two eggs without sperm. The complementarity between men and women, with each relying on the other to accomplish what one alone cannot do, is chiseled into the blueprint of every cell.

The egalitarians, who want to assert that anything men can do, women can do equally well, and vice versa, are patently silly. Sure, there are some women who can match or surpass the athletic prowess or strength of some men. But there are some biological things men cannot do that women can. Get pregnant. Give birth. Nurse. Those are the obvious low-hanging fruits. Not limited to what they conceal under their bathing suits, though, the differences between men's and women's bodies are quite significant. His is better suited for lifting heavy things and fending off foes. Hers is suited for nurturing and sustaining new life. With his broad shoulders, strong back, and narrow hips, the man is biologically programmed to fulfill these three tasks: provide, protect, procreate. His very stature has prepared him for the masculine tasks. Hers is well equipped for her feminine calling.

But it's not just that the man and woman complement each other biologically. They also have complementary roles. The man is husband; the woman is wife. He is father; she is mother. Those roles aren't interchangeable. When describing the roles of husbands and wives as exemplified by the perfect Husband, Christ, and His perfected Bride, the Church, St. Paul gives these tasks to wives: "Submit to your own husbands . . . and let the wife see that she respects her husband." To the husbands, Paul exhorts, "Husbands, love your wives. . . . Husbands should love their wives as their own bodies. . . . Let each one of you love his wife as himself" (see Ephesians 5:22–33).

I've deliberately omitted some critical parts of this excerpt from Paul's letter to the Christians in Ephesus, which we'll return to later. For now, the point is this: husbands and wives are given different things to do. Notice that wives aren't called to love their husbands, just to respect them.

What men need, then, and what women need are different. A wife needs her husband's love. She needs his provision and protection. She needs to feel treasured and cherished. She needs to feel safe from the world outside. She needs to feel secure enough to devote herself to the nurturing task that she alone is equipped to undertake.

Apart from his protection, she cannot completely give herself to this task. If she both has to nurture and care for her children and also keep her household safe, she'll neglect one task or the other. How shameful is any society that asks its women, be they mothers or potential mothers, to take up arms in defense of the nation. No self-respecting husband would ask his wife to head downstairs in the middle of the night to go investigate whatever noise awakened them. Nor would any father enlist his daughters to take care of the school-yard bullies who accosted his son.

Are women capable of fighting and protecting? Sure. But when they have to do so, it's always an indictment of the spineless men who abdicate their responsibilities or clumsily, cowardly naval-gaze while danger approaches. When Barak, commander of the Israelite army, would not go out to battle except if Deborah went with him, she pronounced this judgment against him: "The road on which you are going will not lead to your glory, for the LORD will sell Sisera into the hand of a woman" (Judges 4:9). It's a shameful thing that Deborah has to be the judge. It speaks against the men of Israel at the time—typified by cowardly Barak—that they need a woman to defend them. God intensifies the shame by using another woman to defeat Sisera, the Canaanite commander.

When Sisera's army is defeated, he flees the scene. As Barak is pursuing him, the Kenite woman Jael lures Sisera into her tent, promising, "Turn aside, my lord; turn aside to me; do not be afraid" (v. 18). So he does.

> And he said to her, "Please give me a little water to drink, for I am thirsty." So she opened a skin of milk and gave him a drink and covered him. And he said to her, "Stand at the opening of the tent, and if any man comes and asks you, 'Is anyone here?' say, 'No.'" But Jael the wife of Heber took a tent peg, and took a hammer in her hand. Then she went softly to him and drove the peg into his temple until it went down into the ground while he was lying fast asleep from weariness. So he died. And behold, as Barak was pursuing Sisera, Jael went out to meet him and said to him, "Come, and I will show you the man whom you are seeking." So he went in to her tent, and there lay Sisera dead, with the tent peg in his temple. (vv. 19–22)

Women are strong. When men are absent, a woman will courageously step into the breach to defend her family. And woe to the man who threatens a woman's children! But the responsibility falls chiefly not on her, but on the men given to protect her. No man wants his bacon saved by soft-spoken Jael and her tent peg. That's not a story that Barak is going to tell to his buddies with some embellishment at the local watering hole. Jael doesn't even overpower Sisera in a battle of strength. She's not masculine. Instead, her femininity is what does Sisera in. And this fulfills Deborah's prophecy that Barak's cowardice would be rewarded by being delivered from his enemy by a woman—with a hammer and a tent peg, a glass of milk, and a soft voice. When, years from now, his grandchildren ask him for stories of his military conquests, this will not be the one he tells them first. Or ever. A man needs a helper, someone for him to protect, to shield with his body and life, to shelter with himself.

Apart from his provision, likewise, a woman will step up to the task and provide for herself and her family. But she does so only when necessary, similarly to the man's shame. It's a sad state of affairs when the holy estate of motherhood and the pious work of managing a household are denigrated in favor of outsourcing. Food processing companies take responsibility for making microwaveable meals, and day-care facilities shoulder the work of child-rearing during the daylight hours. Sometimes, these are necessary in a fallen world, but they should never be preferred over the ordinary structure of a family woven into the fabric of creation, still present in our DNA today. When a wife has to leave the care of her children to others so she can get a job that provides a paycheck, it's an indictment of her husband's ability to be the provider. It's contrary to man's nature to be provided for. He needs a companion, a helper for whom he can provide.

In response to or in anticipation of this love, demonstrated by her husband's protection, provision, compassion, and sensitivity, a wife is called to respect her husband. Conspicuously absent from her duties is loving her husband. Despite Paul's threefold admonition for a husband to love his wife, the wife is never called to reciprocate love. Husbands don't need the same kind of love their wives do. A man needs his wife's respect, not her love—at least, not in the same way that he is called to love her.

Without a companion, Adam can be neither husband nor father. So God made a helper for him. This is more a statement about Adam's deficiency alone than it is about the nature of the woman God created for him. "Helper" isn't a bad word, implying, somehow, that the woman is less than the man; it implies neither superiority nor inferiority. She's not less, just different. Being man's helper does not subjugate the woman to the man's rule; rather, the woman fills the man's deficiency.

The Hebrew word *'azar*, translated "helper," is an honorific title. Elsewhere, the Lord Himself is identified as man's helper: "Behold, God is my *helper*; the Lord is the upholder of my life" (Psalm 54:4). "The LORD is on my side; I will not fear. What can man do to me? The LORD is on my side as my *helper*; I shall look in triumph on those who hate me" (Psalm 118:6–7).

In the same way that God accomplishes for man what is impossible for him to do alone spiritually, the creation of woman as man's helper—the one given to him to complete him—allows for man to accomplish what would have been impossible for him to do alone. In the garden, this God-created difference works perfectly (for a brief time), and no one complains that God prefers humans of one sex over the other.

A MAN NEEDS BROTHERS

Even if a man is given the good, godly gift of celibacy and needs no complement, no helper, it is still not good for him to be alone. He needs a friend. And this need is not fulfilled by a wife, a helper. In fact, his friend cannot be one of the opposite sex. A man needs another man.

Doubtless, that sentence gives you a moment of pause. To say that a man needs the close friendship of another man or a couple other men sounds preposterous to heterosexual men and patently obvious to homosexual men. Such is the effect of our hypersexualized society, which has emasculated men by removing normal, intimate friendships between men and replacing them with the eroticized union of two men as lovers.

You don't have to thumb far back into the photo albums of history to find pictures of men walking together while holding hands or draping their arms over each other. They weren't lovers, though their love for each other presumably ran deep. When men worked together in male-only professions, studied together in all-male schools, or fought side-by-side in combat, they developed deep bonds—abiding friendships unlike what men have nowadays.

Christian apologist C. S. Lewis describes the four kinds of love humans experience.[7] *Storge* is the affection between a parent and child or between siblings. It is familial love. *Eros* is love between a man and a woman. It is procreative, sexual love. *Agape* is the love God displays for mankind by offering Jesus on the cross to obtain forgiveness for the sins of mankind. It is unconditional, perfect love. And the love between two men that binds them together in deep friendship is *philia*, a long-lost concept in our contemporary society. Today, we negatively classify a close friendship between two guys as a "bromance," and we assume there must be sexual attraction, *eros*, between them. But historically, these are distinct kinds of affection.

Abraham Lincoln, for instance, is known to have shared a bed with his close friend Joshua Speed, until the latter got married and left Lincoln lonely and depressed. Some today accuse Lincoln of closeted homosexuality, but this is reading history through our modern, distorted, Freudian lens that gives every relationship sexual undertones. Although such bed-sharing today would cause the rumor mill to churn, in the bygone days of close male friendship, it had nothing to do with one's proclivities for homoeroticism.

Even Lewis, who lived from 1898 to 1963, lamented the loss of friendships between men due to homophobia. Friendship is distinct from the relationship between a man and a woman or

7 See C. S. Lewis, *The Four Loves* (New York: Harcourt, Brace, 1960).

between a man and his children. Whereas a man and a woman are joined by attraction, two men are joined by a common task. Unlike romantic lovers who are bonded together by facing *toward* each other, two men are bonded together side-by-side, facing out toward the world. Their devotion to each other flows from their devotion to a common task. Lewis describes the origin of this affection:

> Long before history began we men have got together apart from the women and done things. We had time. And to like doing what must be done is a characteristic that has survival value. We not only had to do the things, we had to talk about them. We had to plan the hunt and the battle. When they were over we had to hold a *post mortem* and draw conclusions for future use. We liked this even better. We ridiculed or punished the cowards and bunglers, we praised the star-performers. We reveled in technicalities. . . . In fact, we talked shop. We enjoyed one another's society greatly: we Braves, we hunters, all bound together by shared skill, shared dangers and hardships, esoteric jokes—away from the women and children.[8]

This kind of affection has the capacity to forge together in close companionship men who would otherwise seem very different.

Consider David and Jonathan, two highly unlikely candidates for close friendship. David, of course, was the shepherd boy—the youngest and least kingly in appearance of Jesse's sons—whom God chose and Samuel anointed to be king of Israel. Saul, the first king of Israel, was still reigning when David was chosen,

---

8 Lewis, *The Four Loves*, 63–64. *The Four Loves* by C. S. Lewis copyright © C. S. Lewis Pte. Ltd. 1960. Extract reprinted by permission.

but God rejected him because he turned away from the Lord (1 Samuel 15:11).

Jonathan was Saul's oldest son and presumably would have been the heir to the throne, had Saul not been rejected as king. Although monarchy was new to the Israelites, they didn't have to spend much time observing the neighboring kingdoms (whose having a king was what inspired the Israelites to want a king in the first place) to know that, typically, the oldest son inherits his father's throne. But then God chose David instead.

After his anointing as the next king, David triumphed over the gargantuan Goliath, and Jonathan and David became close friends. Their friendship was such that

> the soul of Jonathan was knit to the soul of David, and Jonathan loved him as his own soul. And Saul took him that day and would not let him return to his father's house. Then Jonathan made a covenant with David, because he loved him as his own soul. And Jonathan stripped himself of the robe that was on him and gave it to David, and his armor, and even his sword and his bow and his belt. (1 Samuel 18:1–4)

Although David was successful in whatever battle Saul sent him into, and Saul even set David over his army, eventually, Saul grew jealous of the people's praise of David. Gradually, Saul's hatred for and envy of David grew into a murderous rage, and he devoted the last years of his life to pursuing David in order to kill him.

In short, the should-have-been second king of Israel and the divinely-appointed alternate king make for unlikely friends, let alone friends as close as they were. But on multiple occasions, Jonathan was instrumental in shielding David from King Saul's jealous ire; and when Saul and his sons died in battle, David lamented Jonathan's death, saying, "I am distressed for you, my brother Jonathan; very pleasant you have been to me; your love to me was extraordinary, surpassing the love of women" (2 Samuel 1:26).

Love surpassing the love of women? Does this make David and Jonathan sound like closeted homosexual lovers? To the modern ear, probably. Unfortunately, gay activists have misappropriated the intimacy between David and Jonathan to their own cause, making them unwilling champions for a kind of homoerotic false-love that they never shared.

Perhaps the growing number of homosexual unions between men says more about the loss of the freedom of all men to have intimate friendships with one another, and less about the growing freedom men have to express these contrary-to-nature desires publicly. The loss of platonic, nonsexual, intimate friendships between males has left boys and young men confused. They desire this platonic intimacy with other men, but our sexually perverse culture tells them this is an unrealistic expectation. Not only is a man's friendship with a woman expected to be sexual, but his desire for friendship with another man is also expected to be expressed in sexual, homoerotic ways.

A man is programmed to desire intimacy with another man. He wants *philia*. He is not, however, programmed to enjoy *eros* with another man. Why is it more acceptable in our culture for a man to put his reproductive organ in another man's waste-expelling orifice than for two men who have no such unnatural desire to join their hands together while walking? Certainly, some men are homosexual. Their desires, however sinful and contrary to nature, are more than the simple desire for close friendship with and acceptance from another man. Yet there are also men who find themselves attracted to each other in a good, God-pleasing, masculine way but who unnecessarily and harmfully succumb to social pressures to make their friendship erotic. This is not what men need in a friend.

In short, it is simultaneously difficult yet more important than ever to cultivate this kind of friendship. A man needs a brother or two—friends whose bond runs deeper than watching football or drinking beers together. He needs an intimacy that exposes him and makes him vulnerable. He needs a fellow man to challenge him, to correct him, to sharpen him as iron sharpens iron, as the proverb goes (Proverbs 27:17). There's a delicate balance, though, in forging such a friendship. It must be intentional, not accidental. But it cannot be forced. The best places a man can look for a friend like this are the places he already inhabits: work, school, the domains of hobbies, or the playing field of sports. Where there is a common goal, a unified direction for two men to fix their faces, there can be this sort of friendship.

A MAN NEEDS A FAMILY

Nowhere do a man's three drives to procreate, provide, and protect express themselves more fully than in the rearing of children. When a man takes a wife, as the account of creation suggests, he leaves the protection and provision of those whose union brought him into the world, his parents.

Ordinarily, this union is procreative. It makes babies. Somewhere in the last century, the norm for our society has been to divorce the baby-making possibility from the baby-making function. We've wanted to have the pleasure of sex without any of the masculine drives to procreate, protect, and provide. We've made sex about pleasure, and in so doing, we've robbed it of its genuinely masculine procreative nature. The marital union—sex—is where a man's potential to procreate, protect, and provide for his family come to their fullest possibility. The joy of sex is not just the orgasm, but the surrender of a man's self-centered will to God's will, yielding himself to the deep calling within him to procreate, protect, and provide. Sex is designed to be risky for a man. Safe sex is a joke, an impossibility. If God blesses this union, it will produce a child who will rely on this man to protect and provide for him or her, forever undoing the man's self-safety. That's inherently risky.

It's no wonder, then, that our feminized society has become comfortable with separating the sexual act from the possibility of receiving the God-ordained gift of children. Society argues that you should wait to procreate until you are able both to protect and provide for that child and his mother. Thus the masculine callings to protect, provide, and procreate get pitted against one another. The gifts of sex, marriage, and children, intended in the Garden of Eden to be given together, are likewise played against one another.

Nothing could be more selfish or less masculine than using a latex barrier to withhold a part of yourself in the sexual union, dosing your wife with chemicals that treat her gift of feminine fertility as a disease against which she needs to be medicated, or otherwise holding back your procreative powers so that you can continue to enjoy life where children do not impose on your self-centeredness. Contraception lets men continue to be self-centered boys. And women simultaneously wonder why the pool of marriage-minded men grows smaller every year as they pop pills and implant devices that let men continue to play like boys. A child, even the possibility of a child, would cause a man to reevaluate all the one-night-stands and right swipes on Tinder. Sex is supposed to be risky to the little boy inside every man, the self-centered narcissist who is the most important person in his world. It's not meant to be safe.

A man, thus, needs children. He needs human beings who will depend on him to live for their own good, no longer for his. In a way that leaving his parents and marrying his bride simply cannot, having a child is intended to shatter a man's self-centeredness. If a man leaves his wife, she suffers, but her security is not endangered. If a man leaves his child, the child is not only deprived of his natural right to his two biological parents, but the child is also exposed, at risk of hunger, and in danger of predators around.

Children give meaning to other aspects of a man's life. His work, his labor for a paycheck, is transformed by the need to provide for another person. First, when he takes a wife, but more so when she bears children for him, his nine-to-five slogging away is imbued with new meaning. Someone now depends on this work. For a man, his job is meaningful anyway. Right or wrong, he derives much of his identity from what he *does*. When two men greet each other, one of the first questions they ask is "What do you do?" In other words, "What's your job?" But no matter what it is, a man's job is what enables him to fulfill his biological drive to provide. He has to work to support his family. Even if the work is mundane, when he has a family, a man's work is never merely for himself.

Moreover, a man needs children to help him conquer the world. His offspring are his closest tribe. He passes his worldview onto them, and they carry this worldview into the world under the banner of their father's name. A man can only affect those in his sphere of influence. Children expand a man's influence exponentially.

Can you see the blessing of children then? They destroy a man's boyish selfishness and call him to be a man. And they take one man's influence and expand it beyond what he could ever reach. They force his hand to play the man. And they are his legacy, his conquest of the world around him. "Train up a child in the way he should go; even when he is old he will not depart from it" (Proverbs 22:6).

But what about those men from whom the gift of procreating is withheld? What about men who are infertile or whose wives are barren? They, with nearly unified voice, can confess better than most men that children are gifts from God. And they uniquely know the pain of not having received that gift. Barrenness in men is a cross to bear. Like any other cross laid on him, it will teach a man to be prayerful and dependent on God. It will teach him that his identity is not in having sons or daughters but in being, by virtue of having been baptized, a son of the eternal, heavenly Father. And yet, like any cross, like any affliction, it hurts.

This faulty virility can cause a man to question his masculinity. If he cannot procreate, can a man be fully masculine? Yes. Masculinity is reflected in his being open to God's gift of children, not in his ability to make babies. When God withholds that gift, it does not impugn a man's masculinity. When the sexual act is unselfish—intended to be procreative—then even when wombs remain barren, it is nevertheless masculine. Masculinity means giving. In a way, a man without children is no different from a man without a wife. His masculine journey has the same goal as a man with a family; he has to learn to live for others. He has to learn to give.

This also gives a man in an infertile marriage courage to face the shame inherent in bearing this cross. As he questions his own masculinity and virility, he probably assumes others do as well. But if he learns to give, if he learns to find his identity more in his ability to give than to take, he can endure whatever shame or embarrassment there may be (real or imagined) in bearing this cross, because he will find his masculine identity in what he can do for others, not in what others think of him.

Even a man without a wife and children is nevertheless called to live his life for the good of others. Those without children can still serve as fathers. The plague of absent fathers can be met by this small but mighty army of men who know they are called beyond the self-indulgence of boyhood, who desire the vocation of fatherhood but have not been given the gift of biological children. Moreover, you can add not just your voice to the cause of defending unborn children whose mothers are considering abortion. You can add your life to the defense of theirs by adopting children.

If God has not given you biological offspring, take your innate desires to protect and provide outside the walls of your home. Become a Sunday School teacher or a Scout leader. Volunteer at a women's crisis pregnancy center. Read to children at the library. Check your self-centered nature at the door and find a child or a group of children for whom you can be a surrogate father, of sorts. You can do what men with families cannot. You can step into the breach and fight for children in need of father figures. It sometimes takes greater courage and gumption to identify the needs of others around you who don't share your genes, to venture into your community in search of ways your manliness can be of service to others. But you will be of service to others, and by receiving your work to protect and provide for them, they will shape you into a better man.

Children are a beacon call for a man to be a hero. As soon as you have children who depend on you, your place in the world is magnified, especially in their world. You have a desire as old as the man-of-dirt, Adam, to be the "Man of Steel" in the world. You want to be a hero. Children need a hero. Contrary to popular thinking, having children does not mean you have to settle down. Rather, you have to step up, rise to the occasion, don your cape, set your own wants and needs aside, and fulfill your calling to procreate, provide, and protect.

A MAN NEEDS A TRIBE: THE COMMUNION OF SAINTS

It remains "not good" for man to be alone. In addition to a wife, a friend, and a family, a man needs other men. He needs a tribe. He needs to belong. And he needs to be initiated.

This kind of tribe can exist anywhere. Men find companionship in work societies, fraternities, church men's clubs, sports teams. What men need are other men to challenge them, encourage them, discipline them, correct them. But these tribes are dwindling in popularity. People don't join clubs or groups anymore.

Calling for a renewal of masculinity and manliness, Robert Bly, poet and early spokesman of the burgeoning men's movement of the late eighties and early nineties, describes the path from boyhood to manhood in his celebrated and critiqued epic narrative of the masculine journey, *Iron John*.[9] Ancient societies, Bly contends, had an initiation rite for boys becoming men. Many times they would be taken away from their nuclear families by the men of the tribe to participate in some kind of ritual that would mark the transition from boyhood to manhood. Bloodshed, fasting, hunting, tests of strength or endurance, and other rites of passage that today would be considered hazing if done by other boys and child abuse if inflicted by older men served as trailblazers on his journey.

---

9 *Iron John: A Book About Men* (Reading, MA: Addison-Wesley, 1990).

Bly observes that the transition from boyhood to manhood doesn't simply happen by itself. Boys need older men to initiate them and welcome them into the society of men.[10] Men are the catalysts to make other men from the raw material of boys. Unfortunately, the interaction between older men and boys seeking to become men is largely missing in our culture. In a society fixated on youth as the ideal, we try to distance ourselves from our elders. We segregate ourselves by age and thus deter boys from inheriting the collective knowledge of what it means to be a man from their elders. Those of our grandparents who don't take the hint and retire to communities of people in their age demographic in Orlando or Albuquerque are eventually scuttled away to pleasantly euphemized "senior living" centers.[11]

Boys cannot help other boys transition into men. The transition from girlhood to womanhood is not the same as the transition from boyhood to manhood. Boys need older men to teach them how to be men. Without older men, there will be no mature young men. Manliness continues in the collected wisdom from previous generations. It requires mentors.

If society is losing clubs and organizations, then one of the last places where boys can encounter older men is in the Church. As the local communion of saints—the fellowship of those who gather around shared pulpit, font, and altar—the Christian congregation has the potential to be a training academy for boys becoming men. But this can only happen if the older men take the time and care to catechize these boys in the dying art of being a man, of living one's life for the good of others.

Men need a tribe. Boys need a band of men to initiate them into manhood. Men need a band of brothers where they

10 Bly, *Iron John*, 15.

11 Bly, *Iron John*, 16.

can belong. Alone is not good. It takes other men to cultivate masculinity in others. A tribe gives a man a place where he can share his identity with others on a similar quest, working toward a common goal.

BIBLICAL MASCULINITY: ADAM'S CALLING

When God shaped Adam out of the *'adamah*, placed him into the garden, and made a helper for him, He gave Adam several holy callings. The first man was the first prophet, the first priest, and the first king. He was the head of his fledgling family and entrusted with the responsibility to rule in the place of the Lord over his family, the garden, and the whole of creation. Adam was the lord of creation. This was a high calling, a lofty estate. And for a few, bright, shining moments, everything was right in the world. Man was good. "And God saw everything that He had made, and behold, it was very good" (Genesis 1:31).

Adam's tasks were oriented toward the world around him. Give names to the animals. Be fruitful and multiply. Procreate. Preach the Word God has given you to your wife. Protect her from acting contrary to God's commands. Provide for her. Do the same for your eventual offspring. Do nothing for your own good. Care more for her good and their good than your own. This is dominion. You are a means to an end. The end is the good of creation, the survival and success of others around you. Love them. Serve them. Be a man.

The sun set on the sixth day. On the seventh day, because God was finished, He rested and invited the man and woman to join Him in His rest. Genesis 2 ends with this idyllic declaration: "The man and his wife were both naked and were not ashamed"

(v. 25). No shame. No sin. No failure to live up to their holy callings. Everything was very good. For a moment.

BOOT CAMP

NOT SO FROM THE BEGINNING

1. God gives mankind dominion over His creation, entrusting them to do His work for His creatures. *Dominion* means "lordship." How does the Lord care for His creation? What does this mean for Adam's work in creation?

2. It is not good for man to be alone. What are you doing to cultivate and care for these necessary relationships?

   A helper:

   A friend:

   Children:

   A tribe:

   If you have not been given these relationships, how can you exercise your masculinity while bearing this cross?

3. How have modern-day distortions of these relationships made masculinity more difficult to cultivate and exercise?

MAN DOWN

"You should be women, And yet your beards forbid me to interpret That you are so."

—Banquo in Shakespeare's Macbeth

"Manhood is the defeat of childhood narcissism."

—David Gilmore, Manhood in the Making: Cultural, Concepts of Masculinity

There's a lot of action that happens in the white space between the end of chapter 2 and the beginning of chapter 3 in Genesis. It goes from describing the goodness of creation to introducing the serpent who "was more crafty than any other beast of the field" (Genesis 3:1). That word translated "crafty" can have both a positive and a negative connotation. When it's a desirable attribute, it's often translated as "prudent," as in Proverbs 12:16 and 23, where the fool and the prudent man are set in antithesis to one another. When it's intended in a negative sense, the translators prefer something like "crafty," as in Job 5:12, where God is the adversary of the crafty man and thwarts his plans. In calling the serpent "crafty," then, the reader is to understand an adversarial relationship between the serpent and the Creator, between the fallen angel and the Creator's creations.

Somewhere in that narrow white space, a whole lot of chaos goes down. Although the timeline is uncertain, between the "very good" at the end of the sixth day of creation and Satan's arrival in the garden as a serpent, something seems to happen that Jesus later described as Satan falling "like lightning from heaven" (Luke 10:18). He rebelled against God. This is not some kind of cosmic dualism, where good and evil are the balanced yin and yang, as if God and Satan are eternal arch rivals. Satan is a fallen angel, part of the creation. His power, though often underestimated today, doesn't hold a candle to the Almighty. When he does go toe-to-toe with an adversary, it's the archangel Michael against whom he fights, until on Good Friday he is finally defeated by the blood of the Lamb and the testimony of the martyrs (Revelation 12:7–12).

Because his rebellion fails to take the throne room of the triune God, and he is unable to take the place of the Creator, Satan takes aim at the Creator's handiwork. If he cannot triumph, he can at least spoil the goodness of creation and take some humans to hell with him. So he dons the form of a serpent to lure Adam and his bride into a similar rebellion against the Creator. In a perfect inversion of the order of creation, the serpent, a creature, comes to the woman, who eats and gives to her husband, who then also eats; thus the pair set themselves over God and His command. How is it just a few verses earlier in chapter 2? God is over all. He sets Adam in His place and makes a suitable helper, a woman, for him. God places the remainder of creation under their shared dominion, that they might exercise loving care over it.

ORDER OF CREATION	ORDER OF THE FALL
God	Serpent
Man	Woman
Woman	Man
The rest of creation	God

The fall into sin is disorder, chaos. Nothing is as it should be, as God created it. "Order" in the expression "order of creation" is less about chronological order and more about placement, everything in its proper place.

The serpent's seduction crosses the boundary that God had fixed for mankind. Being a creature means living within the prescribed limits. But the serpent was persuasive. Maybe God hadn't said . . . Or, maybe God was wrong or lying. Maybe He had withheld something good from them capriciously. Maybe life would be better on the other side of the boundary. Only one way to find out. The action of outward rebellion was born in the original sin of unbelief, doubting God and His Word, preferring to be their own gods and set their own rules and limits. So the woman and then the man joined the devil in his doomed-to-fail rebellion against the Source of Life. Thus death logically ensued.

DISORDERED MASCULINITY

From that moment, mankind was permanently altered. All Adam's future descendants inherited his sin and his dying. It was the greatest mass murder ever perpetrated. "Sin came into the world through one man, and death through sin, and so death spread to all men because all sinned" (Romans 5:12). One man. This whole rotten mess, death and all the precursors of death (cancer, depression, nearsightedness, broken families, and stubbed toes), lies at the feet of one man: Adam.

SELF-SERVING

Yes, Paul tells Timothy that it was the woman, not the man, who was deceived (1 Timothy 2:14). That's her sin; Adam's was different. Notice how the story plays out. The serpent approaches the woman, engages her in this back-and-forth about the trustworthiness of God's Word. The devil first twists what God had spoken, but she's well catechized enough not to fall for that.

I used to try to get mileage out of the woman's answer, accusing her of adding to God's Word. It sure seems like she does. "We may eat of the fruit of the trees in the garden," she answered, "but God said, 'You shall not eat of the fruit of the tree that is in the midst of the garden, neither shall you touch it, lest you die'" (Genesis 3:2–3). At least in the initial giving of the prohibition, the Lord nowhere included "touching it" in the otherwise simple command not to eat from the tree in the middle of the garden. Did she add something to God's Word?

Remember, God gave this command to Adam before He made a helper fit for him. God never told Eve any such thing. If she's misquoting God, it's as much her pastor's fault as her own. It was Adam, after all, who had preached to and catechized his wife in the Word. What Adam spoke to her was the Word, to be sure. Whether he or she added the bit about also not even touching the tree doesn't matter. It's good advice. The preached Word is still the Word. The problem isn't any addition. The problem is that no one intervened to send the serpent packing at the first words out of his lips.

Finally, after another go-round, the woman succumbs. Won over by the lie, "You will not surely die," and the seduction of being her own god, "She took of its fruit and ate, and she also gave some to her husband who was with her, and he ate" (v. 6).

Did you catch that? Adam isn't away at the office, walking in the front door half a second too late to stop his wife's rebellion. He isn't having a come-to-Jesus encounter with the preincarnate Christ or getting a tour of the more remote regions of Eden only to arrive back on the scene mere moments too late to arrest the downfall of all mankind and keep creation on the straight and narrow. He's right there.

Right. There.

There's Adam's sin. He stands idly by as his wife is enticed into sin. He abdicates his calling to be her *protector*, to kick the serpent to the curb and risk his own hide rather than expose her to any harm. Instead, he's just *standing there*!

It's the first science experiment, with Adam in a lab coat and his wife as the guinea pig. Adam will test the veracity of God's Word with the life of his wife. When the one who elicited the first recorded words of humanity, Mrs. Bone-of-My-Bones-and-Flesh-of-My-Flesh, eats and doesn't immediately keel over, struck dead by the God who gave her to him in the first place, Adam joins the rebellion. He eats too.

Before Eve's doubting or eating, Adam had already shrugged the mantle of masculinity. Somehow and for some reason, his interests grew selfish. He no longer looks out for his wife. He's distracted or simply detached from his calling. Whatever the case, the first distortion of biblical masculinity is for a man to be self-serving. Since then, all of Adam's descendants have been looking out for themselves more than serving the needs and wants of those entrusted to their care.

SELF-CENTERED

Immediately upon their sin, "The eyes of both were opened, and they knew that they were naked" (Genesis 3:7). It's not that their eyes didn't work before. It's just that they were previously closed to this new reality. Before their fall into sin, they didn't know their own nakedness, because their eyes didn't normally incline downward, to self-centered examination.

But now, with eyes weighed down by his transgression, where does Adam's gaze go? Away from his wife, away from creation, away from the gifts and callings of God that surround him, down to his own private parts. This is the very nature of sin, to be fixated on oneself.

St. Augustine, fourth-century bishop of Hippo in North Africa, is perhaps the first to observe this about the nature of sin: sin replaces *amor Dei*, "love of God," with *amor sui*, "love of self." Martin Luther expounds on this, saying that the nature of man since Adam's fall is to be *incurvatus in se*, literally "curved in on oneself."

Look at the immediate loss of Adam's ability to function as a man. His eyes exist not for looking at himself or looking after his own needs. They exist to see his wife. His very posture, if post-fall posture is anything like his physical stature and posture before the fall into sin, has his gaze directed outwards. It takes a weakening of back and neck muscles for his head to slouch downward, to discover his own nakedness and shame. Suddenly, what previously did not matter is now of utmost importance.

This self-centeredness demonstrates how much man has lost in this act of defiance against his Creator. Luther says, "The most serious loss consists in this, that not only were those benefits lost, but man's will turned away from God. As a result, man wants and does none of the things God wants and commands. Likewise, we have no knowledge about what God is, what grace is, what righteousness is, and finally what sin itself is" (LW 1:141). Our knowledge is deficient. Our eyes do not work as intended. We no longer perceive or know the world or God as we ought.

Adam's nakedness and shame leave him exposed and vulnerable. (His wife presumably has a similar reaction, but we'll leave pontificating on the fairer sex to those with firsthand experience.[12]) He needs clothing to hide himself from the eyes of others and even from his own gaze, lest he be overwhelmed with guilt and shame. Therefore, he and his wife whip up some dapper duds from fig leaves, which will likely only last until the first cosmic airing of *What Not to Wear* decrees that bloodless fig leaves are insufficient to cover guilt and shame. Thus, God substitutes clothing made from the skin of an innocent animal, who presumably shed not only blood but also his very life, as flayed creatures are not long for this world.

Ever since that moment, every man's gut instinct has been to consider his own needs above the needs of others, while at the same time exposing the guilt and shame of others before tending to his own. Adam's calling to put others above himself has devolved into narcissistic naval-gazing, and all of his sons have had the same disordered tendency.

SELF-PRESERVING

The effects of sin are magnified once the Creator walks into the garden to find His lost creatures. Their nature changes so dramatically and they become such enemies of God that the mere sound of His walking in the garden elicits panic in them. So they hide.

Adam and his wife are scared of God. Of God! Their Creator! This alone shows their predicament. God has done nothing harmful or wrathful toward them. He hasn't changed, but they have. They have become His enemies because of their desire to be their own gods.

12 Once you've mastered the essence of masculinity, or at least slogged your way to the last page of this tome, pick up a copy of CPH's *LadyLike: Living Biblically* (2015) by the highly competent and eminently capable Gilbert sisters (Rebekah Curtis and Rose Adle). Gather all their advice on what it means to live as a lady, and then stop doing those things. Unless, of course, you are a lady.

A manly solution for Adam would have been to take ownership of the catastrophe he caused—even defend his wife from any accusation against her by God—and face the consequences. But what does the first man, the icon of masculinity, do?

> The LORD God called to the man and said to him, "Where are you?" And he said, "I heard the sound of You in the garden, and I was afraid, because I was naked, and I hid myself." He said, "Who told you that you were naked? Have you eaten of the tree of which I commanded you not to eat?" The man said, "The woman whom You gave to be with me, she gave me fruit of the tree, and I ate." (Genesis 3:9–12)

This is how far Adam has fallen from his identity as a man. The only one Adam seems genuinely concerned to protect is himself. God's call to the hiding duo was never for His own benefit. It's not that He turned His back momentarily and the man and woman got lost somewhere in a dark corner of Eden. His call "Where are you?" is purely for Adam's benefit, that he would acknowledge his place and see the wretchedness of his estate. When hiding proves futile, as was inevitable, Adam has a litany of excuses.

First, it's Eve's fault. Instead of taking responsibility for his emasculated looking-on while his wife was seduced and deceived by the serpent, Adam abdicates his call to protect her yet again. "She gave to me and I ate! What could I do? It's totally not my fault."

Second, in Adam's estimation, it's ultimately God's fault. "The woman, *whom You gave to me* . . ." It's as though he's saying, "If we're being honest, God, I was doing quite a bit better before You knocked me out and excised a chunk of my side to make a helper. If You hadn't given me a wife, I would not have been lured into rebellion against You. So, in the interest of precision, I simply don't think it's fair to blame *me*. Also, we should talk about what a terrible idea free will was . . ."

Adam's goal is self-preservation. He throws his wife under the bus and lays the fault at God's feet. This is effeminacy, *malakia*, which we first encountered in chapter 1. The essence of man is to protect others. The essence of an effeminate man is to protect himself. Since this moment of Adam's playing the blame game, every man has been an honest heir of this deficiency.

In a remarkably short period of time, Adam's nature changes completely. It's entirely corrupted. Now, he serves himself more than others. He looks to himself and caters to his own whims and desires. Effeminacy now comes naturally. Masculinity does not. Self-preservation is his new instinct. Protecting others is an acquired skill. And, worst of all, he looks after his own protection and preservation, even at the expense of his wife or his Creator. This is not a real man anymore.

DYSFUNCTIONAL "MANHOOD"

Since the moment Adam sought to cover his nakedness with fig leaves, the easiest way to impugn another man's masculinity—from the junior high playground to the corporate boardroom, and even to the *Gemütlichkeit*[13] at pastors' conferences—has been to question the size or quality of his reproductive organs. The act of procreation, once a source of pride and no shame, has now become (rightly) confined to bedrooms, behind closed doors. Sin and sex are related at a fundamental level. As soon

13 The fraternity, conversation, and *ahem* drinking at the evening-end of any good pastors' conference.

as they sinned, Adam and Eve sought to hide their genitals. And since then, the Bible has had an odd fascination with the male "member."

CONSEQUENCES OF SIN

After the fall into sin, God quickly doled out promises and curses. From the top down, in the same order of the fall, He started with the serpent and concluded with the man.

To the serpent: "Cursed are you above all livestock and above all beasts of the field; on your belly you shall go, and dust you shall eat all the days of your life. I will put enmity between you and the woman, and between your offspring and her offspring; he shall bruise your head, and you shall bruise his heel" (Genesis 3:14–15).

There is no promise here for the serpent. He receives only curses. You are cursed. Dust is your fare every day of your life. You will be at odds with the woman. Her offspring will crush your head, though you will strike His heel. The phrasing is somewhat awkward, as ordinarily the promise of seed or offspring is given to the man, but this is nevertheless a promise of a Savior. Thus, every instance of sexual union between Adam and Eve would be seasoned with hope for the Savior, the Serpent-Crusher.

To the woman: "I will surely multiply your pain in childbearing; in pain you shall bring forth children. Your desire shall be contrary to your husband, but he shall rule over you" (v. 16). What was originally natural, pain-free, and unencumbered by complications or frustrations now reels with the consequences of sin. Childbearing was never intended to be painful or deadly; the pain, bloodshed, and occasional death that now take place during birth are the effects of sin. But God declares that childbearing will also be the solution to sin. Every delivery, even every act of conception will bring with it hope: *maybe this is the child who will crush the serpent's head.*

To the man: "Because you have listened to the voice of your wife and have eaten of the tree of which I commanded you, 'You shall not eat of it,' cursed is the ground because of you; in pain you shall eat of it all the days of your life; thorns and thistles it shall bring forth for you; and you shall eat the plants of the field. By the sweat of your face you shall eat bread, till you return to the ground, for out of it you were taken; for you are dust, and to dust you shall return" (vv. 17–19).

Adam's curse derives from the fact that he listened to his wife. Instead of protecting her, caring for her, and serving as her head, he stood by, simply observing, treating her as his lab rat. He failed his call to protect and provide for his wife. Because he failed to play the role of the man, Adam's curse encompasses even the place of his origin. The dirt, the *'adamah*, will reel from the effects of his sin. No longer will the soil be good and naturally fertile. Now it will bear thorns and thistles. It will need to be cultivated, hoed, and weeded. And it will cost man his sweat, blood, and—occasionally—his life. The dirt is symbolic of Adam's nature. No longer will it function as intended. It will incline toward weeds; he toward sin.

Finally, God confirms what the man and woman knew immediately when they sinned. Their reproductive organs need to be covered. The once holy work of procreating now is to be done in private, and it will be fraught with complications, frustrations, and failings.

CIRCUMCISION

Several generations after God wrapped Adam's nakedness in the skin of a freshly-killed animal, He pulled back the loin cloth again to mark the promise of the coming Offspring. In Genesis 12, the Lord promised to a man named Abram that He would make of him a great nation (v. 2). He intensified this promise in chapter 15, saying Abram's "very own son" would be his heir (v. 4), and his offspring would be as numerous as the stars in the heavens (v. 5). But time wore on, and Abram and his wife Sarai had no children. They therefore figured that perhaps divine promises needed a little human intervention to help them along. So Sarai gave Abram her servant girl Hagar that he might impregnate her and have a son of his own.

Hagar conceived and bore Abram a son, Ishmael. But just any son was not what the Lord had promised. His Word needs no human cooperation to come to completion. So in Genesis 17, the Lord appeared a third time to Abram. He reaffirmed His promise to make Abram the "father of a multitude of nations" (v. 4) and changed his name from Abram ("great father") to Abraham ("father of many") (v. 5). Then, the Lord gave newly-named Abraham the sign of His eternal covenant with him:

> This is My covenant, which you shall keep, between Me and you and your offspring after you: Every male among you shall be circumcised. You shall be circumcised in the flesh of your foreskins, and it shall be a sign of the covenant between Me and you. He who is eight days old among you shall be circumcised. Every male throughout your generations, whether born in your house or bought with your money from any foreigner who is not of your offspring, both he who is born in your house and he who is bought with your money, shall surely be circumcised. So shall My covenant be in your flesh an everlasting covenant. Any uncircumcised male who is not circumcised in

> the flesh of his foreskin shall be cut off from his people;
> he has broken My covenant. (vv. 10–14)

This is, admittedly, a little odd. To circumcise is literally to "cut around" the penis, removing the foreskin. God cuts His covenant into Abraham's flesh—and not just any flesh, but the flesh of his penis. From then onward, every Jewish male was to be circumcised on the eighth day of his life. There's a bit of word play here too. If a male is unwilling to submit to the cutting *around* as a sign of the covenant, he is to be cut *off* from the people of God.

The circumcised penis is less than the intact penis. God has a piece of human flesh removed. Was this a result of Abraham's trying to fulfill God's promises for Him by sleeping with the servant girl? Probably not. Although, once ninety-nine-year-old Abraham's penis healed and he engaged in intercourse with also-renamed Sarah, it not only felt different, but it also looked different. This private act of procreation was marked with God's sign, reminding Abraham of the promise.

God made good on His promise to give Abraham and Sarah a son. Then, when that son (Isaac) was eight days old, they circumcised him too. This served as a reminder that God would still use sex to fulfill the promise He made in the Garden of Eden to send an Offspring to save His people from their sinful rebellion and forever crush the serpent's head. Every procreative act from then on was a reminder of this promise. The man's "manhood" is marked with the sign of the covenant. Part of the flesh of man has been removed as a reminder of the work of the Divine to accomplish what man cannot.

Circumcision is unavoidably weird. And, as a sign of the covenant, it only marks the males. The sowing of seed through the sexual act is the work of the man. The woman's work is to receive. The very essence of masculinity and femininity is preserved in the marital sexual congress. Men give. Women receive. But the man's giving is circumscribed by the marking of the covenant. His participation in procreation is overshadowed by the promise of the Seed of the woman to liberate God's people from sin and death.

After the Seed of the woman, the promised Messiah, is born, though, circumcision no longer remains a sign of anything. It pointed toward a male child who would be born to redeem the Lord's people. To insist on circumcision for spiritual reasons after the enfleshment of the Son of God is to deny that He is the fulfillment of this promise. So St. Paul pronounces, "I wish those who unsettle you [by requiring circumcision] would emasculate themselves!" (Galatians 5:12). In other words, don't just cut *around*; if you want to insist on making Christians follow laws that were designed to point forward to Christ, you might as well cut all the way *through*. This is not unlike the word play God used when He set up the sign of circumcision. Better to cut it off than to be cut off from God's people.

PHALLIC FIXATION

Given Adam's immediate attention to his exposed male member upon his fall into sin, it shouldn't be surprising that the boy bits get quite a bit of attention in the Old Testament. There's a curious fascination with masculinity and the penis that makes some of the Old Testament sound more like junior-high locker room banter than the Spirit-inspired Word for God's people.

The status of a man's testicles can exclude him from the Israelite assembly for worship. Among the descendants of Aaron, those excluded from drawing near to offer sacrifices in the tabernacle include "one who has a blemish . . . a man blind or lame, or one who has a mutilated face or a limb too long, or a man who has an injured foot or an injured hand, or a hunchback or a dwarf or a man with a defect in his sight or an itching disease or scabs or crushed testicles" (Leviticus 21:18–20). Even among the animals to be sacrificed, the regulations are remarkably similar, excluding any whose testicles are bruised, crushed, or cut (22:24).

God reiterates His laws just before bringing His people into the Promised Land, saying that the status of the male organ and testicles matters not just for the priests and the sacrifices, but also for the rest of the male worshipers. "No one whose testicles are crushed or whose male organ is cut off shall enter the assembly of the LORD" (Deuteronomy 23:1). How strange, right? Why is so much emphasis placed on the condition of the private parts of Jewish men? Why must priests and the animals for sacrifices be fully intact males? Why are those who gather with the assembly required to be trimmed and intact? Because the promised Messiah, the final High Priest and the perfect Sacrifice, the awaited Seed of the woman, would be fully and completely male.

There's another peculiar prohibition in the Book of Deuteronomy that bears mentioning in a book about reclaiming biblical masculinity. When a wife wants to break up a fight between her husband and another man, if she doesn't want to have her hand cut off, she should not attempt to put an end to the fisticuffs by grabbing her husband's adversary's genitals: "When men fight with one another and the wife of the one draws near to rescue her husband from the hand of him who is beating him and puts out her hand and seizes him by the private parts, then you shall cut off her hand. Your eye shall have no pity" (25:11–12). This is a ceremonial law, of course, designed to set apart the Israelites from the nations around them, to make them the odd men out. Therefore, it is no longer applicable to those who are defined not by their cultural peculiarities but by their identity in Christ. There's no longer a need to lop off your wife's hand if she saves your bacon by taking hold of the situation. Nevertheless, it's a law that fits within the peculiar fascination of God and His covenantal people with the male reproductive organs.

As frequently happens in locker rooms populated with insecure adolescent boys or simply when men want to diminish the stature of another man, there's even a bit of euphemistic banter in the Bible about the size or status of other men's members. The taunting woe against the Chaldeans mocks them with the words "You will have your fill of shame instead of glory. Drink, yourself, and show your uncircumcision!" (Habakkuk 2:16). Part of the shame, in addition to the outpouring of the Lord's wrath against them as enemies of His people, will be their physical inadequacy.

There's also the peculiar interaction of Rehoboam and Jeroboam in 1 Kings 12. At the twilight of his life, King Solomon turned from worshiping the Lord and allowed worship of the false gods of the neighboring countries. Thus, the Lord vowed to take the territory and lordship of ten tribes of Israel away from his son and heir, Rehoboam (ch. 11), and give them to Jeroboam, one of Solomon's servants. Solomon, therefore, tried to kill Jeroboam, but he escaped into Egypt (v. 40). After Solomon's death, Jeroboam came back from exile to ask for Rehoboam's mercy to reduce the oppressive load Solomon had imposed on the Israelites before his death. Not knowing how to answer, Rehoboam sent the envoy away for three days. He then sought the counsel of his father's advisors, who told him, "If you will be a servant to this people today and serve them, and speak good words to them when you answer them, then they will be your servants forever" (12:7). But Rehoboam rejected this advice and instead asked his friends. They advised, "Thus shall you speak to this people who said to you, 'Your father made our yoke heavy, but you lighten it for us,' thus shall you say to them, 'My little finger is thicker than my father's thighs'" (v. 10). If you understand that the word translated "thigh" or "waist" is elsewhere used as a euphemism for that which hangs between a man's thighs, you catch the drift of what these guys want Rehoboam to say. "My little finger dwarfs my dad's manhood! You thought things were bad under Solomon? I'm a bigger man than he. You ain't seen nothin' yet."

Likely no one can adequately explain the Lord's exceedingly odd rebuke for His people through the prophet Ezekiel in Ezekiel 23. However, in a discussion of penises in the Old Testament, we would be remiss not to deal with this: "Yet she increased her whoring, remembering the days of her youth, when she played the whore in the land of Egypt and lusted after her lovers there, whose members were like those of donkeys, and whose issue was like that of horses" (vv. 19–20).

God compares the divided kingdom, now Israel in the North and Judah in the South, to two made-up sisters, Oholah and Oholibah. (Comparisons of idolatry to adultery are frequent and quite appropriate throughout Ezekiel's prophecy.) Oholah, or the Northern Kingdom, "played the whore" with her lovers, the Assyrians. But things didn't end well for Oholah or for the Kingdom of Israel, sacked by the Assyrians in 722 BC.

Undeterred by her elder sister's whoring and subsequent destruction, Oholibah "became more corrupt than her sister in her lust and in her whoring, which was worse than that of her sister" (v. 11). She lusted after the Assyrians. She lusted after the Chaldeans. And then, remembering her youthful indiscretions with the Egyptians (remember, the Israelites were slaves there), with her memories magnified by the progress of time, she recalled the donkey-sized members and horse-quantity issue of her lovers there, and lusted for them as well. The tl;dr[14] version is that adulterous idolatry doesn't go any better for Oholibah. The Southern Kingdom of Judah was destroyed by the Babylonians in 586 BC. Not even the big show of masculinity from the Egyptians could protect poor Oholibah. Her lovers became her destroyers. What she needed was fidelity to her first Lover, the Lord Himself, who exemplifies the masculine work of protecting and providing.

Even before there was a medical diagnosis and a blue pill to identify and fix physical dysfunctions of manhood, there was a gradual descent from the perfect masculinity that appeared for a brief, shining moment in Eden. Death entered. Lives got shorter. Suffering and sickness entered the healthy, happy creation. People lost original righteousness, and with it, it seems, the full functionality of their bodies too. Damaged manhood could exclude a man from serving in the temple or even assembling there for temple rites and worship. But sex was marked with a sign of God's promise to provide a Savior for His people. The Savior would be a man just like Adam, the first man. So this interest in the organs that, in part, make a man a man, has the function of pointing forward to the Man to come, to fulfill the promise God made in the garden.

Man's struggle to be genuinely masculine is as old as the fall, which is just a week or so shy of being as old as the world. (More on this to come later.) Since that first man abdicated his responsibilities to protect and provide, all the rest of us who've inherited his sin along with his Y chromosome have been heirs to this struggle.

14 That's millennial speak for "too long; didn't read."

You can get a sense of this struggle in the numerous ways the enemies of God's people are threatened with emasculation. It's not good for a man to be womanly, to be made less than a man.

- "In that day the Egyptians will be like women, and tremble with fear before the hand that the LORD of hosts shakes over them" (Isaiah 19:16).

- (To the Ninevites) "Behold, your troops are women in your midst. The gates of your land are wide open to your enemies; fire has devoured your bars" (Nahum 3:13).

- "A sword against her horses and against her chariots, and against all the foreign troops in her midst, that they may become women!" (Jeremiah 50:37).

- "The warriors of Babylon have ceased fighting; they remain in their strongholds; their strength has failed; they have become women" (Jeremiah 51:30).

Even strong warriors are reduced to women when the Lord bares His arm to fight for His people.

Since that fateful moment in the garden, masculinity has been as much of a challenge as it is a holy calling. It no longer comes naturally. But we're in this together, man. Press on. Hope is not far away.

BOOT CAMP

MAN DOWN

1. Disordered masculinity is self-serving, self-centered, and self-preserving. How do you observe these sinful tendencies in yourself? In the way society portrays men?

2. What are the manly opposites of these disordered traits?

3. Circumcision was God's way of marking people, albeit only the males, as His own. Read Colossians 2:8–15. To what practice of the Church did circumcision point forward? According to St. Paul, what benefits has this "circumcision made without hands," the putting off of your sinful flesh in Holy Baptism, accomplished?

4. What is meant by the "order of creation"? How is the fall disorder?

THE DESCENT OF MAN

"In adversities we should shew ourselves like men and pluck up good spirits."

—Martin Luther, The Familiar Discourses of Dr. Martin Luther

"There has got abroad a notion, somehow, that if you become a Christian you must sink your manliness and turn milksop."

—C. H. Spurgeon (1834–92)

Being a man in a fallen world; fighting against your own sinful inclinations to be self-serving, self-preserving, and self-centered; and heeding the call to procreate, protect, and provide for your family and community in a God-pleasing way would be difficult enough if you had everyone around you cheering you on. But you don't. In fact, masculinity is under assault from all directions. Many people want you to fail in these tasks, to abdicate your call, to abandon your post, to chuck masculinity into the dustbin of history and take up the mantle of effeminacy under the banner of egalitarianism. As if it weren't hard enough for man to fight against his sinful flesh to exercise genuine, biblical masculinity, now he also has to contend against forces that believe this masculinity is harmful to the world.

WHICH CAME FIRST: THE CHICKEN OR THE FEMINIST?

It's easy to shrug off masculinity. It's hard work to be a man. It's not natural, not since the fall, anyway. Although your genes make you genetically a man, your reproductive organs hang (proudly or shamefully) on the exterior of your corpus, and your endocrine system produces testosterone that makes your muscles bigger than your sister's or your mother's, using those male traits in an authentically masculine way is not programmed into your genes. It requires a daily struggle against your selfish nature.

Given that it's easier by nature to be effeminate than masculine and to be selfish rather than serving, it's easy to understand why men seem not only reticent for this duty, but also glad that women no longer expect them to conform to this higher calling. Remember the curses doled out after the fall? To Eve, God declared, "Your desire shall be contrary to your husband, but he shall rule over you" (Genesis 3:16). Submission to Adam's authority no longer comes naturally. Genuine femininity no longer comes naturally to the ladies either. So both sexes are complicit in the loss of these divinely ordained roles. Adam doesn't mind letting Eve run things if that means he gets to check out and play video games or spend evenings absorbed in the buzz of beer and *SportsCenter*. Eve doesn't mind Adam's abdication if it lets her compete on an equal footing, put on a pantsuit, and get a job in Corporate Eden. The way is broad and easy that leads to egalitarianism.

So, which came first? Adam's abdication or Eve's usurping? The coward or the shrew? The chicken or the feminist? Did men stop knowing what it meant to be men first? Or did women first begin to disabuse men of the qualities that made them intrinsically masculine, qualities like power, courage, impulsiveness, and independence?

Men have certainly lost their moorings. Assigning blame perhaps matters less than identifying a solution and moving forward. And being a man and playing the victim card have never been compatible. But moving forward will require us to know what we're up against and to identify how far we've fallen from the masculine ideal.

THE F-WORD

Feminism is a word that covers quite a breadth of meaning. And, as a philosophy of a movement, it spans quite a timeline, with different phases, or "waves." Depending whom you ask, feminism began in roughly the nineteenth century as a reaction against the Victorian notions of a "feminine ideal" that included certain roles and expectations for women, as well as a push for women to have the same rights as men. What most consider the "first wave" of feminism was the drive in the late nineteenth and early twentieth centuries for equal rights for women in the political sphere. The movement climaxed with the passage of the Nineteenth Amendment of the Constitution, granting women the right to vote.

This was hardly the end of the movement, as population-control front-woman Margaret Sanger and others rode the coattails of the movement to treat women as people and gain societal acceptance for the use of birth control and, eventually, abortion. Freeing women from the biological consequences of sex and the burdens of unwanted motherhood through legal access to chemicals or devices that isolated sex from procreation paved the way for women to be "liberated" from distinctly feminine roles and emancipated from needing a man for any other purpose than sexual pleasure.

Yet merely having the same political rights as men did not achieve the goal of setting women free from the cultural expectations that the inherent differences between men and women equip them for different roles and responsibilities within society. After what seems to the outside observer of the feminist movement like a hiatus at the end of World War II, the so-called second wave of feminism began in the 1960s with the goal of liberating women from roles imposed on them by society and biology. Betty Friedan's *The Feminine Mystique* of 1963 became the manifesto for the next wave of the feminist movement. Friedan wanted to shatter the image of a woman finding happiness and fulfillment through the roles of wife and mother.

Although, on paper and in theory, women had gained equal standing with men in the realm of rights, they nevertheless faced societal obstacles and cultural barriers (not to mention some biological ones) to doing anything a man could do. It was this second wave of feminism that changed abortion from a question of the rights of unborn human beings to a question of the reproductive rights of a woman, leading to the decriminalization of abortion in 1973.

A third wave of feminism emerged in the 1990s as a criticism of the second wave's apparent failure to accomplish enough for minority women and as a critique of the binary understanding of gender, which was still implicit in feminism of the sixties and seventies. This third wave of feminism has advocated for the rights of lesbian and minority women, as well as paved the way for conversations about the rights of homosexuals and transgenders.

A WOMAN NEEDS A MAN . . .

Although it's important to understand the effects of feminism, for our purposes in exploring masculinity, we're less concerned about the effects the different waves of the feminist movement have had on women and more concerned with their effects on men. Treating women as equals in the political sphere—giving them ordinary human rights like owning property and participating in our republican democracy—hardly seems controversial today, though this has shifted our understanding of the building blocks of society from *families* to *individuals*. If voting is determined by age, for instance, instead of by owning property or being under a father's household rule, there is less incentive to keep a family together in order to have a stake in the community.[15]

At the risk of overgeneralizing, we can tease out the effects of feminism's waves by examining the way each wave viewed men. The first wave of feminism saw men and women as equals and fought for women to be given the same rights in society as men. The second wave of feminism saw men as unnecessary and sought to liberate a woman from the notion that she needed a man in her life. The third wave of feminism and feminism still today sees men as inferior to and less capable than women.

BOYS ARE STUPID?

In second-wave feminism, the creed became "A woman needs a man like a fish needs a bicycle." The point was clear. Fish don't need bicycles. Women, therefore, don't need men. But the thought that men are unnecessary has now changed.

15 For a more thorough treatment of the harmful effects even of first-wave feminism, see the article "Emancipated Surf" by Rebekah Curtis in the March/April 2016 edition of *Touchstone Magazine*.

No longer are men simply superfluous in a woman's quest for happiness and fulfillment. Now they're detrimental. The tenor of feminism has changed from "Men are unnecessary" to "Men are bad." The slogans have changed. The women whose cars sported bumper stickers with "A woman needs a man like a fish needs a bicycle" are raising daughters wearing shirts that say, "Boys are stupid; throw rocks at them."

Apparently empowering girls and enabling them to be strong and independent of men is no longer sufficient. Is respect for the sexes a zero-sum game? Can only one sex be esteemed, and only at the expense of the other? We would balk at a shirt worn by a man that advocates violence toward women, so why is it acceptable for a girl to wear a shirt saying that boys deserve to have rocks thrown at them by virtue of their Y chromosomes and inherent stupidity? Imagine the outcry if boys showed up to school donning shirts saying, "Girls are annoying; push them down the stairs." That dog don't hunt.

So why the shift in feminist ideology from rights for women to male bashing? On the one hand, there's a nearly universal cry among young, unmarried women, wondering "Where have all the good men gone?" On the other hand is the insinuation that men simply *aren't* good. Men are simultaneously being upbraided for traits that are inherent to their masculinity and then excoriated for not possessing the traits that real men should have and real women desire.

In January of 2012, when the *Costa Concordia* ran aground, tilted, and began to sink, albeit partially, off the shore of Tuscany, reports started to emerge of the men who pushed aside women and children to get to the lifeboats first. News outlets lamented the loss of masculinity and chivalry that, in ages past, would have seen "women and children first" into the safety of lifeboats. In her book *Men on Strike*, Helen Smith responds,

> The guys' behavior is a culmination that has been years in the making. Our society, the media, the government, women, white knights and Uncle Toms have regulated and demanded that any incentives men have for acting like men be taken away and decried masculinity as evil. Now they are seeing the result. Men have been listening to what society has been saying about them for more than forty years; they are perverts, wimps, cowards, assholes, jerks, good-for-nothing, bumbling deadbeats and expendable. Men got the message; now they are acting accordingly. As you sow, so shall you reap.[16]

If the goal is equality—for the fair treatment of women—no one can disagree. If the goal is sameness—flattening differences between men and women and arguing that anything a man can do, a woman can too—logic and simple observation will testify otherwise. If the goal is to exalt women by denigrating men and diminishing masculine traits, women will, as Smith says, reap what they sow. Men will rise or sink to the expectations made of them. If expected to be men, they will be. If expected to be selfish jerks, they will be.

Which came first, a loss of the masculine ideal or a rise in feminism? And which has had a more deleterious effect on our present state of masculinity? It's difficult to say. Both have left us in our modern-day predicament. Men are confused. They've lost a sense of what it means to be men. Thus, men are less desirable to women as lifelong companions, and women are questioning whether they need a man at all. Men have forgotten what the calling to be a good man entails; while women, at the

16 Helen Smith, *Men on Strike: Why Men Are Boycotting Marriage, Fatherhood, and the American Dream—and Why It Matters* (New York: Encounter Books, 2013), 120–21.

same time, have sought to disabuse men of those qualities that are unique to masculinity—traits like courage, sacrifice, power, desire, and impulsiveness.

CITY OF THE SAME

This two-pronged attack on masculinity—the abandonment by men of their callings to be leaders, protectors, and providers alongside the battle cry of the feminists to push beyond mere equality into the domain of female privilege and male-bashing—has constructed a new kind of society. In this new society, City of the Same, there are new rules and new structures.

THE LAW OF THE LAND

In City of the Same, people are quintessentially individual. There are no assigned roles; each person is free to choose roles based on his or her proclivities and preferences. Articulating any differences between men and women is anathema. Men can do what women can do; women can do what men can do.

In City of the Same, the nurture of children is entrusted to the community more than to a mother and a father. It is often said that it takes a village to raise a child; well, in this new society, the village is better equipped to raise a child than the biological parents.

In City of the Same, there are universal virtues, not masculine or feminine virtues. All people, regardless of gender, are to be nice, tolerant, accepting, loving, hardworking, and open-minded. In City of the Same, feminism has triumphed. Men neither hold any position of prominence or esteem nor are they called to do anything extraordinary.

In City of the Same, you will be ostracized for thinking that there are some jobs better suited for men than women and some tasks that women are more capable of accomplishing than men. It is a thought crime in City of the Same to expect men and women to behave differently.

In City of the Same, not even biology determines a person's fate. Sex characteristics (the hardware) are alterable with hormone therapy and sex-reassignment surgeries. You are free to find the gender you prefer, and you have far more than the antiquated binary choice of male or female from which to choose. In this city, neither biologically-assigned gender nor its natural sexual expression is fixed. You are free to be what you feel like and have sex with whomever you prefer.

In City of the Same, diversity of people with uniformity of thinking is the only creed. Believe what we tell you. Disobedience is intolerable.

THE NEW SCHOOLHOUSE ORDER

In the schoolhouse of City of the Same, boys are taught to behave like girls. Rambunctiousness is discouraged. If you cannot control your sons, there are medications we can prescribe.

Boys are taught alongside girls and expected to learn like girls, sitting still—not fidgeting—reading, listening, quietly absorbing. Yet, while these are desirable characteristics for those who possess them, many boys do not. By nature, boys move. They're active. They're like a hypercaffeinated, manic adult wrapped in the thin veneer of child's skin. They fidget. They hum. They drum. They stand and pace. Their attention seems to wander.

Teachers in City of the Same—most of whom still remain women, though this is purely a product of their own choices and not any latent maternal or nurturing instincts—have no time or patience for dealing with frenetic boy energy. Thus, the solution is to excise it, to treat it as a malfunction of normal humanity, to medicate against it and prescribe Ritalin to take the edge off.

Being a boy is not a disease, though rates of diagnoses for ADD or ADHD and medication prescribed to keep boys sedentary and calm seem to suggest otherwise. Depending on the statistic, rates for ADD and ADHD are three to six times higher for boys than girls. Either there's something attached to their prepubescent Y chromosomes that predisposes little boys to fidgety distraction or those symptoms we're medicating against are merely part of the psyche of little boys. But in City of the Same, different traits are symptoms of a failure of the society to iron out inconsistencies between the sexes. Medication is preferable to coming up with a different educational approach for boys versus that for girls. Sameness is the motto, even if it takes chemicals to get boys to behave in feminized schools.

HOME SWEET HOME

In City of the Same, it matters little whether there is a father *and* a mother in the home. A parent is a parent, and differences between what men and women bring to the rearing of their children are ignored for the sake of equality.

There is no appreciable difference between husbands and wives. The role of each spouse is simply to love the other, until that love proves too difficult, of course, and then no-fault divorces are quite common and acceptable in City of the Same. Love is synonymous with affection, and, in this egalitarian utopia, when it's over, it's over. In City of the Same, each participant in this relationship prefers to be called a "spouse," as this covers over any expected differences between the male spouse or the female spouse. Once the shift from husband and wife to coequal spouses was effected, and the procreative function of marriage was eliminated, it was only natural and expected that the marital union be opened to any two (but why stop there?) people who are committed to one another with an appropriate level of affection. Male and female are equal and interchangeable in City of the Same.

Moreover, in this paradise, there are no prescribed household roles. This makes the quest for a spouse more difficult, as complementarity is resigned outside the ordinary categories of biology. Although different anatomy was once an adequate indicator to know that another person would make a suitable lifelong helper, now City of the Same must rely on intricate computer matrices to pair its inhabitants with lifetime mates. (Can we even say "mates" anymore, if the mating function is merely accidental to marriage?)

It's no longer a question of who does the laundry, who does the dishes, and who gives the lawn mower its annual tune-up. All tasks, like all people, are essentially the same, whether in the economics of the household or the upbringing of children. The lament in City of the Same about a single mother is no longer that her children are deprived of their father, but that she is deprived of the help another body could provide. Biological connection to children or complementarity characteristics to mom's are nothing to be prized anymore. All she needs (if she will acknowledge any need at all) is another set of hands. If more hands on deck are all that's desirable, though, as long as the hands are connected to bodies that love the bodies from which other arms and hands proceed, there's no reason to arbitrarily limit the number of adult participants in the household to two. More hands make lighter work. And, in City of the Same, the less you have to work, the more successful you must be.

ZOMBIES IN THE STREET

The streets in City of the Same are populated with those who used to have certain, productive means of occupying their time. Now that men are the same as women, there are displaced men wandering the streets. This is an unfortunate development, and one that shows the infancy of this noble experiment. As the city matures, these men will find their rightful new places. Although women are liberated and empowered in this new society, some men have had difficulty adapting to their redefined roles. There are three kinds of men of whom to be wary.

The effeminate man has succumbed to the societal pressures around him to be "nice." He is the perfect candidate for citizenship in City of the Same, but he's been displaced. Since everyone is the same, he has lost his male uniqueness, his distinct masculinity. Sure, he's nice. Sure, he's accommodating. But he's nearly accommodated himself out of the picture. He's unnecessary. Instead of inhabiting the house where he used to serve as a capable and competent breadwinner, he's lost in the streets, wandering around without an identity. His past girlfriends told him that if he were nicer, softer, more open to new roles and revisions of what it means to be men and women, he would fit better in this emerging society. But now he's lost. His acquiescence to the culture has left him adrift, without any meaning or purpose.

This soft man is quick to bend to the whims of the culture or an assertive woman. He's not quite like the man we profiled in the first chapter whose vice is *malakia*. That guy was purely selfish. This soft, effeminate man is not. He's quite selfless. He wants to give, to help, to serve. But he has lost his masculine moorings that teach him what the essence of giving, loving, helping, and serving are.

Now he simply rolls over to the demands of women and culture around him. Although these traits were originally praised in City of the Same, he finds himself unable to cope. Lacking purpose for his life, without a responsible way to harness his strength and ambition, he has nothing to do but wander the streets of the city and wait for someone to tell him what to do next. Eventually, he'll be the perfect fit in City of the Same, but until then, he's got some masculine energy to unlearn or simply repress.

The man-child, on the other hand, has never quite acquired those masculine sensibilities. He remains, for all intents and purposes, a boy. It's not that he's malicious in his immaturity. It's just that no one has ever expected anything of him. He's a product of the emerging City of the Same, wherein he's never been taught what masculinity means. He's fixated on himself, his own wants, desires, pleasures, and predilections.

In part, his existence has been manufactured by his culture. Whereas boys need some kind of rite of passage to know they've become men, in this new city, those kinds of rites have been eschewed as antiquated relics of a bygone era. In that past era, perhaps, to the detriment and subjugation of women, boys were brought through some ordeal to make them men. But in the new city, a man's drive to procreate, protect, and provide is actually disruptive to societal order. These are desires that ought not be drawn out or expressed.

Men as men no longer matter in City of the Same. If a man's physical prowess, courage, and ability to risk himself for the good of others are no longer prized qualities, why can't he just hang out in the basement of his parents' house playing World of Warcraft and getting a moderate beer buzz? If no one needs him, he should be free to indulge his selfish inclinations. What's the incentive for a man to grow up and see himself as a means for the ultimate good of others when this involves an unavoidable element of sacrifice and self-abandonment? If no one expects this anymore, don't give it.

Finally, there's *the compensating man*. He's naturally an outsider in City of the Same. He refuses to be the same. He feels the dull ache of something missing in his life, as society has asked him to suppress his masculinity. So he compensates. Masculinity for him becomes a caricature. Instead of protecting, masculinity is just about the superficial evidence that he could protect, if called on: big muscles. Or maybe, lacking these and the mirror in the gym in front of which he can happily prance, he settles for the evidence of his ability to be a provider, should anyone actually ever call on him to provide: big tools. Although a big truck is not a substitute for big muscles, it will have to do in a pinch.[17]

Hypermasculinity is really not masculinity at all, any more than those big-head pictures the caricaturist draws of you at the amusement park are really a true-to-life depiction of what you look like. Caricatures nevertheless abound. Hypermasculinity is the result of desperate men trying to respond to a culture that has asked them to be more like women than men, to be passive, soft, receptive, and meek. So, expectedly, they've responded by moving in the opposite direction. The powers who rule over City of the Same do not understand the real essence of masculinity, so their attempts to curtail man's posture and prowess are met by heel-digging-in reactions that retreat into a fake version of masculinity.

17 This is spoken from experience. When no one at the gym is as fixated on my biceps and trapezius as I am, I hope that they will at least notice the old school F-350 dually with the dump bed I climb in to drive home. Your lifted Silverado with the 24-inch rims and low profile tires is cute, and I'm sure your girlfriend likes having to be hoisted into it, but when you need to do some actual work, you can call me.

The hypermasculine man is incredibly insecure.[18] Masculinity is not simply about power, prowess, or the ability to procreate. Masculinity is not about how strong you are, how big your paycheck is, or how many women you can bed. Those are peripheral to the heart of masculinity. The hypermasculine man is almost worse than the soft, feminized man because his depiction of masculinity converts others against the cause of masculinity. If, seeing him, they conclude that masculinity is just self-indulgence and insecurity, they will deduce that the feminists are right and the man needs to be tamed and emasculated. The hypermasculine man is volatile and afraid. In City of the Same, he is compensating for what has been taken away from him. But who can blame him?

There are those who hypothesize that the plague of violence in society is really a result of our damaged notion of masculinity. As early as 1973, psychologist Erich Fromm theorized that the man who inflicts violence on others does so due to feelings of powerlessness and impotency; he desires to take control of others in order to compensate for his own powerlessness.[19]

Drawing on Fromm's insight, Peter Langman, a psychologist who has studied school shootings for the past fifteen years, concluded that boys who feel a sense of damaged masculinity resort to external forms of power, like guns and violence, to compensate for the lack of power they feel in themselves.[20] Intentional violence is the opposite of masculinity, but when men watch their natural masculine drives and desires denigrated as harmful to society, who can wonder when they lash out

18 Seriously. Have you *seen* my truck?

19 Erich Fromm, *The Anatomy of Human Destructiveness* (New York: Holt, Rinehart and Winston, 1973), 292.

20 Peter Langman, *Why Kids Kill: Inside the Minds of School Shooters* (New York: St. Martin's, 2009), 28–29.

violently? There's never an excuse for violence. Never. Men have been endowed with power, strength, and courage for the good of others, not for their own good. But when others no longer want the benefit of that masculine energy, it may find a harmful outlet elsewhere. Thus the compensating man of City of the Same finds the expression of his masculinity in wrongheaded or harmful ways, but given the opportunity, he would certainly channel these gifts toward healthier, more helpful ends. Those helpful ends are against the laws of City of the Same, though.

CHURCHES FOR GIRLS

In City of the Same, churches have ceased to be places where men are accepted. Although Christianity is the product of a Man who called twelve other men to follow Him, somehow in City of the Same, pews are largely populated with women.

In his book, *The Church Impotent*, researcher Leon Podles traces a shift in the history of the Church from seeing the role of the individual Christian as distinctly masculine to seeing the role of the Christian today as typically feminine.[21] Indeed, there is something distinctly masculine about being a Christian. St. Paul describes all the baptized as *sons* of God:

> But now that faith has come, we are no longer under a guardian, for in Christ Jesus you are all sons of God, through faith. For as many of you as were baptized into Christ have put on Christ. There is neither Jew nor Greek, there is neither slave nor free, there is no male and female, for you are all one in Christ Jesus. And if you are Christ's, then

21 See *The Church Impotent: The Feminization of Christianity* (Dallas: Spence Pub, 1999).

> you are Abraham's offspring, heirs according to promise. (Galatians 3:25–29)

Why sons? Sons were heirs. In the same way still today that traditionally sons retain the family name and daughters are given the family name of the man they marry (and therewith his property and inheritance), so in Jewish law, it was the son who could receive an inheritance. What Paul says is quite radical, then. It's the answer to the question Jesus is asked repeatedly about how to *inherit* eternal life (Mark 10:17; Luke 10:25; 18:18). It's a foolish question, if ever there was one. You can't *do* something to *inherit* something. It's akin to asking what I can do to inherit the crown of England. Answer: nothing. Sorry, pal, but unless you're born into the right family, you're outta luck.

So, Paul says, Baptism is that rebirth into the right family. It makes you a son of God. Even girls are made metaphorical sons in Baptism because they're made heirs with Christ of the treasures of heaven. Thus, there's an inherent masculinity simply to being made a Christian through the waters of Holy Baptism. Every Christian is a son of God.

There's a femininity to being a Christian too. If the essence of masculinity is to give; a significant part of what it means to be feminine is to receive. Inasmuch as receptivity is the posture of every Christian toward God, every Christian also has a feminine side, though this does not change "sons of God" into "daughters of God." It simply means Christians learn from their Mother (the Church) how to receive from their Father (God).

Moreover, the Church herself is pictured as a woman, the Bride of Christ. These are separate metaphors though. The individual Christian is not the Bride of Christ. Christ is monogamous. He has one Bride. Everyone who is made a part of His Church is a part of His holy, redeemed Bride. This was the normal narrative the Church told and Christians understood for the first thousand years of the Christian Church. Podles locates the shift from seeing the Bride of Christ as Jesus' beloved to seeing the individual believer as the object of His intimate affection in the writings of Bernard of Clairvaux, a twelfth-century French monk.

Although Bernard is not the first to speak of the individual person as the Bride of Christ, his interpretation of Song of Songs as a romance between Christ and the individual believer was a watershed moment in the loss of masculinity in the Church, according to Podles:

> The transfer of the role of the bride from the community to the soul has helped bring about the pious individualism that has dissolved ecclesiastical community in the West. The Church is the bride and the object of the heavenly bridegroom's love, and individuals are the objects of that love only insofar as they are members or potential members of the society of the redeemed. The Church should yearn for the presence of her bridegroom, who consoles her and makes her fruitful in good works and children. This imagery was natural to the Fathers but has been lost. Instead the individual is felt to be the center of God's affections . . . and the only real concern of Christianity is "Jesus and me." . . . For men the consequences have been disastrous. Bridal language used to describe a Christian's relationship with God has homosexual overtones to manly men, unless they engage in mental gymnastics and try to think of themselves as women. . . . Bridal mysticism and the metaphors and attitudes to which it gave rise have placed a major obstacle to men's participation in the Church.[22]

22 Podles, *The Church Impotent*, 118–19.

It's difficult for run-of-the-mill heterosexual men to identify with being Jesus' lover. And many theologians have lamented the fact that much of what passes for music in the Church today are love songs to Jesus with lyrics that could just as easily be spoken by a husband to his wife.

Consider these examples.

Kelly Carpenter's 1999 "Draw Me Close" sets the paradigm for this kind of love song to Jesus. It continues to this day to be covered by various worship bands and is regularly rotated among worship medleys in church: "You are my desire / No one else will do / 'Cause nothing else could take Your place / To feel the warmth of your embrace . . . / You're all I want / You're all I've ever needed / You're all I want / Help me know You are near." My wife would swoon if I spoke to her that way. I'm not sure Jesus has the same head-over-heels reaction.

Although already a decade old, "How He Loves" by John Mark McMillan has been covered by numerous contemporary Christian music artists and endures as a popular worship song. Sing along if you know it. "So heaven meets earth like a sloppy wet kiss / And my heart turns violently inside of my chest, / I don't have time to maintain these regrets / When I think about the way / That He loves us / Whoa, how He loves us / Whoa, how He loves us / Whoa, how He loves . . ." Not even Bernard of Clairvaux spoke of the affection Jesus has for Christians culminating in a "sloppy, wet kiss."

Michael W. Smith's "Breathe" has Christians singing over and over again, "I'm desperate for you . . . I'm lost without you." Matt Redman's "Let My Words Be Few" contains these few words: "The simplest of all love songs / I want to bring to You, / So I'll let my words be few / Jesus, I am so in love with You." The song "Madly" by Passion Band repeats the line, "We are madly in love with you."

Then there's the always-creepy "In the Secret" by the band MercyMe: "In the secret, / In the quiet place / In the stillness you are there . . . I want to touch you / I want to see your face / I want to know you more." Ew. Taken out of the context of worship, this sounds more like the petition of a horny, desperate teenager—not words you would sing to a God in the presence of whose holiness, people regularly fall down in fear and cry out for mercy (Isaiah 6:5; Matthew 2:11; Mark 3:11; Luke 5:8; Revelation 5:8).

Admittedly, these songs are not the newest nor presently the most popular praise and worship songs. The last few years have actually seen a remarkable upswing in the theological depth of such songs, with many new songs simply being innovative takes on older hymns. Perhaps partly as a reaction to the sappy, vacuous love songs to Jesus, lots of new worship songs are refreshingly cross-focused and Christocentric. But these "Jesus, be my boyfriend" songs persist in too many praise and worship playlists. And what self-respecting guy wants to fall in love with Jesus?

Even the language of popular Christianity has been softened and feminized. What is the very essence of Christianity in many, if not most, Evangelical churches? A relationship with Jesus. This language is both absent in the New Testament and a foreign tongue to the modern man. In his important study on the role modern churches have on the church-going habits of men, David Murrow notes, "When Christ called disciples, he did not say, 'Come, have a personal relationship with me.' No, he simply said, 'Follow me.' Hear the difference? Follow me suggests a mission. A goal. But a personal relationship with Jesus suggests we're headed to Starbucks for some couple time."[23] What's a "relationship" with Jesus entail anyway? Will guys have to talk about their feelings? Although the word itself is quite unspecific (you could have an adversarial relationship with Jesus, for instance), as it's used in Evangelical parlance, "relationship" seems to imply the kind of eros love of a couple facing one another, looking into each other's eyes. It's not the friendship of two men laboring side-by-side, disciples following Jesus, heading in the same direction.

CHURCHES FOR DUDES

In a reaction against the feminization of Christianity, some churches on the outskirts of City of the Same have run to the other end of the spectrum. To their credit, they do not confess the false egalitarianism to which churches in City of the Same are required to subscribe in order to participate in the local ministerial alliance; they probably don't have the coquettish praise babes leading choruses of "Jesus I am so in love with you"; and they do encourage men to take roles as servants in the work and witness of the congregations and as the spiritual leaders of their households. But instead of settling on a confession of genuine, biblical masculinity, they embrace the other extreme of hypermasculinity. In these churches, being a pious Christian is virtually synonymous with being a "dude." Gun raffles on Father's Day? Check. Celebrating beer guts, big trucks, and hot wives? Check, check, check. Calling other men wimps or worse for failing to possess the right mix of swagger, bravado, and bullishness? Check. Sermon series that exhorts men to "grow a pair"? Pair of checks. Coarse language, overplayed bravado,

23 David Murrow, *Why Men Hate Going to Church* (Nashville: Nelson Books, 2011), 165. Copyright © 2011 by David Murrow. Used by permission of Thomas Nelson. www.thomasnelson.com.

and bullying machismo are the norm in these churches that cater (pander?) to guys.

Part of their assessment of society is correct. They rightly identify the fact that men are different from women, that they have roles different from those of women, and that they need to *man up* and live up to the biblical ideal of a man. Although the term *malakia*, softness/effeminacy, which we treated in chapter 1, is both biblical and more theologically precise than whatever insults get bandied about in the liturgies of these churches, we can, in fact, agree with the underlying premise that creation doesn't work correctly when it's disordered, when men and women, creation and the Creator, are in the wrong places.

The problem with these churches deliberately constructed outside City of the Same is not what they complain about. The problem is their solution. Men cannot reclaim their masculinity, as if it were something taken from them. They can learn to live as men. Masculinity is not about asserting one's rights. It's about using one's rights, power, courage, wisdom, etc., in serving those a man is given to serve.

It's difficult to filter the truths about masculinity from the hypermasculine hype. The contention that being a Christian is distinctly masculine is true—more on that later. But asserting that you've got to extol big trucks, big guns, and big bravado to get men to believe in Jesus? That's just pandering. And it's a far cry from *real* masculinity that sees strength and prowess (and, sure, trucks and guns, if you've got 'em) as tools to be wielded for the good of others.

The hypermasculine distortions of both masculinity and Christianity continue in the churches that have organized resistance against the feminized forces in City of the Same. In another suburb of the City are the churches that use cage fighting to sell people on Jesus. In 2009, a church in the St.

Louis area brought in a chain-link octagon for their "Easter in the Octagon" series. The point? Jesus didn't tap. Through His death, He emerged victorious and resurrected from the cage match with sin, death, and the devil. White paraments and Easter lilies were conspicuously absent, but no punches were actually thrown.

That's not the case with the seven hundred fight ministries profiled in the 2014 documentary *Fight Church*. There, the fight is the draw. Pastors moonlight as MMA fighters and host fight training during the week in the church's worship space. Profiled in the film is Pastor John "The Saint" Renken (19-28-3, 1 NC), a former MMA professional turned preacher, who says,

> Lost people are watching MMA, so I think that's where we should be.... I think that the vast majority of the problems we're having in our culture today are because we don't have a warrior ethos. We have a bunch of cowards. We've taken away their God-given attributes of aggressiveness, of competitiveness ... almost like they act like females.[24]

Competition and sport—even violent sports—are indeed manly, but they aren't precisely masculine. Knowing how to fight, how to defend oneself and others, is a skill necessary for a man to fully accomplish the calling to protect, should that need ever arise. But fighting sport has no place in the Church. It's just a gimmick. And it doesn't actually foster godly, giving masculinity.

Our made-up society is not that fictional. Most of the details of City of the Same have already come into existence. The zombie

24 John Renken, video interview by Bob Woodruff and Ben Newman, "In Jesus' Name, Throw Punches: 'Fight Church' Christian Ministries Believe in Fight Clubs," ABC News, October 3, 2014, abcnews.go.com/US/jesus-throw-punches-fight-church-christian-ministries-fight/story?id=25953786.

men who have abandoned their posts are as much to blame as the feminists who have diminished their masculinity. They're real, though. Real caricatures of how men ought to be. As such, they're aberrations. And they stand in the way of every man trying to cultivate and practice genuine masculinity.

The City of the Same, however, cannot survive—not if it relies on an egalitarian work force to maintain its infrastructure. Masculinity—male power and prowess harnessed for the good of others—is essential to society. Even those who disparage masculinity have to acknowledge masculinity bears some good fruits. The feminist Camille Paglia, who irritates other feminists, opines,

> When I cross the George Washington Bridge or any of America's great bridges, I think—*men* have done this. Construction is a sublime male poetry. When I see a giant crane passing on a flatbed truck, I pause in awe and reverence, as one would for a church procession. What power of conception, what grandiosity: these cranes tie us to ancient Egypt, where monumental architecture was first imagined and achieved. If civilization had been left in female hands, we would still be living in grass huts. A conceptual woman clapping on a hard hat merely enters a conceptual system invented by men.[25]

Paglia rightly sees the difference between men and women, though not all the rest of her colleagues in academia agree. The ivory towers of the universities in the City of the Same seem to rise above the plane of distinct gender differences into the ether where the air is thin, memory is short-lived, and imagined

25 Camille Paglia, *Sexual Personae: Art and Decadence from Nefertiti to Emily Dickinson* (New Haven, CT: Yale University, 1990), 37.

utopias have greater substance than the brick and mortar edifices in which they are dreamed. Anthony Esolen, Professor of English at Providence College, has, from a different perspective than Paglia's, observed,

> The feminist professor drives in her car, invented by men, made out of metal that men have wrested from the earth and rendered usable in infernal foundries, powered by fuel even more dangerous to draw out of the earth or the sea and to transport to distant places; she drives along roads laid by men and repaired by men at all hours and in plenty of bad weather, arriving at the building where she teaches, whose foundations were laid by men with backhoes, sledge hammers, and shovels, whose walls were set in place by men scrambling upon scaffolds, doing work that will ruin their backs by the time they are fifty; and she gives not one thought to them as she, at twice their pay, proceeds to her class in Women's Studies, where she teaches young women with smooth hands how the great monster Man has done nothing but oppress his sisters throughout all of human history, until the advent of Betty Friedan or Germaine Greer, those great titans of intellect.[26]

Who poured the foundation and laid the bricks of the ivory towers from which the feminists with their words are constructing the alternative City of the Same? Men. A society without them will soon crumble. Instead of maligning masculinity as essentially harmful or losing the exercise of masculinity in the

26 Quoted from a personal conversation I had with Dr. Esolen during which he had to endure a van full of my hungry, road-weary children. Not only was he able to hold forth eloquently on numerous topics, but he was also able to convince these children and their skeptical parents to try pizza with anchovies. Quote used with permission.

hypermasculine overreaction, we must teach men and free them to exercise their manly traits for the good of society.

MEN WITHOUT CHESTS

The result of man's slowly eroding notion of what masculinity is, coupled with society's assault on masculinity, has hollowed man out at his very core. Sometimes we speak of emasculating a man as simply removing his external genitalia. But C. S. Lewis thinks it's something more central to his identity that is removed. In *The Abolition of Man*, his critique of Britain's educational system, Lewis laments the growing plague of "men without chests."

> Such is the tragi-comedy of our situation—we continue to clamor for those very qualities we are rendering impossible. You can hardly open a periodical without coming across the statement that what our civilization needs is more "drive," or dynamism, or self-sacrifice, or "creativity." In a sort of ghastly simplicity we remove the organ and demand the function. We make men without chests and expect of them virtue and enterprise. We laugh at honor and are shocked to find traitors in our midst. We castrate and bid the geldings be fruitful.[27]

For Lewis, the chest is the mediator between the belly and the head. It's the instrument by which the head governs the body, or the rational part of man that controls the visceral part of man. It's the chest that makes a man a man. His thoughts are

27 C. S. Lewis, *The Abolition of Man* (New York: Touchstone, 1996), 36–37. Copyright © C. S. Lewis Pte. Ltd. 1943, 1946, 1978. Extract reprinted by permission.

not substance, just spirit. And his drives are purely animal. It's a chest, then, the mediating influence between reason and instinct, that makes a man a man.

In the sad irony of our predicament, in taking away the chest of masculinity, all we have are the extremes. On the one hand, man can agree with the radical feminists that his masculinity is harmful and needs to be renounced. Cerebrally, he can live and exist in a world without indulging his masculine drives. On the other hand, man can simply be the sum of his unchecked, unbridled animalistic drives. This yields the kind of faux-manliness that is hypermasculinity. Either way, without a chest, without a way to channel his desires and drives for the good of others around him, he is selfish and self-absorbed. He is an heir of his first father, Adam. But, as Lewis wrote, who can blame him? We've robbed him of his chest, and then we've complained when he simply acts in his own self-interest.

PORNOTOPIA

The effects of the degradation of masculinity are no more apparent than in the prevalence of pornography. In case you hadn't noticed, pornography is everywhere. Gone are the days when pornography was predominantly accessible by purchasing it in a brown paper bag from the convenience store. Now, anyone with an Internet connection has almost immediate access to a deluge of digital debauchery, in all flavors and perversions you can imagine, and thousands more you cannot.

Porn epitomizes the state of masculinity today. Men have forgotten how to be men, how to live their lives for the good of others. And women have stopped expecting men to behave like men and serve them as men. So men are set free from any constraints that would keep them from indulging in a pornographic binge any time they have a free moment in the day. Although pornography use is not restricted to men, seeing other people as objects is distinctly anti-masculine. Sin knows no boundary between the sexes, though even in their pornography usage, the proclivities of men and women differ. Generally speaking, men prefer visual stimulation through pictures or videos, while women gravitate toward the erotic in story.

The most comprehensive, recent statistics on pornography are available from Covenant Eyes, a provider of Internet monitoring and filtering software. The following data can be downloaded from their website.[28]

Porn by the numbers

1. From 2001 to 2007, Internet porn went from a $1-billion-a-year industry to $3-billion-a-year in the US.

2. From July 2009 to July 2010, 13 percent of all Internet searches were for erotic content.

3. Men who view pornography at least once a month: 18- to 30-year-olds, 79 percent; 31- to 49-year-olds, 67 percent; 50- to 68-year-olds, 49 percent.

4. Women who view pornography at least once a month: 18- to 30-year-olds, 76 percent; 31- to 49-year-olds, 16 percent; 50- to 68-year-olds, 4 percent.

28 "250+ Facts and Stats About Pornography," Covenant Eyes, www.covenanteyes.com/pornography-facts-and-statistics.

5. 32 percent of teens (ages 13–17) admit to intentionally accessing nude or pornographic content online. Of these, 43 percent do so on a weekly basis. Only 12 percent of parents knew their teens were accessing pornography.

6. 9 percent of 13- to 18-year-olds have sent a sext. 17 percent of 13- to 18-year-olds have received a sext.

7. 8 percent of 14- to 24-year-olds have participated in a webcam chat during which someone else performed sexual activities.

8. In a study of college students in 2009, 51 percent of male students and 32 percent of female students first viewed pornography before their teenage years (12 and younger).

9. 63 percent of adult men have looked at pornography at least one time while at work in the past three months; 38 percent have done so more than once. 36 percent of adult women have looked at pornography at least one time while at work in the past three months; 13 percent have done so more than once.

10. 64 percent of self-identified Christian men and 15 percent of self-identified Christian women view pornography at least once a month (compared to 65 percent of non-Christian men and 30 percent of non-Christian women). 37 percent of Christian men and 7 percent of Christian women view pornography at least several times a week (compared to 42 percent of

non-Christian men and 11 percent of non-Christian women).

11. In 2002, of 1,351 pastors surveyed, 54 percent said they had viewed Internet pornography within the last year, and 30 percent of these had visited within the last thirty days.

Doubtless, no matter when you read this book, these statistics are already out of date. The porn industry is growing. And it's growing because men have stopped acting like men.

Although the porn producers want you to believe it does, viewing porn doesn't make you the alpha male. This is the lie that keeps pornography big business. Porn preys on distorted masculinity. Men have lost other affirmations of their masculinity; porn gives women who seem interested, willing. But those girls don't want you. Your money, yes. You, no. Men and boys have lost the knowledge of how to give, how to live for the good of someone else. They've become selfish. They've grown accustomed to taking. Porn gives them something easy to take. It feeds their already-broken desires.

Even for people who don't view pornography, porn typifies the loss of masculinity and femininity in society. Lust is the currency of the day. Sex is about taking. College hookups, Tinder, and pick-up artistry are no different from pornography in their embrace of the culture of broken masculinity. They simply reduce the distance between the object and the objectifier. Lust is the perfect epitome of selfishness, and, thus, the antithesis to masculinity.

Modern man, if being truly masculine is his goal, is in a perilous predicament. Two equally destructive monsters threaten on opposite sides: emasculation like the six-headed Scylla, dashing manly traits into the rocks of feminism and egalitarianism, and hypermasculinity like the whirlpool Charybdis, pulling man to his self-interested destruction. The course seems pretty hopeless, which is perhaps why so many men have checked out. In fact, every one of us has failed to live up to this holy calling. Everyone except One. In Him, men have hope.

BOOT CAMP

THE DESCENT OF MAN

1. What's the difference between equality and sameness? Can men and women be equal in the world and equally valued by God without steamrolling the differences between the sexes?

2. What evidence do you see that Christianity in the West has been feminized?

3. A "man without a chest" is self-interested, acting to please only himself. What is the source of this plague of chestless men acting more for their own good than for the good of others?

4. How has a feminist society paved the way for the pornification of our culture and the widespread availability and use of pornography?

5. How is pornography the opposite of masculinity?

ECCE HOMO: BEHOLD, THE MAN!

"Awake, mankind! For your sake God has become man."

—*St. Augustine, Sermon 185*

"We have very efficiently pared the claws of the Lion of Judah, certified him 'meek and mild,' and recommended him as a fitting household pet for pale curates and pious old ladies."

—*Dorothy Sayers, Creed or Chaos*

Who even knows what manliness looks like? If everyone—*everyone!*—since Adam has been less than the ideal man, what's the point in even trying? Is masculinity an unobtainable ideal, a nice principle on paper, but not something actually attainable or doable? Well, . . . kinda.

All of us with external genitalia and Y chromosomes have had a rough go of it since Adam's effeminate rebellion. Selfishness has come more naturally to us than service; taking more easily than giving. It's as if we're all stuck in a pit. Some of us may have a better idea than others what this masculinity business is supposed to produce, but not one of us is doing well when compared to the ideal. If it were just up to us as a band of brothers to push one another up out of the mire, no one would get out. Masculinity needs a higher ideal, a better example. But first, we've gotta get out of this hole.

TAKE A KNEE, BOYS

> In the beginning was the Word, and the Word was with God, and the Word was God. He was in the beginning with God. All things were made through Him, and without Him was not any thing made that was made. In Him was life, and the life was the light of men. The light shines in the darkness, and the darkness has not overcome it. . . . And the Word became flesh and dwelt among us, and we have seen His glory, glory as of the only Son from the Father, full of grace and truth. (John 1:1–5, 14)

The importance and profundity of this cannot be overstated: the Word became flesh. In my study, I have a framed page of the beginning of the Gospel according to St. John from an old Latin Bible, a couple hundred years old. Written in red in brackets at verse 14, it says, "[*hic genuflectitur*]" or "genuflect here." And then verse 14 is in all caps: "*ET VERBUM CARO FACTUS EST*." How strange, right? Before typing with the caps lock key was the preferred way for the technologically obtuse to send emails that you immediately want to delete, it was used here to maximize the visual impact of this verse. "THE WORD BECAME FLESH." And the rubric in the text of Holy Writ commands the reader or hearer to genuflect. In other words, take a knee, boys. The incarnation is so significant that it arrests the reader in the middle of his reading and elicits this act of reverent worship. To bend the knee is to worship the God who took human flesh.

That's what John confesses. Who is the Word? Who is the one with God, who is God, who was with God in the beginning, through whom all things were created? The Second Person of the triune God, God the Son. He is the Word. He is eternal, just as God the Father and God the Holy Spirit are eternal.

And then, the eternal Second Person of the one, true, triune God descended from His eternal throne to take up residence in the womb of a young, virgin girl. God became man. Suddenly, for all of us descendants of Adam, there is hope.

There is an old tradition in the Sunday morning church service to bow the knee at the words "and was made man" in the Nicene Creed. This is presumably why that page from the Bible includes this stage direction at John 1:14. The tradition of genuflecting at the words of the creed that confess the incarnation—the enfleshment—of the Son of God was so well-established by the time of the Reformation that in a Christmas Day sermon, Martin Luther could include this story:

> The following tale is told about a coarse and brutal lout. While the words "And was made man" were being sung in church, he remained standing, neither genuflecting nor removing his hat. He showed no reverence, but just stood there like a clod. All the others dropped to their knees when the Nicene Creed was prayed and chanted devoutly. Then the devil stepped up to him and hit him so hard it made his head spin. He cursed him gruesomely and said: "May hell consume you, you boorish ass! If God had become an angel like me and the congregation sang: 'God was made an angel,' I would bend not only my knees but my whole body to the ground! Yes, I would crawl ten ells down into the ground. And you vile human creature, you stand there like a stick or a stone. You hear that God

> did not become an angel but a man like you, and you just stand there like a stick of wood!" Whether this story is true or not, it is nevertheless in accordance with the faith (Rom. 12:6). (LW 22:105)

Imagine if your pastor used a sermon illustration like that! "I heard a story the other day about the devil going to church . . ." After describing the devil's sucker-punching the guy, the pastor concludes, "I can't say whether this actually happened, but it certainly agrees with what we confess about Jesus."

God became man. Fully man. Perfect man. The Creator is a human being. It's difficult to say it more beautifully than this verse from the fifth-century poem, *Carmen Paschale.*

> Behold, the world's creator wears
> The form and fashion of a slave;
> Our very flesh our maker shares,
> His fallen creatures all to save. (*LSB* 385:2)

God was an embryo. And a zygote. And a blastocyst. And a fetus. And an infant. And a toddler. And an adolescent. And a teenager. And a young man. And a man.

God has flesh and bones. DNA and Y chromosomes. Skin and teeth. Two arms, two eyes, two legs, two lungs, one penis, and two testicles. In the person of Jesus, God is a man.

That's worth taking a knee in humility and using the moment to contemplate the profundity.

CIRCUMSCRIBED AND CIRCUMCISED

Certainly, you've heard the assertion that we should not put God in a box. What those who cite this maxim intend to say is this: don't limit what God can do. I guess it's similar to the saying, "Don't put a period where God placed a comma." Apparently, God likes run-on sentences and comma splices and is a little claustrophobic when it comes to cardboard cubes.

If the point of the saying is that God is bigger, more powerful, more grandiose, more awesome, or whatever, that's certainly true, but so what? It's not like God is in danger of getting stuck in a metaphorical box of human thought. The greater danger is not putting the Creator of all things within limits. The greater danger is not finding the Creator when He puts Himself in a box in order that He may be found, simply because some well-meaning but dead-wrong friend saw it on a bumper sticker and warned you not to put God in a box. If God puts Himself in a box, you should get over your fear of boxes.

This is what we confess about the incarnation. God became man. The Creator limited Himself to the box of human flesh, the bounds of skin and bones. The One who has the whole world in His hands now has hands roughly the size of your dad's. If God puts Himself in a box, you darn well better look for Him in that box. If you want to find God, look in the box. If you want to know God, you've got to know Jesus, the incarnate God.

In the garden, Adam and Eve's transgression was that they crossed the boundary established for them, breaching the limits of creatures and trying to make themselves their own gods. So the Creator's solution to their boundary transgression was to place Himself within their bounds. The incarnation circumscribes the Second Person of the Trinity to the body of Jesus. He has a specificity and a locatedness. For a time, He was carried in the specific place of His mother's womb. Then, having given birth, she wrapped Him in swaddling clothes and placed God into the box of the manger, a feed trough. The account of the evangelists, the Gospel writers, is one of specificity. Jesus went places. He did things. He spoke to people. Sometimes they touched Him. In Jesus, you can find God. God, who by His nature is constrained by neither time nor place in the incarnation, is bound to a specific time and place.

And then, when He was a mere eight days outside of the womb of His mother, the circumscribed God became the circumcised God. After the angelic chorus had subsided and the shepherds had returned to their sheep, St. Luke recorded, "At the end of eight days, when He was circumcised, He was called Jesus, the name given by the angel before He was conceived in the womb" (2:21).

Even if the second verse of "Away in a Manger" is correct, and "no crying He makes" when He was born (though it's doubtful, since He was a real human baby, and crying is one of the two spiritual gifts God gives to all babies), when that flint knife removed the foreskin of the divine Baby, you better believe He screamed. The silent night was broken by the cry of the Word become Flesh who then had slightly less flesh than He had on the seventh day of His life *ex utero*.

On the eighth day of Christmas, then, the Church Year gives to you the Feast of the Circumcision and Name of Jesus. You thought it was just New Year's Day? Nope. January 1 is the day on which Christians worldwide celebrate the simultaneous naming and cutting off of the foreskin of the incarnate Word. Why? The French hymnwriter Sebastien Besnault describes it like this:

His infant body now
Begins the cross to feel;
Those precious drops of blood that flow
For death the victim seal. (*LSB* 898:3)

Get it? On the eighth day of His life, the infant Christ submitted to a Law that for His own sake He never needed to obey. He did what the Law required for the sake of every other man who had or would fail to keep the commandments of God. By shedding blood as He received the name that means "He will save His people from their sins" (Matthew 1:21), He pointed forward to the way that He would fulfill that name by shedding His blood in His death on the cross. Already as an infant, His body began to bear the weight of the cross.

Although the details of Besnault's life are largely lost to the passage of time, we do have one other hymn he wrote, "Felix dies quem proprio" or "O Happy Day, When First Was Poured." I'll give you one guess what it's about. Hint: It's happy for you, but not for Someone Else. Monsignor Besnault had a peculiar fascination with this event. Here are the first three verses:

O happy day, when first was poured
The blood of our redeeming Lord!
O happy day, when first began
His sufferings for sinful man!

Just entered on this world of woe,
His blood already learned to flow;
His future death was thus expressed,
And thus His early love confessed.

From Heaven descending to fulfill
The mandates of His Father's will,
E'en now behold the victim lie,
The Lamb of God, prepared to die![29]

This is the reason God instituted circumcision: to point forward from the fall to the fulfillment of the promise that the Seed of the woman would crush the head of the serpent. Every act of coitus pointed forward to this Son, born miraculously without the sexual union of a man and a women. Every man who had sacrificed the foreskin of his manhood in order to be marked with the sign of God's covenant had hope in this eight-day-old Boy. And now, the Son of God sheds the blood from His baby boy bit as the first of His work to fulfill every letter and dot of the Law.

What happened thereafter to the detached foreskin of the Lord has sparked more than a little lore in the history of the Church, as you might imagine. More than ten reliquaries have claimed to possess the Holy Prepuce of Christ. And one theologian speculated that when Jesus ascended into heaven, He took his detached foreskin with Him; then, through some astronomical sleight of hand, it became the rings around the planet Saturn. Sheesh.

The point of the circumcision of Jesus is not in locating the removed flesh or attaching some kind of weird cultic devotion to the removed prepuce. The point is that part of His flesh was removed, cut into, in order to mark Him as the One who would give the entirety of His flesh on the cross.

29 Sebastien Besnault, "O Happy Day, When First Was Poured," translated by John Chandler in *Hymns of the Primitive Church* (London: John W. Parker, 1837), no. 48.

BEHOLD, THE MAN

Although we will return to the perfect example of manliness Jesus exemplifies in His earthly ministry in the next chapter, the perfect demonstration of his masculinity is in the event foreshadowed by His circumcision. More important than His masculinity is simply the fact that Jesus is a man, a human. He is God, as He has been eternally in the mysterious union with God the Father and God the Holy Spirit. But now God is a man; and a man is God.

"His infant body now Begins the cross to feel; Those precious drops of blood that flow For death the victim seal." Bleeding is not a characteristic of God. But in the man Jesus, God bleeds. For that matter, all the other ordinary things of being a human being are not intrinsically part of what it means to be God. God doesn't use the bathroom, wipe His nose, or shout in pain when He accidentally hits His thumb with a hammer. But in Jesus, God poops, blows His nose, and exclaims in pain when He misses the head of the nail.

God has become man, taken on the flesh of mankind in the womb of His virgin mother, so that He can offer His body as the sacrifice to pay for the self-centeredness of all men and women since the failure of Adam and Eve in the garden. This was the plan behind the promise, "I will put enmity between you and the woman, and between your offspring and her offspring; He shall bruise your head, and you shall bruise His heel" (Genesis 3:15). This was the reason God issued His Law atop Mount Sinai, so that the only solution for human disobedience and rebellion would be the perfect obedience of one Man. This was the cause for the ceremonial and civil laws that made the Israelites stand out as weirdos among their neighbors, so that one Israelite could be the Way that all men would regain access to the God of Israel.

The Savior of mankind from sin and death would need to be man in order that He could render perfect obedience to the Law. And He would need to be God in order for His death to be sufficient to pay for the sins of every human being in the history of the world. In Jesus, God and man are one. Not like Superman, one man with two identities who sometimes exists as the Man of Steel and other times hides himself in the guise of Clark Kent. Not like Dr. Jekyll and Mr. Hyde, who are two personalities within the same person. Not like a mythological demigod, the offspring of god and a mortal. Jesus is fully and perfectly both God and man.

So, thirty-three years after His first bloodshed, Jesus brought to culmination the perfect plan of God to redeem men from their bondage to selfishness. At least three times, He announced to His disciples His plan to go to Jerusalem; to be handed over to the Gentiles; to be mocked, shamefully treated, and spit on; to be flogged; to be killed; and finally to rise from the dead (Luke 18:32–33).

> Then Pilate took Jesus and flogged Him. And the soldiers twisted together a crown of thorns and put it on His head and arrayed Him in a purple robe. They came up to Him, saying, "Hail, King of the Jews!" and struck Him with their hands. Pilate went out again and said to them, "See, I am bringing Him out to you that you may know that I find no guilt in Him." So Jesus came out, wearing the crown of thorns and the purple robe. Pilate said to them, "Behold the man!" When the chief priests and the officers saw Him, they cried out, "Crucify Him, crucify Him!" (John 19:1–6)

Despite being vilified by the Apostles' Creed, Pontius Pilate becomes a bit of an unwitting prophet in the crucifixion story.

After requesting that Jesus be delivered to him by the regiment of temple guards, Pilate examined Jesus. He tried to have the murderous rebel Barabbas released in Jesus' place. When the crowd insisted on Jesus' blood, Pilate had Jesus flogged, mocked with a fake robe and painful crown, and abused by the soldiers. Then he brought out to the crowd blinded by bloodlust the One who took on flesh in order to shed His blood for them, and whose circumcision as an eight-day-old infant foreshadowed that day. And he announced, "Behold, the man!"

The Man.

The God-man. The incarnate God, the Word of God with human flesh and bones. The Seed of the woman who was promised to crush the head of Satan and destroy his tyranny. The One named Jesus/Joshua/Savior because He would save His people from their sins. The only One ever to have obeyed God's Holy Law perfectly. The One intent on giving His life as payment for all of His human creatures' rebellion. The long-awaited descendant of King David to reign forever over the new heavens and new earth. Behold, the Man.

All this happened according to Jesus' prediction. Everything is according to His plan and will. All these events are divinely orchestrated, as a composer and conductor collude to get different musicians with diverse instruments to create the sound of one masterpiece, one symphony.

NOT GOOD; THEREFORE, A BRIDE

On the sixth day of the very first week since the creation of time, from the fertile soil of Eden, the Creator formed a man. But before the day could conclude with the declaration that all was "very good," the loneliness of the man was declared "not good." So after knocking Adam out with a deep sleep, God extracted from his side the necessary source material to manufacture a helper. Having fashioned a bride for the man, God presented her to him, eliciting Adam's "At last! Bone of my bones and flesh of my flesh!" (see Genesis 2:23).

On the sixth day of another week,[30] the God who had formed Himself into a man from the virgin soil of His mother's womb fell into the deep sleep of death.

> Since it was the day of Preparation, and so that the bodies would not remain on the cross on the Sabbath (for that Sabbath was a high day), the Jews asked Pilate that their legs might be broken and that they might be taken away. So the soldiers came and broke the legs of the first, and of the other who had been crucified with him. But when they came to Jesus and saw that He was already dead, they did not break His legs. But one of the soldiers pierced His side with a spear, and at once there came out blood and water. He who saw it has borne witness—his testimony is true, and he knows that he is telling the truth—that you also may believe. For these things took place that the Scripture might be fulfilled: "Not one of His bones will be broken." And again another Scripture says, "They will look on Him whom they have pierced." (John 19:31–37)

And so that the God-man might not be alone, because alone He would have no one to be the recipient of His limitless love, from the spear-wound in His side, God the Father extracted the necessary source material—blood and water—with which

30 Just in case you have one of those calendars ripe for the recycling bin by virtue of its placing the second day of the week—Monday—at the beginning, or you have otherwise forgotten to count beyond the fingers of one hand, that's *Friday*, fellas.

He made a Bride, a Church, for the Man and presented her to Him eternally.

It was not good for God to be alone. He did not want to destroy the whole mess of His creation, wrecked by humanity's sinful rebellion. And it would have been in vain to call men up to Himself by their obedience to His Word. Instead, God came to men. God became Man. Behold, the Man.

HOPE FOR MAN

Let's take a radical departure from the trajectory of every other book on masculinity out there and from where you probably thought we were headed.

If you're honest with yourself, you'll probably come to the point of being able to admit your failings as a man. There are people you have hurt whom you were supposed to help. You have given in to lust, the mentality of taking, as a way of looking at women. You have been selfish with your time, selfish with your money, selfish with your energy. You've spent too much time looking out for yourself and not enough time looking out for others. There were situations that called for courage, and you were paralyzed with fear. There were crises that demanded you to intervene for the good of others, and you protected your own skin. You have taken more than given. You have consumed more than produced. You have wanted praise for a job well done.

You have been soft. You have succumbed to the effeminacy of protecting yourself and looking after your own needs. You have been selfish, self-centered, self-protecting. Even if outwardly the world esteems you manly enough to write a book on the subject, a careful examination of your interior life reveals a heart and a will bent toward softness, effeminacy, and selfishness. Or maybe you're not like me. But, then, what are you still doing reading this book? The first step is admitting the problem.

The second step is learning who's to blame. Although we've spent a fair amount of time and ink examining who's to blame in our society-wide feminization of men, it won't do to pass the blame for your own struggles with masculinity onto someone else. That's the same self-preserving blame game Adam sought to play that began this ceaseless struggle with manliness. Sure, there are plenty of factors that have brought us here collectively. And the deck is stacked against you in our culture. But the real problem with you is not someone else. The real problem with any man is that man himself. As soon as you take ownership of your problems, you're closer to a solution than you've ever been before.

At your core, you probably know this is not how men were designed to be. Selfishness is a corruption of humanity. Effeminacy is a corruption of man. A selfish person is not fully human. An effeminate, self-interested man is not fully a man.

The hope for man, then, is to be fully man. The solution for your masculinity is in the One who was both fully and completely divine and fully and completely man. But in order to be fully masculine, you've got to be in touch with your feminine side.

The essence of man is to give. The essence of woman is to receive. Admitting that you are not fully man as God created man to be was the first step. The second step was to allow the blame to be placed at your own feet. The third step (don't worry, there aren't twelve) is to receive the benefits of the life and death of the one perfect Man. Although we criticized the Jesus-is-my-boyfriend mentality of some strains of pop Christianity in the last chapter, something about being a Christian seems a little feminine.

In a sense, women make better Christians than men, and the lamented lack of men in the pews could be attributed to this feminine energy at the heart of Christianity. The masculine drive to fix, to do, to take action will do nothing toward making a man a Christian. Inasmuch as the only hope to be fully able to live as a man is to be in Christ, the God-man, a man has to be receptive, but not in the sense of feminine receptivity. A man isn't called to become like a woman in order to be a Christian.

The illustration Scripture uses is not of receptivity as a woman receives from a man, because even her act of receiving is nevertheless an act of her will. The written Word uses death and resurrection to illustrate how the incarnate Word works. As long as a man lives, he will persist in his masculine drive to do and to accomplish. Only when he dies will he stop striving. Dead men are finally free to be fully acted on passively. Only dead men can be resurrected. So St. Paul describes it:

> And you were dead in the trespasses and sins in which you once walked, following the course of this world, following the prince of the power of the air, the spirit that is now at work in the sons of disobedience—among whom we all once lived in the passions of our flesh, carrying out the desires of the body and the mind, and were by nature children of wrath, like the rest of mankind. But God, being rich in mercy, because of the great love with which He loved us, even when we were dead in our trespasses, made us alive together with Christ—by grace you have been saved—and raised us up with Him and seated us with Him in the heavenly places in Christ Jesus, so that in the coming ages He might show the immeasurable riches of His grace in kindness toward us in Christ Jesus. For by grace you have been saved through faith. And this is not your own doing; it is

> the gift of God, not a result of works, so that no one may boast. For we are His workmanship, created in Christ Jesus for good works, which God prepared beforehand, that we should walk in them. (Ephesians 2:1–10)

Dead men don't participate in being resurrected. They don't have do-it-yourself salvation schemes. They're not very adept at *doing* much of anything. Admitting that you can't be a good man by your own doing is admitting your spiritual need for resurrection. You're dead. Trying harder is not the answer.

Fortunately, this Man is Christ, the one who was Himself raised from the dead and also is in the business of raising the dead. His crucifixion was not His defeat. It was His triumph over sin and death. Nor was His death on the cross His end. Thus, in Him, your death is not your end. If you're willing to accept the diagnosis of being dead, then there's a Man capable of raising the dead, of giving life to those who, because of their death, are purely receptive to His gifts.

Dead men make no decisions. Receiving this grace, which Paul says is given freely as a gift, does not depend on your asking for it or deciding to make it yours. Simple receptivity is the posture required for God to make you alive in Christ.

New life in Christ, the perfect human, is where you can find hope to be fully human. Selfishness is a perversion of both masculinity and femininity, and it renders you subhuman. Being dead apart from Christ is not simply the plight of men. It's the plight of all descendants of Adam and Eve, men and women alike. The ladies struggle with genuine, godly femininity just as much as you grapple with genuine, godly masculinity. Effeminacy—*malakia*—is just as destructive to femininity as to masculinity. "Dead in the trespasses and sins" applies to everyone, regardless of chromosomes. So also the hope for being fully human through the new life bestowed through Christ is for dudes and dames alike.

This new life sets a person free from the destructive, humanity-lessening selfishness of sin. This is the hope for men and women in Christ. Women can be free to be women. Men are free to be men. In the person and work of Jesus, the perfect Man, who removes sin by bearing the full list of mankind's transgressions on His body on the cross (Colossians 2:14), flawed, imperfect men have hope. With forgiveness and new life in Christ, effeminacy is removed. You are free to be fully human. Free to be fully and unapologetically masculine. This is who you were created to be.

RECEPTIVE SPIRITUALITY

God works this new life for you principally through the waters of Holy Baptism. There, in the otherwise placid waters of the baptismal font, the rebel against God, the sorry excuse for a man, comes to a violent end. It certainly doesn't look that way to anyone who's witnessed a Baptism, but each time it happens, someone drowns. This is how the apostle Paul describes the event:

> Do you not know that all of us who have been baptized into Christ Jesus were baptized into His death? We were buried therefore with Him by baptism into death, in order that, just as Christ was raised from the dead by the glory of the Father, we too might walk in newness of life.
>
> For if we have been united with Him in a death like His, we shall certainly be united with Him in a resurrection like His. We know that our old self was crucified with Him in order that the body of sin might be brought to nothing, so

> that we would no longer be enslaved to sin. For one who has died has been set free from sin. Now if we have died with Christ, we believe that we will also live with Him. (Romans 6:3–8)

In Baptism, we were crucified with Christ, united into His death, and buried with Him. But the violence is not the end of Baptism, because, once the sinner has been drowned in the microflood of Baptism, a new man emerges from the watery grave. He is forgiven and free, released from his slavery to sin, from his inability to do good, from the decay of his flesh. Again, however, those realities are hidden behind what we can see, and the life even of the baptized man is still a struggle against his old rebellious inclinations.

And it is a struggle. But the essence of Christianity is not a man growing up into greater independence and self-reliance. Quite the opposite. Jesus lauds the littlest, most helpless humans—babies, those who had to be carried to Him by their parents—as model Christians (Matthew 19:14; Mark 10:14; Luke 18:16). This is difficult for men—driven to produce, protect, and provide for others—to comprehend, let alone accomplish. But, like entrance into the Church, none of this depends on a man's ability. Maturation in this new life in Christ is cultivating the art of *dependence* on Christ and His gifts.

John Kleinig describes progress in this Christian life as a *reversal* from how we normally live our lives:

> As we mature in faith, we move away from pride in ourselves and our own achievements to a gradual awareness of our spiritual failure and Christ's work in us as we entrust ourselves to Him. We move away from the conviction that we are self-sufficient to the repeated experience

> of spiritual bankruptcy. We move on from delusions of our spiritual importance to a growing sense of our utter insignificance and the glory of God. We move on from delight in our own power to the painful recognition of our spiritual weakness. We are brought from our self-righteousness to the increasing consciousness that we are sinful. In each of these painful realizations, we recognize the glory of God. Christ fills our emptiness and justifies us by grace. In short, the power of Christ is made perfect in our weakness (2 Corinthians 12:9).[31]

Growth into "mature manhood" (Ephesians 4:13) is not growth in independence, prowess, productivity, or any of the other metrics by which we evaluate masculinity outside the Church. What is valuable and necessary for a man in all of his other godly callings—father, husband, worker, citizen, and so forth—is of no value in his growth as a Christian.

It amounts to a paradox, then: if a man wants to be a man in all other aspects of his life, if he wants to be free to be fully masculine, if he wants to be set free from selfishness and effeminacy, if he wants to cultivate manly virtues in his vocations, he has to learn to be anti-manly toward God. He has to be submissive. He has to be receptive. He has to be passive. He has to be given to. He has to be completely dependent. He has to be a beggar, which is the posture of every Christian who prays, "Lord, have mercy."

In this surrender, you will find the freedom to be a man.

31 John W. Kleinig, *Grace Upon Grace: Spirituality for Today* (St. Louis, MO: Concordia, 2008), 33.

GOOD FRIDAY COMPLEMENTARITY

There's no egalitarianism, no sameness, no interchangeability in the marriage between Christ and His Bride, the Church. Christ and His Church are complementary. They perform distinctly different roles. In the Church, Christ is clearly man. His Bride is clearly woman.

Christ pursues His Bride. His Bride is sought by her Groom.

Christ gives His gifts to His Church—gifts of faith, forgiveness, Baptism, the Lord's Supper, His Word, preachers, the community of believers, and more. His Church receives His gifts, gives her "amen," her "yes," to what He delights to give.

Christ dies to create His Bride. His Church is created from His side in the washing of water and the Word.

Christ feeds His Church with His body and blood in the Lord's Supper. His Church is fed by His gracious, giving hand.

Christ gives; His Bride receives. This sets the pattern for the dynamic between men and women, particularly husbands and wives, for the rest of time. His death frees men and women, husbands and wives, sons and daughters, from their natural selfishness. He is the vicar, the stand-in, the substitute. His death sets His Church free.

Although His death is vicarious, Christ is no victim. He lays down His life intentionally for the good of the whole world. And He is also the victor, triumphing over sin and death by His death and resurrection. For those set free from sin and death, Christ is an icon of perfect righteousness. He is a perfect man. He exemplifies what a perfect man does. Those set free from their former effeminacy by Christ's sacrifice will also find in the God-man, then, the perfect paradigm of masculinity. That's where our journey takes us next.

BOOT CAMP

ECCE HOMO: BEHOLD THE MAN

1. What comfort can you draw from the profound fact that the Second Person of the triune God became completely and perfectly man?

2. Remembering Luther's story of the day when the devil went to church and saw a man who refused to bow to Christ at the "and was made man" of the Nicene Creed, imagine what the devil would find if he showed up in most Christian worship services today. Would he find humans reverently adoring Christ for His condescension to don human flesh, to become one of us? Or would he want to gut punch the "boorish asses" who fail to grasp the magnificence of the confession that God became man?

3. How have you failed to live up to the ideal of masculinity? How have you been selfish or self-preserving?

4. How can you find freedom to be a man in the distinctly unmanly disciplines of Christianity: submission, dependence, helplessness, passivity, and receptivity?

GOD DOWN. MAN UP.

> *"By man death has gained its power over men; by the Word made Man death has been destroyed and life raised up anew."*
>
> —*St. Athanasius, On the Incarnation of the Word*

Jesus is the perfect man. And He is perfectly God. By His incarnation, His death on the cross, His resurrection from the dead, and His ascension into heaven, He has obtained for the rest of us men full forgiveness for our sins. He obeyed the Law in our place. And yet, He suffered in our place. He is our substitute. He is the animal in the garden whose life was ended, blood spilled, and skin procured to make coverings for Adam and Eve (Genesis 3:21). He is the ram caught in the thicket who died instead of Isaac (22:13). He is the year-old unblemished Passover lamb whose blood marked the doorframes of God's people, whose death shielded them from the angel of death, and whose flesh was completely consumed by eating or by fire (Exodus 12:4–10). He is the whole burnt offering, with its blood splattered on the altar and its corpse completely consumed by fire, which renders a sweet smell to God (Leviticus 1:3–9). He is the bull and the two goats on the annual Day of Atonement, the bull and sacrificial goat killed to atone for the sins of the people, and the scapegoat sent outside of the city, into the wilderness with the sins of the people confessed over him (Leviticus 16). He is the servant of the Lord who was pierced, crushed, and wounded for the sins of the people, whose wounds provide healing and forgiveness for the people of God (Isaiah 52:13–53:12).

In every way, Jesus is the perfect substitute for the sins of all mankind. This way of speaking about Christ, which is the dominant, controlling theme of Scripture, depicts Christ as the vicarious satisfaction of the justice of God, the fair punishment for sinners. In other words, Scripture depicts Christ as the *vicar* for mankind. *Vicar* means "substitute." The beautiful, comforting Word of God is this: you don't have to die for being a jerk, a failure as a man, a sinner. Jesus did. In your place. As your substitute.

The Bible is not a how-to manual. The central story is about Christ crucified for sinners. Jesus rejected any who would go to the Old Testament to find in it anything but a story about Him (John 5:39). He explained that everything written in the Scriptures was about the suffering, death, and resurrection of the Christ, and that the goal was repentance and forgiveness for all people (Luke 24:44–47). Any attempt to reduce the Bible to a guidebook for how to live is not only wrong, it's also idolatrous. It replaces Christ at the center with something else, with moralism. The point of the Word, the goal of Christianity, is not to teach you how to be a good person, or a good man. The goal is repentance and forgiveness, given freely to sinners because of the substitutionary death of the God-man, Jesus.

And yet, it is also wrong to limit the work of Jesus to a mere vicar. He is also the victor over the enemies of mankind. He is the perfect icon of what it means to be a human being. He is the only example of what it means to be a perfect man. We call this theme of Scripture a *Christus Victor* motif. Jesus wins. He destroys mankind's oppressors, the real axis of evil: sin, death, and the devil. When He sets men free from their selfishness, their effeminacy, He also becomes their example for how to live as His renewed, restored creatures. He gives new life, and He exemplifies how that life is to be lived.

Do you want to be a man? Do you want to know how to live like a man? Look to Jesus.

MAN UP: THE LIFE OF JESUS

The creeds move quite quickly from the incarnation and the birth of Jesus to His suffering and crucifixion. Rightly so. The mission of Jesus culminates in His death on the cross. But the journey He takes to the cross is hardly idyllic and pleasant. And all along the way, Jesus' interactions with other people are awkward at best and hostile at worst. Jesus is no disciple of Dale Carnegie, author of the best-selling *How to Win Friends and Influence People*. Originally published in 1936, Carnegie's book is one of the best-selling self-help books in history. But, apparently, Jesus never read it.

Carnegie counsels his readers how to handle people in such a way as to minimize conflict: don't criticize, show appreciation, see things from their perspective. He advises how to get people to like you. He has twelve ideas for how to influence people to your way of thinking. Among them: avoid arguments, never call another person wrong, be friendly, be sympathetic, and let other people think their motives are higher and nobler than they might actually be. Finally, some of Carnegie's advice for leaders: show others their mistakes indirectly, let other people save face, use encouragement, make others happy about your suggestions.[32] Reading the Gospels, you'll quickly see that Jesus

32 Dale Carnegie, *How to Win Friends and Influence People* (New York: Simon and Schuster, 1936).

does pretty much the opposite of what Carnegie says a good, influential leader should do.

Jesus' mission, of course, is not to win friends or influence people. He is God in human flesh. He is God come down to His creation. His mission is to die to save people and enliven them with His resurrected life in Holy Baptism. What friendship has light with darkness (2 Corinthians 6:14)?

NO MORE MR. NICE JESUS

The sole remaining virtue for modern man is niceness. Gone are the masculine virtues of courage, wisdom, industry, resolution, self-reliance, discipline, and honor. The ancient cardinal virtues of prudence, justice, temperance, and fortitude have long been forgotten, to say nothing of the theological virtues of faith, hope, and charity. All that matters is that a man is nice. Mothers hope for their daughters to find a *nice* man. Teachers reprimand students who are not *nice*. One of the cardinal sins in civilized society is to *not* be *nice*.

Niceness, however, is not a Christian virtue. Niceness is not masculinity. Niceness is nothing. It's akin to the word *tolerance*, which is pop-culture speak for "Let me do whatever I want." Against the cult of niceness, especially as it has infiltrated the Church—both in thoughts about virtue and masculinity and also in conceptualizations of Jesus—stands the real example of the incarnate Son of God. "Nice" is neither what men are called to be, nor is it an appropriate description of Jesus.

What is this niceness, anyway, that's so desirable in modern society? Does it mean that a man is agreeable, mild-mannered, not mean or harsh? Those aren't undesirable qualities, but nice today is more a synonym with milquetoast: unassertive and spineless.[33]

Nice is not the same as *good*. Jesus is good, perfectly good, to be sure. But he's not nice. He's no Caspar Milquetoast. He's the incarnate God. And, if you cross Him, you won't find Him spineless, ineffective, or agreeable.

Jesus the Family Man

Consider Jesus' interaction with members of His own family.

When His mother presses Him at a wedding to intervene in order to prevent the groom from facing the fate of being known as the guy who ran out of wine at his wedding, Jesus' reply seems brash to the woman who bore Him in her womb and nursed Him at her breast: "Woman, what does this have to do with Me? My hour has not yet come" (John 2:4). This is neither disobedience nor dishonor, however; for, as the writer of Hebrews makes clear, Jesus was completely without sin (4:15). Nevertheless, for Jesus to treat His mother as just another disciple in need of his gentle correction is anything but nice in the modern sense of the term.

And then, having corrected His mother's false expectations, how does Jesus respond to His mother's petition? He fixes the problem! But He doesn't just calm the crisis. He commands the steward to fill six twenty- to thirty-gallon stone jars with water and to draw some out and take it to the master of the feast. What he tastes is not second-rate, bottom-shelf swill. Jesus doesn't do half-measures. It's the choicest vintage ever to cross the human palate. And it's not just a couple bottles of

33 Originally, the word *nice* was not a "nice" way to be thought of. In the earliest uses of the word in English, dating back to the 1300s, the word *nice* meant "foolish, simple, silly, or ignorant." I suggest that we ought to think of the nice guy in terms of the word's original meaning. It's not desirable to be *nice*.

the good stuff. Anyone still sober enough to do the math can calculate that that's 120–180 gallons, or 600–750 bottles of wine. Even if one were already three sheets to the wind and numbers are too much to handle, just know that that's enough to keep the party going for a few more days, at least. Jesus is no tame or timid winemaker. This is not nice; it's reckless. But there's plenty of wine for a good time.

Later, in His hometown of Nazareth, Jesus read from the prophet Isaiah, "The Spirit of the Lord GOD is upon Me, because the LORD has anointed Me to bring good news to the poor" (61:1). He then announced to the crowd that this Scripture was fulfilled even as He spoke it, that He was in that precise moment preaching this good news of forgiveness to them, the poor in spirit. But the crowds reacted violently and began to grumble, "Is not this Joseph's son?" And instead of diffusing the situation, Jesus intensified it. No prophet is welcome in his hometown, He rebuffed. And sometimes it's the outsiders, like the widow from Zarephath and Naaman the Syrian, to whom God shows favor instead of the insiders. So, the hometown crowd of Jesus' family and friends drove Him out of town and tried to throw Him off a cliff (Luke 4:16–30). Not the reaction you'd imagine would be given to a nice, hometown boy.

At another time, a would-be Hallmark-card-creator, wanting to extol Jesus' mother for the good works she had done for Him, said, "Blessed is the womb that bore You, and the breasts at which you nursed!" But Jesus interrupted her, redirecting the praise to different organs of Mary: her ears. He said, "Blessed rather are those who hear the word of God and keep it!" (Luke 11:27–28). It was through the hearing of the Word, after all, that Mary had conceived by the power of the Holy Spirit. And it was through the ongoing hearing of the Word that His mother remained in the company of His disciples. Still, were Jesus a bit nicer, He could have indulged the praise for His mother's work to give flesh and life to the Son of God. But He didn't.

There's also a peculiar lack of niceness and charm in the call of Jesus just a bit later in Luke when Jesus tells the crowds seeking to follow Him, "If anyone comes to Me and does not hate his own father and mother and wife and children and brothers and sisters, yes, and even his own life, he cannot be My disciple. Whoever does not bear his own cross and come after Me cannot be My disciple" (14:26–27). That's certainly not *nice*. The point is clear, though. If good gifts from God—family, friends, children, possessions, or anything else—become more important than the Giver of the gifts, then even they are idols. In comparison to the devotion Jesus demands to Himself, all other affections must be rejected. "Nice" would be to make room for divided devotion, allowing gifts to reign alongside the Giver in a man's heart. But that's not the nature of the Word made flesh, the incarnate God.

Jesus in the Community

Jesus hardly put on a more respectable air when conducting Himself outside of Nazareth. At least twice He played the role of temple-wrecker. Right after His interaction with His mother and the wedding guests, when He performed His first miracle, Jesus went up to Jerusalem for the annual Passover celebration. Finding the temple courtyard filled with people profiting off the sale of animals for the ritual sacrifices, Jesus did what any respectable God with human flesh would do. He wove a whip out of cords[34] and, treating the profiteers as belligerent animals, He

34 Where, pray tell, did He get those? Are the raw materials for a whip just part of the everyday carry for the Son of God?

used the whip to drive them and their herds out of the temple. Then He overturned the tables of the money-changers and gave them a verbal tongue lashing (John 2:13–17).

This isn't an unfortunate story in the otherwise nice-guy narrative of Jesus, one lone exception in an otherwise serene biography of the God Man from Nazareth. At the end of his account of the Gospel, St. John noted, "There are also many other things that Jesus did. Were every one of them to be written, I suppose that the world itself could not contain the books that would be written" (21:25). But he's pretty clear about his agenda: "These are written so that you may believe that Jesus is the Christ, the Son of God, and that by believing you may have life in His name" (20:31). In other words, this temple vandalism event is recorded so that you can know and believe that Jesus is the incarnate God. This isn't Jesus meek and mild. It's the wrath of God against those who would use those worshiping Him to turn an easy buck.

Nor was this just a one-time event. St. Matthew records a repeat of the event when He entered Jerusalem for the final time, for the Passover celebration that would culminate in His offering Himself as the Lamb of God to forever take away the sins of the world. Again, He drove out the sellers and buyers, overturned the tables of the money-changers, and rebuked them all, saying "It is written, 'My house shall be called a house of prayer,' but you make it a den of robbers" (21:12–13).

When summoned to the house of his friend Lazarus who was sick and dying, Jesus, the apparent foil to the American nice-guy archetype, took His sweet time getting there. He deliberately waited two extra days. In so doing, the One who raised from the dead the son of the widow from Nain and the daughter of the synagogue official named Jairus let His friend Lazarus die. Sure, Jesus raised Lazarus from the dead after he had been in the grave for four days and had begun to putrefy and stink (John 11:1–44). But the sadness caused to Mary and Martha, the sisters of the dead Lazarus, sadness that could have been easily avoided had Jesus heeded the call to come while Lazarus was still sick, kinda makes Jesus seem like a jerk. His actions seem more like those of a playground bully or someone with a superhero complex who creates a crisis in order to swoop in at the last minute to save the day. Not exactly nice.

Interactions with His Adversaries

Maybe Jesus is merely misunderstood among His family and hometown and just a bit standoffish at times, but when it comes to His interactions with the Pharisees, chief priests, scribes, elders, and other Jewish leaders who are opposed to Him, He seems deliberately aggressive at times.

It's fairly well-known that Jesus and the Jewish religious leaders have an adversarial relationship. Nice guys often find themselves in these kinds of predicaments. If they're adept at the skills of niceness, they can usually roll over and let their adversaries call the shots and get their way, without causing too much of a ruckus. Jesus, however, is not one to roll over and take it. He not only holds His own in encounters set up to test Him (Matthew 19:3; 22:35; Mark 8:11; Luke 10:25), but sometimes He also takes to the offensive, inciting His adversaries to respond.

For instance, while Jesus is teaching in the synagogue one Sabbath, He encounters a man with a withered hand. He knows the thoughts of the scribes and Pharisees. He knows they are watching to see if He will heal on the Sabbath and thus have a reason to accuse Him of being a rebel and a scofflaw. So what does He do? He pokes the hornets' nest. He calls the man into the midst of the crowd and asks those gathered, "Is it lawful on the

Sabbath to do good or to do harm, to save life or to destroy it?" When they have no answer, Jesus heals the man (Luke 6:6–11). As St. Mark records it, Jesus looked at them "with anger, grieved at their hardness of heart" (3:5). That's strong, assertive, even angry on the Son of God's part; it hardly seems nice.

Often, Jesus' words with these opponents are pointed and (gasp!) seem a little mean. He calls them a "brood of vipers" (Matthew 12:34), an "evil and adulterous generation" (v. 39), "hypocrites . . . blind guides . . . blind fools . . . blind men . . . hypocrites . . . whitewashed tombs . . . sons of those who murdered the prophets . . . serpents . . . brood of vipers" (23:13–36). These epithets need to be preceded by "Trigger Warning: Strong, Offensive Language." Growing up, your mother would have told you not to hang out with people who talk like that. Let's just say these don't become Sunday School lessons. What Jesus says barely passes for mixed-company language. It's not polite. It seems unbridled and untamed. It's not very nice.

Words for His Disciples

But those are His adversaries, you say. It makes sense for Jesus to be a bit standoffish with those who are opposed to Him. Yet the way He treats His disciples, those following Him, willingly learning from Him, receiving His instruction openly and gladly, is even less friendly.

Jesus has a nickname for His disciples in Matthew's account of the Gospel. It's hardly a flattering way to describe those committed to His instruction. Like many nicknames, it's a word Jesus made up. Occurring nowhere in Greek until His usage, Jesus regularly calls His disciples *oligopistos* (singular) and *oligopistoi* (plural). It's a combination of the words for little/few (*oligos*) and faith (*pistis*). Essentially, Jesus calls His disciples "littlefaiths," which is not exactly a very encouraging thing for a nice guy to call the people learning from Him.

First, in the Sermon on the Mount, Jesus criticizes those who worry about clothing, food, or drink. God cares for the sparrows, providing food and drink enough for every day He gives them life and breath. He makes sure that the roadside lilies are well-clothed as long as He permits them to live. Why, then, would any human being, worth far more to the Creator than sparrows or lilies, worry about whether the heavenly Father will provide for him? "But if God so clothes the grass of the field, which today is alive and tomorrow is thrown into the oven, will He not much more clothe you, you *littlefaiths*?" (Matthew 6:30).

Later, Jesus is in a boat with His disciples when a storm arises. He is sleeping peacefully in the stern (where you steer the boat) when the fear of the storm and panic over a sleeping Jesus converge to create unbridled fear. The disciples pray to the God asleep at the wheel, "Save us, Lord; we are perishing" (8:25). But before He rebukes the wind and the waves in order to save His disciples from the temporary peril of the storm, He delivers another rebuke with more enduring consequences: "Why are you afraid, you *littlefaiths*?" (v. 26) And then, once He rebukes the wind and the waves, the magnitude of the immediate calm stands in sharp contrast to the smallness of the disciples' faith.

In another episode that combines the themes of *Deadliest Catch* with *Fear Factor*, Jesus feeds ten thousand plus with the lunch of one little boy clever enough to have brought food for the day-long confirmation class. Afterwards, the disciples leave the scene in a boat while Jesus finishes praying by Himself. He then strolls out onto the water to catch up to His disciples, who again are buffeted by the wind and waves of the Sea of Galilee. The ever-impetuous Peter challenges Jesus to bid him walk out on the water to Him, to prove that Jesus is really Jesus. But when Peter "[sees] the wind," he is afraid and begins to sink. This time, Jesus saves the rebuke until after He immediately takes Peter by the hand and saves him from drowning, "You *littlefaith*, why did you doubt?" (14:31).

Jesus uses this cute little nickname twice more as St. Matthew records His interactions with His disciples, once (16:8) when they freak out at not having any food (having forgotten how He fed the five thousand men plus women and children [14:13–21] or the four thousand men plus women and children [15:32–39]) and again (17:20) when they question why they were unable to drive out from a boy a demon that was making him mute. This last time follows on the heels of an even more stinging lament from Jesus, who complains about the lot of His apostles, "O faithless and twisted generation, how long am I to be with you? How long am I to bear with you?" (17:17). Gentle Jesus, meek and mild? Hardly.

Peter again finds himself the object of Jesus' not-so-nice rebuking when he thinks he can play the hero and prevent Jesus from suffering crucifixion at the hands of the Gentiles. In Matthew 16, Peter makes a bold confession of the faith, proclaiming Jesus to be "the Christ, the Son of the living God" (v. 16). This is so sublimely beautiful and true that Jesus praises it by calling Peter's confession the rock on which He will build His Church. Later, Jesus tells His disciples that He is on His way to Jerusalem to suffer at the hands of the chief priests and scribes, to be crucified, and to be raised on the third day. But on-this-rock Peter thinks he can intervene and protect Jesus from such a fate, saying, "Far be it from You, Lord! This shall never happen to You" (v. 22). This elicits the rebuke from Jesus: "Get behind Me, Satan! You are a hindrance to Me. For you are not setting your mind on the things of God, but on the things of man" (v. 23). Holy smokes! Overreact much, Jesus?

As you can see, Jesus never treats His apostles with kid gloves. He's stern at times. And He refuses to mince words. But not just with those closest to Him; sometimes Jesus' rough treatment extends to those outside His inner circle of twelve men.

How about Jesus' treatment of the Canaanite woman who approached Him in Matthew 15? True, she's an outsider. Her very existence is evidence of the Israelites' failure to obey the commandment of the Lord to kill all the Canaanites when entering the Promised Land (Deuteronomy 20:17). But then the Israelites committed an even more egregious sin, not merely letting them live, but eventually marrying the Canaanites and adopting their false gods as gods to be worshiped alongside the God of Israel. So when this woman comes along, her lineage reminds the Israelites (or should, at least) of their past transgressions and their failure to worship the God who had delivered them from slavery in Egypt and brought them to the Promised Land.

How does she approach Jesus? She has this beautiful, succinct prayer, wherein she addresses Jesus as the Messiah, which most Jews were unable to articulate so clearly. She prays, "Have mercy on me, O Lord, Son of David; my daughter is severely oppressed by a demon" (v. 22). What a perfect prayer! Short, sweet, with an address to Jesus as Messiah, and completely selfless, not for herself but for her daughter. How does the Nice Guy Savior respond? He doesn't. He ignores her. The silence is deafening. The crowd is hushed by the awkwardness of this interaction. But she persists. She keeps crying out. It gets so uncomfortable for the rest of the crowd that the disciples have to intervene. "Send her away; she keeps crying out after us" (v. 23). So Jesus answers, "I was sent only to the lost sheep of the house of Israel" (v. 24). Ouch. Not a Jew? Not for you.

"C'mon, lady," you want to intercede. "Save face and go home. You gave it a good shot." But she doesn't. She prostrates herself at Jesus' feet and prays, "Lord, help me" (v. 25). Then comes the worst blow from Jesus against this poor woman: "It is not right to take the children's bread and throw it to the dogs" (v. 26). A dog. A dog! How is that any way to treat one of your followers?! But she doesn't need a divine nice guy. She needs a Savior. So she assents to His diagnosis. "Yes, Lord, yet even the dogs eat the crumbs that fall from their masters' table" (v. 27). Then Jesus praises her faith as great and heals her daughter (v. 28). A *nice* guy would have done that as soon as she asked, not put her through the wringer the way Jesus did.

It's little wonder that when this is the Gospel reading (which it is on the Second Sunday in Lent), the hymn of the day isn't this little ditty, which just narrowly missed inclusion in every single Christian hymnal ever published. Sing along to the tune of *What a Friend We Have in Jesus*:

What a jerk she has in Jesus,
Doesn't even seem to care!
When this woman came and pleaded,
He ignored her fervent prayer.
He seems cold and kind of racist;
She just didn't get the news.
Sure, she calls Him Son of David,
But He only came for Jews.

She has trials and temptations?
See her daughter anywhere?
She should rightly be discouraged,
Figure Jesus doesn't care.
When she kneels in prayer before Him,

Surely now He'll help her up.
Jesus knows her sinful sickness;
He calls her a Gentile mutt.

Are you weak and heavy laden,
Cumbered with a load of care?
If you think that you deserve it,
He'll ignore your stupid prayer.
If you come in deep contrition
Knowing sin should silence prayer,
By His cross He'll show you mercy;
You will find a solace there.

How about Jesus' interaction with the Jews in John 8? This is a back-and-forth Jesus has, not with Jews adversarial toward Him, but with the Jews *who believed in Him* (John 8:31–59). Here's how that conversation goes.

> ***Jesus:*** *If you abide in My Word, you are My disciples. You will know the truth; the truth will set you free.*
>
> ***Believing Jews:*** *We are Abraham's offspring and have never been anyone's slaves.*
>
> ***Jesus:*** *You may be Abraham's offspring, but you seek to kill Me because My Word finds no place in you. You learned this from your father.*
>
> ***Believing Jews:*** *Like we said, Abraham is our father.*
>
> ***Jesus:*** *If you were Abraham's children, you would not try to kill someone who preaches the truth of God to you. Abraham didn't*

do that. You are doing the works of your father.

Believing Jews: *At least we're not bastards, born of sexual immorality, like You. God is our Father.*

Jesus: *No, God is not your Father. If God were your Father, you would love Me. Your father is . . . (wait for it) . . . the devil. He was a murderer from the beginning. He hates the truth and is the father of lies. The reason why you do not hear the Word of God is that you are not of God.*

Believing Jews: *Now we know You have a demon.*

This goes on for a while longer, escalating until the point where these believing Jews want to stone Jesus to death. You would probably want to stone Him, too, if this Guy *in whom you believed* treated you this way. What's the deal, Jesus?! It's like He has a death wish.

Elsewhere, Jesus says, "Do not think that I have come to bring peace to the earth. I have not come to bring peace, but a sword. For I have come to set a man against his father, and a daughter against her mother, and a daughter-in-law against her mother-in-law. And a person's enemies will be those of his own household. Whoever loves father or mother more than Me is not worthy of Me, and whoever loves son or daughter more than Me is not worthy of Me. And whoever does not take his cross and follow Me is not worthy of Me" (Matthew 10:34–38). A sword? Families divided? Not worthy of Me? That's not nice-guy language. But it's Jesus' language.

One regular, anti-nice-guy characterization of Jesus, as Jesus Himself characterizes it, is, "The Son of Man has come eating and drinking, and you say, 'Look at Him! A glutton and a drunkard, a friend of tax collectors and sinners!'" (Luke 7:34; Matthew 11:19). Accused of gluttony and drunkenness. Rightly identified as a friend of tax collectors and sinners. That's not nice-guy status. That's awkward and off-putting. But that's Jesus.

Hopefully by now, you're getting the point. Jesus is not a nice guy. Were He a pastor, these brash, offensive words and actions would merit more than a few phone calls from concerned parishioners to His ecclesiastical supervisor about this "bull in a china shop" who lacks the social graces and niceties we've come to demand of our clergymen. Not far off are the letters to the seminary threatening to withhold contributions until the faculty exercise better control to ensure that guys like this rough-around-the-edges Nazarene aren't unleashed on congregations hoping and praying for a *nice* pastor.

No, Jesus is not a nice guy. But He's good. That's something more important than niceness. Why Jesus does what He does, says what He says, engages people in the way that He engages them is for a purpose. This is the lesson for masculinity. No, you don't get to drive people out of congregations with a whip. But you should make a firm defense for what is good, even if it irritates people. No, you don't get to needlessly call people names. But you should avoid mincing words when the choice is between hurting someone's feelings and allowing evil to continue. Ideally you'll be able to save face, guard feelings, *and* defend and do what's good. But always err on the side of good instead of nice.

Jesus is good, good to the core, good in everything He does. He does not sin. And yet He doesn't fit the mold of a twenty-first-century emasculated nice guy. He hates injustice, offense, and false righteousness. He won't tolerate anything that separates His people from Him. He will fight against false doctrine. He is intensely compassionate. He perfectly and completely loves all the people He has to treat with rough language. His goal in everything is their good, their salvation. When He offends, He does so in the same way that the Word of God is offensive. The Law, which calls all men sinners, is offensive. Moreover, the Gospel, which declares that men are saved from their sinfulness and, ultimately, from themselves, is even more offensive. The cross is always an offense. It is not nice. But it is good.

MAN UP: THE DEATH OF JESUS

We have no surviving photographs of Jesus. As of yet, no one has been able to locate His Instagram account. No one took selfies with Him. Suffice it to say, we don't know what He looked like.

And yet, I find myself irritated with effeminate depictions of Jesus, with gentle poses, delicate hands, soft facial features, and slender limbs, unencumbered with masculine musculature. No one knows how big Jesus' muscles were, whether He was a bodybuilder, a powerlifter, or a CrossFitter. But inasmuch as Jesus was a perfect, full-bodied *man*, he should be depicted as a perfect, full-*bodied* man. We don't know Jesus' personal record on the bench. But whatever His strength, it has one goal. His strength, His life, exists so that He can spend it in His death. Jesus' goal from the moment of His incarnation, even from before His enfleshment, all the way back to the garden, has been to give His life as a ransom for mankind.

STRENGTH TO SPEND; LIFE TO GIVE

A strong, chiseled, muscular corpus of Jesus on a crucifix is a perfect icon of how a man should live in the world, fulfilling His vocations. Shredded physique, macho muscles, bound and nailed to a cross. Dying. Jesus' strength doesn't exist to save

His own skin. It exists in order to give His life, to lay down His life on His own terms. This is what men are supposed to do.

Although He seems to save His own hide on numerous occasions, Jesus is no coward. When, under the shelter of His guardian Joseph, Jesus fled to Egypt to escape from Herod's sword, and all those baby and toddler boys gave their lives as the price to protect the life of the infant Christ, it wasn't to flee death. It was to flee someone else's timeline for His death. So, too, as we discussed above, when the crowd in Jesus' hometown of Nazareth sought to take Jesus out and throw Him off a cliff, Jesus left (Luke 4:29–30). It's not that He wasn't willing to give His life but that He was unwilling to die according to the timeline or will of anyone other than Himself and His Father. Twice the Jews tried to pick up stones to kill Jesus for what they perceived as blasphemy on His part (John 8:59; 10:31). Twice Jesus evaded them. He would die, but He would not die on their terms.

This is how the strength of masculinity is to be exercised. Strength exists for the protection of others. Prowess exists for the provision for others. Power is not about taking back what may have been taken from you, but about being able to give of your own life on your own terms.

Speaking of how He was going to give His life in the violent death of asphyxiation through crucifixion, Jesus promised, "And I, when I am lifted up from the earth, will draw all people to myself" (John 12:32).

Here, then, is the new meaning of the expression, "Man up!" and the title of this book.

Every other time, "Man up!" is an exhortation to those with Y chromosomes and external genitalia, those biologically male, to start acting like men. It is simultaneously an indictment and an exhortation. Quit whatever unmanly thing you're doing, and be more manly. Although this book is such an accusation and exhortation as well, it is not principally that. First and foremost, it is a book about Jesus. Although we've taken a circuitous route to get here, this is where we've been headed.

A call to "man up" apart from a real example of manliness is bound to fail. Before I exhort you to man up, I want to exhort you to look at the Man on the cross.

This is masculinity. Jesus is fully and completely God. This is how St. Paul describes Jesus, incorporating what most believe is an existing hymn about Christ into his letter to the church in Philippi.

> Have this mind among yourselves, which is yours in Christ Jesus, who, though He was in the form of God, did not count equality with God a thing to be grasped, but emptied Himself, by taking the form of a servant, being born in the likeness of men. And being found in human form, He humbled Himself by becoming obedient to the point of death, even death on a cross. Therefore God has highly exalted Him and bestowed on Him the name that is above every name, so that at the name of Jesus every knee should bow, in heaven and on earth and under the earth, and every tongue confess that Jesus Christ is Lord, to the glory of God the Father. (Philippians 2:5–11)

Fully and completely God, what does Christ do? He makes Himself nothing, takes the lowest form, the form of a servant, a slave. He did not consider His equality with God the Father and God the Holy Spirit a thing to be held onto, but emptied Himself, being born in the likeness and the flesh of a man. He descended to the lowest and most shameful point, humbled Himself to endure, not just death, but the most humiliating kind of death, the death of a criminal on a cross.

A crucifix with a burly, ripped Jesus confesses this sublime paradox. Jesus has every power in the world (far more than even the most hulking specimen of a man), and what does He do with it? He spends every ounce of His strength in His death, not for His own sake, but for yours.

This is masculinity.

"Man up!" then, is first of all an exhortation to consider the work of the perfect Man, the incarnate God, Jesus Christ. Look at Him, the Man up on the cross. His death on the cross serves to draw all men—and women—to Himself. His death has reconciled mankind to God the Father. Therefore, God has exalted Him and given Him the name that is above every other name, the name at which every knee must bow.

So, men, have this mind of Christ as your own. To be masculine is to have this mind of Christ Jesus. It is to acknowledge your power and your prowess and to see these as gifts to be employed in the service of others. Genuine, Christlike masculinity is the opposite of effeminacy. Christ's manliness knows no *malakia*, no self-preservation. It is perfectly self-giving, selfless, self-denying, self-emptying. Thus, it is purely good.

FATHER, FORGIVE THEM

Manliness can never be mere insistence on rights, taking back whatever a feminized culture has taken or whatever you by your own selfishness have surrendered.

Masculinity is a fight, but it's as much about picking the right battle as it is about winning the fight. Jesus knew the nature of His fight. He came not to topple earthly kingdoms and to set up His own regime, though many among the crowds who followed Him wanted Him to. But He continued to confound them with His journey toward the cross. His fight was far bigger than earthly powers that oppressed the people of God.

When He was arrested in the Garden of Gethsemane, He put up no resistance. In fact, when Peter thought that with his sword he could win another day of freedom for Jesus, Jesus rebuked him and told him to put his sword away. Swords are no match for the kind of power Jesus had at His disposal: "Put your sword back into its place. For all who take the sword will perish by the sword. Do you think that I cannot appeal to My Father, and He will at once send Me more than twelve legions of angels?" (Matthew 26:52–53).

When the mob brought Him before the kangaroo court of the high priest Caiaphas, Jesus gave no defense for Himself. His silence evoked rage from those who looked on. Why wouldn't He say something? Finally, urged in the name of the living God to answer, He assured them that He was indeed the Christ, the Son of God, and from then on, they would "see the Son of Man seated at the right hand of Power and coming on the clouds of heaven" (Matthew 26:64). His display of power, though, the demonstration that He was truly divine, was for another day.

Again, when Jesus appeared before Herod, He was silent (Luke 23:9). Before Pontius Pilate, though He answered one question, He still did not defend Himself. This was not the battle. This was the plan. To lay down His life intentionally, willingly, was His mission.

Then, from the cross, Jesus broke His virtual silence, speaking seven times. The first saying set the tone and made clear the reason for His suffering. There, with criminals flanking the sinless Son of God, the Creator of all things, the eternal Word made flesh, Jesus prayed for those who captured Him, who lusted for His blood, who sought His death, who beat Him, who spat on Him, who mocked Him, who nailed Him to the cross, and who mocked Him from below. He prayed, "Father, forgive them, for they know not what they do" (Luke 23:34).

This was the fight.

Against sin and death, Jesus would fight to the death. Against those enemies who held His people captive, Jesus would spend every last ounce of energy and drop of His blood.

He would fight for those who fight against Him. He would love them despite their fierce hatred against Him. And He would win. His death was the triumph over His enemies. He conquered the captors of His people in the perfect selfless offering of Himself as the ransom.

So He prayed for forgiveness. He won forgiveness on the cross. And He seeks to deliver His forgiveness through the ongoing work of His Church. The cosmic war has been won, sin and death defeated. Although the battle against sin seems daily to rage for each individual believer, Jesus has won. On the First Sunday in Advent, the Gospel reading for which is Jesus' entry into Jerusalem to die on the cross, Martin Luther preached, "This King is and shall be called sin's devourer and death's strangler, who extirpates sin and knocks death's teeth out; he disembowels the devil and rescues those who believe on him from sin and death."[35]

Forgiveness, for which Jesus prayed from the cross, is His victory over sin, death, and the devil. Even as He was giving up His life on the cross, His words were a selfless prayer for those who were crucifying Him. Even when they sought His death, Jesus sought their good. This is perfect masculinity.

To emulate this example of manliness is to give perfectly, to forgive instead of harboring resentment. This example of

35 Martin Luther and Eugene F. A. Klug, *Sermons of Martin Luther: The House Postils*, vol. 1 (Grand Rapids, MI: Baker Books, 1996), 5.

Jesus as the icon of perfect manhood teaches men to pick their battles. What's worth fighting for? The good of others, the lives of others, the forgiveness of others. What's not worth fighting for? Yourself, your own interests, your own wants or needs. You have been given your life—and new life in Christ—to be of service to others. The cross is the perfect example of selflessness and strength put into the service of others.

MAN UP: THE REIGN OF JESUS

Having laid down His life willingly and for the good of all humanity, whom He loves and treasures, for whose sake He had taken on human flesh in the first place, Jesus didn't remain dead.

MAN UP FROM THE GRAVE

Never before had this happened. Never before had one who was dead triumphed over death. Sure, there had been other resurrections, but none quite like this. Other resurrections were wrought by an external power. Elijah raised the son of the widow from Zarephath (1 Kings 17:17–24). Elisha raised the son of the Shunammite woman (2 Kings 4:35), and a dead man was raised when his corpse fell on the bones of the dead Elisha (13:21). Jesus raised three people: the son of the widow of Nain (Luke 7:13–15), the daughter of the synagogue official named Jairus (Matthew 9:25), and his friend Lazarus (John 11:43–44). Later, Peter raised the garment-maker Tabitha (Acts 9:36–42), and Paul raised the young man who dozed off during his sermon and fell out the window to his death (Acts 20:9–12).

Jesus' resurrection was distinctly different. His resurrection was different because His death was different. All those other resurrections were preceded by "natural" deaths. Although death is distinctly *un*natural, because it was not a part of the creation that God declared "very good" and only came about when Adam and Eve rebelled against the Source of Life, every other death has been rightly deserved as the fair consequence for sins. "The wages of sin is death" (Romans 6:23).

But when the sinless Son of God died, the formula was broken. Previously, all those who died were sinful. Although lamentable, their deaths were fair. Sin meant death. But Jesus had no sin of His own. He didn't die because of His own rebellion or impurity. He died because of all other past, present, and future transgressions of God's Law. So, though Jesus died, death never had a rightful claim to Him. His resurrection was guaranteed. His death so completely broke the power of death that as soon as Jesus died, many of those who had died trusting in the promise of God to forgive their sins and raise them to life *rose*. The shock wave from the death of the only sinless human being ever rumbled out through Jerusalem, causing death to lose his grip on numerous others, simply by virtue of the death of God on the cross.

Following His death but before His resurrection, Jesus descended into hell, the abode of the dead and the damned, and proclaimed victory to them there. His resurrection on the third day simply confirmed His limitless power over death. As He promised, no one took His life from Him. He had power and authority to lay it down as well as power and authority to take it back up again (John 10:18). So He did. He rose.

The fact that this resurrection was so unlike other resurrections, unlike anything ever in the history of the world to that point, struck fear in the hearts of those who encountered the news of Jesus' rising from the dead.

First, an angel who was "like lightning" descended from heaven and rolled back the stone that had sealed Jesus' tomb.

He then perched himself atop the stone and made the band of soldiers fall down as though they were dead (Matthew 28:2–4)! These were grown men trained in the art of war who presumably had witnessed many of the horrors of men fighting one another in duels to the death.

The women who found the stone rolled away and intrepidly entered the tomb where Jesus had lain dead were nearly equally afraid when two men in dazzling white appeared. Luke reports that "they were frightened and bowed their faces to the ground" (Luke 24:1–5). Not struck as though dead like the soldiers, but their reaction is similar.

St. Mark's account of the resurrection (ch. 16) includes a similar encounter. The angel in the tomb announced to the women who had come to anoint Jesus' body that they needn't be afraid because Jesus had risen. He exhorted the women to tell Jesus' disciples (and Peter!) that He would meet them in Galilee, as He promised. Then, "They went out and fled from the tomb, for trembling and astonishment had seized them, and they said nothing to anyone, for they were afraid" (v. 8). Most scholars believe that Mark's account ends here. But within a few generations, longer endings were added to Mark's account of the Gospel to give readers a more satisfying resolution than a band of scared women.

Can you think of a less manly end to the account of the Gospel? At least St. John recorded the footrace between himself and Peter upon hearing from Mary Magdalene that the tomb that was supposed to be securely sealed and safely guarded was now *empty*. But a bunch of women afraid of the message they had just heard? Where are the men? They weren't even courageous enough to make the Sunday morning trek to the tomb?

Here, then, is the lesson in manliness to be gleaned from looking at the Man who rose triumphantly from the tomb: courage.

In his commentary on the Gospel according to St. Mark, Professor James Voelz argues that this abrupt ending fits with St. Mark's goal of pointing his hearers to the veracity of the Word: "This, then, is what Mark's Gospel is about: *the ambiguity of the evidence, the necessity of believing in the face of such evidence, and the reliability of Jesus' Word.*"[36] The women scared silent by the news of the resurrection are intended as a foil to the courage this event evokes. They obviously didn't stay silent. Their message was not forever stuck in their throats. The way St. Mark leaves these women in fear is intended to *highlight* by contrast the courage of the early Christians in proclaiming this message of a God who died and rose, and who promises to bring His believers into His own death and resurrection through the waters of Holy Baptism.

Jesus' resurrection means your resurrection.

That's the promise of St. Paul: "We were buried therefore with Him by baptism into death, in order that, just as Christ was raised from the dead by the glory of the Father, we too might walk in newness of life" (Romans 6:4).

If you had nothing to lose, would that inspire you to greater courage? If there were no chance that your life would be in peril, would you take greater risks? If your future were guaranteed, regardless of your present, would you have greater confidence?

This is what you have in Baptism. Jesus rose victorious over death. All who have been baptized have His death and resurrection as their very own. Therefore, in your life as a man, you can and should have tremendous courage.

Jesus' bodily resurrection is your bodily resurrection. Someday, what began when you were baptized will be brought to its fullness when you are bodily raised from the dead.

36 James Voelz, *Concordia Commentary: Mark 1:1–8:26* (St. Louis: Concordia, 2013), 55.

This certainty of their having been joined into the death and resurrection of Christ is what has given Christian martyrs throughout the history of the Church courage to face death boldly. They knew that nothing—not persecution, or struggle, or death—could take resurrection away from them, so they gave witness with their lives to this truth: Jesus is God made flesh who died and rose and will return. This a truth so profound that it would be worth dying to believe, even were there no promise of resurrection. How much more confident and courageous are you free to be, then, when you know that death cannot and will not be your end!

This confidence is not just for men, of course. It's for all who are baptized. Baptism means new life in Christ for all believers. But for a man, who is called to live his life not for himself but for the good of others, who is called to spend himself for the good of others, this is a special, necessary source of courage.

You can be free to live your life purely as a man, free from the encumbrances of effeminacy and selfishness, because in Holy Baptism, the resurrection of Christ gave you new, eternal life that will fully and finally be yours when Jesus returns to raise you and all believers form the dead. You are therefore free to live for the good of others. Nothing can shake you. Resurrection is yours. New life is yours. Have courage. Take heart. Man up.

MAN UP INTO HEAVEN

Forty days after He left the grave in the wake of destruction and made a mockery out of death, toppling the devil's regime, Jesus ascended into heaven in order to reign and rule from the right hand of His Father.

Christianity is a very fleshly religion. Jesus didn't ascend into heaven spiritually. He ascended as He was throughout His life: as a real human being.

One of the earliest heresies the Christian Church had to combat was a philosophical/religious movement called Gnosticism. With its origins in platonic Greek philosophy, Gnosticism is so called for its emphasis on obtaining salvation through discovery of secret or hidden knowledge (Greek: *gnosis*). Although Gnosticism is too diverse to have one unifying creed, one of the common tenets of Gnosticism is the preference of the spiritual realm over the material. In other words: spirit good; matter evil. The body is a prison that holds the spirit captive. The goal is release from the body, from matter and material things.

In stark contrast to this stands Christianity, which not only affirms the goodness of the body and matter but also confesses that the eternal God joined Himself to human flesh in the incarnation. The salvation He procured is not a matter of secret knowledge to liberate souls from bodies but of forgiveness and reconciliation for whole persons, with the promise of a future, bodily resurrection.

The fleshly nature of Christianity is highlighted in the bodily ascension of Jesus into heaven. Sure, the rest of Jesus' life does a pretty good job of confessing the goodness of creation and the need for an embodied Savior to bear the sins of all mankind on His body and to give His life in exchange for men. Jesus is the incarnate—enfleshed—God, after all. But having finished His work to redeem mankind, what is remarkable is that Jesus didn't abandon His human body and ascend spiritually into heaven. Although this way of speaking of the body—inherited not from the Scriptures but from ancient Gnosticism—has infected much of the way even Christians speak about death ("That's just a shell of Grandpa." "She's finally free from her body in which she suffered so much."), this is simply not the case with Jesus. He didn't leave His body behind. He didn't stop being truly human at His ascension. He remains as He was from the moment of His conception in His mother's womb: fully God and fully human.

So, take a minute and let that sink in. This has profound implications for any of you who, like Jesus, also has a human body. A human being ascended into heaven. A human being sits at the right hand of God the Father. A human being reigns at the right hand of the Father. A human being will return to this world to judge all the living and the dead. A human being.

This is distinctly good news if you, like Jesus, happen to be a human being.

At the beginning of this book, we considered the question the psalmist posed in Psalm 8: What is man? What man was when King David asked the question in the psalm and what man has become through the work of Christ is a question the author of the Book of Hebrews takes up immediately in the first chapters of that beautiful book.

> [Jesus] is the radiance of the glory of God and the exact imprint of His nature, and He upholds the universe by the word of His power. After making purification for sins, He sat down at the right hand of the Majesty on high, having become as much superior to angels as the name He has inherited is more excellent than theirs.
>
> For to which of the angels did God ever say,
>
> "You are My Son,
> today I have begotten you"?
>
> Or again,

> "I will be to Him a father,
>
> and He shall be to Me a Son"?
>
> And again, when He brings the firstborn into the world, He says,
>
> "Let all God's angels worship Him." (1:3–6)

Although mankind was created lower than the angels, in the incarnation, crucifixion, resurrection, and, finally, ascension of Jesus, God has exalted not just Jesus but all mankind. When Christ ascended, He elevated mankind above the angels. God did not become an angel. He did not die for angels. An angel did not rise from the dead. Angels are offered no forgiveness. An angel does not reign at the right hand of God the Father with all things placed in subjection under his feet.

In the ascension of Christ, all mankind is exalted.

What does this mean for those of us struggling to live as men—this quest for masculinity? Think how this elevates your daily work. You minister to human beings, the pinnacle of God's creation, exalted above the angels, those whose Brother sits at the right hand of God the Father. When you love your wife; when you do the dishes or otherwise adjust your schedule to lighten her load; when you awake in the middle of the night to clean up vomit from a sick kid or change yet another blowout diaper; when you write off a broken window, a wrecked car, a lost investment to maintain patience and mercy toward another person; when you refuse to wrong another person though the opportunity to do so and get away with it arises; when you help those less fortunate; when you hold another's hand; when you smile at a person; when you do anything—big or small—in service of mankind; you confess the goodness of flesh-and-blood human beings and praise the One who descended to don human flesh and ascended with that flesh to the highest place in the cosmos.

These people around you matter. Those whom God has placed into your spheres of influence are holy and exalted. Your work toward them is good and holy. You have a higher calling, simply because Christ ascended with human flesh. Men and women are worthy of your devotion. People matter. God became man. A Man sits on the throne of heaven. Man up.

BIBLICAL MASCULINITY: CHRIST'S WORK

Christ's mission was not to teach you how to be a man. It was to be a man, a perfect Man, and to bear the faults and failings of men, to make their failures His own, and to redeem them with the offering of His life on the cross.

His mission, then, is to make you a man, fully masculine. He makes men fully masculine and women fully feminine. He drowns your failure as a man in the water of Baptism and raises a new man, a man just like He is. Your failures become His. His success becomes yours.

ADAM'S FAILURE; JESUS' SUCCESS

In writing against the aforementioned heresy of the Gnostics, Early Church Father Irenaeus said of Christ: "When He became incarnate, and was made man, He commenced afresh the long line of human beings, and furnished us, in a brief, comprehensive manner, with salvation; so that what we had lost in

Adam—namely, to be according to the image and likeness of God—that we might recover in Christ Jesus."[37]

What man lost through Adam, he can regain in Christ.

Adam was self-serving. He sought chiefly to provide for himself. Christ is the opposite. Nothing He does is attuned to His own needs. In His own words, "The Son of Man came not to be served but to serve, and to give His life as a ransom for many" (Matthew 20:28). Jesus is more interested in serving you than in what you can do for Him. This is why church services are arranged as they are. The goal of the church service is not to serve God, to thank Him, praise Him, and so on. All of these happen, to be sure, but they're not the reason God gathers His people together. The goal of His gathering is for Him to serve us.

The German word for a church service, *Gottesdienst*, confesses what is actually going on as the Church gathers together week after week. Sometimes translated "Divine Service," it's the time when God gathers His people to serve them. The role of the Christian, then, is not chiefly to serve God. It's to be served by God with His gifts of forgiveness and mercy, which He delivers through His Church in the service, so that the Christian can then serve his neighbor.

Christ's service toward you sets you free to serve your neighbor. It sets you free to express this essence of pure masculinity: selflessly serving others. What Christ as perfect God and Man does for you, serving you without expectation of return, without any *quid pro quo*, without any selfish desire for reciprocation, He sets you free to do for others. Serve them just because they need your service, not because you can get anything out of the arrangement. This is pure manliness.

---

37 Irenaeus, *Against Heresies* 3.18 in *Ante-Nicene Fathers*, ed. Alexander Roberts and James Donaldson (Edinburgh: T&T Clark, 1867), 1:446.

Whereas Adam was self-centered, eyes fixed on himself, Christ is focused on those around Him, those whom He came to serve. Immediately upon the fall, Adam's gaze fell down on himself. He became acutely self-aware in a way that he was not before his fall into sin. Christ's gaze, however, is always outward, always toward the rest of mankind, always toward His creation.

Particularly in St. Mark's account of the Gospel, Jesus is always looking around. When Jesus entered the synagogue one Sabbath and the crowd watched Him to see whether He would heal the man with the withered hand on the Sabbath, Jesus, "looked around at them with anger, grieved at their hardness of heart," before healing the man (Mark 3:5). Later, when the crowd told Jesus that His mother and brothers were outside looking for Him, "looking about at those who sat around Him, He said, 'Here are My mother and My brothers!'" (3:34). When the woman touched His garment and He felt power go out from Him, Jesus looked around (5:32). When the rich young man confidently declared that he had kept all the commandments from youth, Jesus, "looking at him, loved him, and said to him, 'You lack one thing: go, sell all that you have and give to the poor, and you will have treasure in heaven; and come, follow Me'" (10:21). A couple verses later, Jesus looked around at His disciples before declaring, "How difficult it will be for those who have wealth to enter the kingdom of God!" (v. 23). When the disciples reacted that it is therefore impossible for anyone to be saved, "Jesus looked at them and said, 'With man it is impossible, but not with God. For all things are possible with God'" (v. 27). Then, after His Palm Sunday entrance into Jerusalem, Jesus went into the temple, "And when He had looked around at everything, as it was already late, He went out to Bethany with the twelve" (11:11).

Jesus is always looking at others, loving them, rebuking them, having mercy on them, being immediately interested in their needs instead of His own. This is distinctly masculine, and it restores what Adam lost. This kind of focus on others is a hallmark of Christ, and the gift for all those restored to full masculinity and manliness through Him. You're free in Christ to see the world as He does, ripe for your service, ready to be given to instead of taken from.

And where Adam's reaction to being confronted with his sin was to try to throw both his wife and the Creator who gave him a flesh-of-his-flesh helper fit for him under the bus, Christ is never even one bit self-preserving. He, rather, is completely self-sacrificing. His life is a gift to give for the good of His Bride, the Church. The cross is His goal, His destination, the reason for His incarnation. Sacrifice is His mission. So, in Christ, redeemed from selfishness by His perfect sacrifice, you are free to sacrifice yourself for others.

In Christ you have both freedom from effeminacy and selfishness, freedom to give and to sacrifice, as well as an example of what this masculinity looks like when it is fully lived for the good of others around you. It's time to reclaim this biblical picture of a man, to make a bold statement about what a man is and should be.

BOOT CAMP

GOD DOWN. MAN UP.

1. How does the example of Christ call you to be more than just another "nice guy"? What's the difference between being nice and being good?

2. What might a good man have to do that a nice guy wouldn't? At what times in your life has being nice prevented you from being good or doing what's right and necessary?

3. Jesus used every ounce of His strength for the good of others. A false view of masculinity sees strength simply as something to be exercised to impress others or to get what you want for yourself out of life. What are your specific strengths? What are ways that these God-given strengths can be employed in the service of others?

4. Jesus was undeterred on His path to the cross. He knew which fights to pick and which to avoid. Given this example of selflessness, what should be the goal of your life? How are you distracted from this ultimate good?

5. How does confidence in the reality of your final bodily resurrection give you courage to face the more difficult aspects of your struggle to be fully masculine?

PART 2

A PORTRAIT OF MAN: ADAM

> *"The beard signifies the courageous; the beard distinguishes the grown men, the earnest, the active, the vigorous. So that when we describe such, we say, he is a bearded man."*
>
> —*St. Augustine, Expositions on the Book of Psalms*

At last, we return to the question we asked at the beginning of our journey. What is a man? What—according to the design of creation and the benefit of recreation in Christ—is a man? What should he be, despite adverse influences on him and on cultural understandings of masculinity? For what good is he endowed with strength and prowess? What is the essence of masculinity? What does it mean to be a man?

Even to believe these questions are answerable or appropriate to ask is countercultural. In a society that wants to make men and women the same, that wants fluidity between biological sexes, that wants to ignore intrinsic differences and focus on interchangeability of men and women, to ask such questions is heresy.

By now, however, the naysayers and PC police have given up hope that this book will say anything they want to agree with. Probably, too, the neo-macho men with their underlying insecurities and their need to be affirmed as men have also grown weary of my stubborn refusal to succumb to the trend and write another "assert your manly rights" diatribe against feminism. Even the church-going crowd, while glad for all the Jesus talk, has most likely grown uncomfortable with talk of Jesus as a biological man who will not bend to pressure from the quilting societies to be a *nice guy*. Therefore, if you've made it to this point of the book and have been okay with my desire to make you uncomfortable and challenge you, you're in an elite group (of just one? Well, thanks, Mom).

So, this is it. A manifesto for being a man.

Before we expound on any of the details, there is one general principle that defines masculinity and orders all the traits that should properly belong to the domain of a man. A man gives. He is strong in order to give. He has authority in order to give. He is given headship in order to give. He is set up with dominion over creation in order to give. He has leadership in order to give. He has power, assertiveness, courage, wisdom, integrity, and tenacity so that he may give of himself to others. At the core of what it means to be a man is to know how to use all the masculine traits and privileges not for the good of himself, but for the good of others.

Just because creation since the fall no longer functions properly does not mean that it *shouldn't* function properly. It just means that it's more difficult to live according to the Designer's ideal. And yet, difficult though it will be, it's good. And it's worth it. What Adam was given to do is what men today are still called to do. Although it seemed to vanish a mere moment after its existence, the picture of Adam in the garden, both as an ideal from which we've fallen and as a goal toward which we're headed anew, serves as a helpful first step in constructing a picture of what modern man should be.

HEADSHIP

In creating Eve from Adam's side and giving her to Adam as a helper, God sets Adam up as the head of his family. This is repeated by St. Paul in his command to wives:

> Wives, submit to your own husbands, as to the Lord. For the husband is the head of the wife even as Christ is the head of the church, His body, and is Himself its Savior. Now as the church submits to Christ, so also wives should submit in everything to their husbands. (Ephesians 5:22–24)

This, of course, is every husband's favorite verse to learn by heart and recite to his wife anytime he's not getting his way around the house. However, his memory is usually a bit fizzy, and he only recalls one word of the three verses Paul addresses to wives. He altogether forgets that Paul devotes a significantly greater amount of ink to what husbands are given to do; but we'll return to that in just a moment. In his truncated memory, what he knows is this: "The Bible says you're supposed to submit to me, so . . ." This assertion is usually followed not by the way a head functions toward a body but by how a bully functions toward his victim. Here, the husband exerts his will as law and coerces his wife into doing what he wants by using the Bible trump card.

This is not headship. Or, at least, this is not healthy headship. When a head is not interested in the good of the body to which it is attached, it is dysfunctional. A head that no longer can do what's in the best interest of the body is diagnosed as sick. There are psychologists, psychiatrists, drugs, and therapies for that. A head in opposition to the body to which it is attached will not long survive.

Manliness does not mean exerting your will over against your wife's. It does not mean Adam got to order Eve around. It means that He existed for her good as much as she was created for his good. Heads are attached to bodies so that bodies can live and function. Marriage is not a competition. Family life is not a contest. The goal of being a man, of having headship in your family, is not to get whatever you want and have your family members serve you as minions. That's disordered. That's not genuine masculinity. That's selfishness.

The headship that is part and parcel of being a man in relationship with others, St. Paul elsewhere describes like this: "The head of every man is Christ, the head of a wife is her husband, and the head of Christ is God" (1 Corinthians 11:3). No man is his own authority. His head is Christ. Even in the Garden of Eden, Adam is never given total and complete authority. He may be the head, but he's under the headship of Christ. And the head of Christ is God the Father; not in the mysterious equality of the Holy Trinity but in terms of how the triune God relates to His creation.

In other words, man is not independent. He's not the boss. His headship is normed and governed by the headship of Christ. Although he exercises authority in his household, he remains a man under authority, under the rule of another. As Christ is not capricious, commandeering, or cavalier in exercising His authority over men, so men must not use their headship as an excuse to be capricious, commandeering, or cavalier in exercising their authority. Headship is not a license to do whatever you want. It is a calling to do what others around you need.

DOMINION

In the garden, Adam is given dominion. The Creator places him in His place to rule over His creation. As a man, Adam exists as a lord in the place of and service of the Lord. Masculinity entails not only lordship within his family but also lordship over the rest of creation.

The Creator parades the animals before Adam so that he can assign to each one its name. To name is the most basic form of dominion. Parents name their children. Teachers give nicknames to their pet students. Pet owners choose a name by which they will summon their pets from digging in the neighbor's flower gardens. Explorers assign names to the places they discover. Scientists who discover a new element or a new species are given the honor of choosing the name. The donor who contributes the most to a building or a sports stadium is given naming rights. To name is to exercise ownership. So Adam is given a unique, privileged place in creation when God entrusts him with the authority and responsibility of naming the animals.

Dominion has often been distorted into exploitation. Just as familial headship can be distorted into a selfish abuse of authority, so can dominion over creation devolve into a disordered desire of the man to use other creatures for his own good instead of seeing himself as the lord for the good of those creatures.

The Creator's dominion is not exploitative. He doesn't create in order to take advantage of His creation or to use creatures or created objects for His own good. So then Adam's dominion—his lordship, standing in the place of the Creator toward the rest of creation—is not exploitative. Adam's dominion exists for the good of others, for the proper functioning and the order of creation.

This dominion, thus, has implications for the way Adam conducts himself as a creature among other creatures. Man is lord of creation. If he stoops to worship any aspect of creation, this is an inversion of the created order. Plants, animals, weather patterns, and minerals are not to be worshiped. Nor are they to be given privilege above mankind. Sometimes trees or mineral deposits need to be burned in order to keep human beings alive. Sometimes animals need to be eaten in order for mankind to survive and thrive. This is a delicate balance, which is why it is entrusted to mankind to exercise wisdom and care in the allocation of resources, the care of animals and plants, and the judgment about what will be used in the service of what.

Care for creation properly belongs not to the godless, the atheists, those who do not acknowledge a Creator but to the man and woman who know their rightful place in the taxonomic order of creation. It should come as no surprise that those who do not submit to the rule of the Creator often find themselves in the inverted structures of the created order, like the philosophy of deep ecology, wherein all living things are placed on the same level. Blades of grass are accorded the same rights as hippopotami. There's no order, no hierarchy. Such a system can never survive, of course. It's a self-defeating philosophy, written on paper produced from the wood pulp of trees.

Dominion is a high calling, a holy estate. Man not only *can* exert his loving authority over creation, he also *must*. Before the fall, this was simple and pleasant. After the fall, in the wake of the curse, man's work is fraught with difficulty and danger. Now the soil will only yield bread by the sweat of the man's brow and, occasionally, the blood from his veins and the life from his body. Farm accidents are the unfortunate result of the fall. No one lost his fingers in a mishap with a combine before Adam's rebellion. But now man continually has to reassert his control over creation to keep the chaos at bay. Apart from his dominion, creation can and will spiral out of control. Human-induced global warming is as much a concern as human-disinterested global chaos. Man must always walk the fine line between harming creation with too much manipulation and harming it with too little control.

Even before God creates a helper for Adam, He places him in the garden to guard and keep it (Genesis 2:15). This is dominion. Man is in control, which puts the management of resources within his purview. Creation depends on man, just as man, with the rest of creation, depends on his Creator. Taking advantage of the dependence of others on him is subhuman, as is abdicating his call to work for the good of the creation around him.

PROPHET, PRIEST, AND KING

PROPHET

Remember Eve's interaction with the serpent in Genesis 3? When the deceiver questions her about eating from the trees in the garden (planting the seed of mistrust in God's Word and doubt toward God Himself), Eve answers, at first, somewhat faithfully, "We may eat of the fruit of the trees in the garden, but God said, 'You shall not eat of the fruit of the tree that is in the midst of the garden, neither shall you touch it, lest you die'" (vv. 2–3). Eve had already heard the prohibition against eating from the tree in the middle of the garden. But God had never issued any such prohibition to her. It was only to Adam that He commanded, "You may surely eat of every tree of the garden, but of the tree of the knowledge of good and evil you shall not eat, for in the day that you eat of it you shall surely die" (2:16–17). The only way Eve could know this—or any—commandment from God is because *someone* told her. Who? The only one to whom the commandment had been given. Adam is entrusted with the Word of God not merely for his own benefit. He is the first man ever called into the office of prophet, the office given to speak the Word of God. Eve has heard the Word of God purely because Adam has preached to her.

Before the fall, Adam was a faithful preacher, the original prophet of God. This, then, is part of what it means to be a man, to proclaim the Word of God to those whom the Lord intends to hear it. As husband and father, it's fairly clear to whom man is called to preach the Word of God. His wife and his children, his family, are his congregation. Before there was a need for pastors, pulpits, or catechisms, the head of his household was the original preacher.

This truth is confessed in the Lutheran Church as each of the Six Chief Parts of Luther's Small Catechism begins with the superscription, "As the head of the family should teach it in a simple way to his household." Every man with a family has the God-given responsibility to instruct his family in the faith, to preach and teach the Word of God to them. If men simply understood this calling, it would likely reinvigorate their church attendance. We bemoan men's abdication of the divine directive to lead their families to the altar, but in egalitizing men and women, in assigning the same roles to mother as fathers, we've stripped men of their responsibility to proclaim the Word to their families. We shouldn't be surprised that they've largely taken the easy way out that's been given to them. Who wouldn't?

It is no easy task to teach the Word. But a man who has a family has an intimate congregation depending on him to fulfill this calling. If he views the Word as something simply for *others*, though, he will never be a faithful preacher. He must catechize himself, preach the fullness of the two-edged Word—unadulterated Law alongside undiluted Gospel—to himself as much as to his wife and children.

And, should a man not yet be given this congregation, he nevertheless remains a caretaker of the Word in society, a preacher of the Word in the world, as well. The deceiver continues to entice people everywhere into his web of deception; but in many cases, the last one to hold the breach, to fight against the devil with his lies, is a man equipped with the Word of God.

PRIEST

Second, Adam is called to be a priest. The prophetic role is to speak for God to His people. The priestly role is to intercede for his people before God. In other words, Adam is given to pray for his family and creation.

By many modern notions of masculinity, prayer is not very masculine. If a man is defined by what he does, he doesn't want to be defined by prayer. Prayer is the admission that a man cannot do what needs to be done. It's submission to a higher authority, an acknowledgment by the one called to be the head of others that he is not his own head.

Prayer is counter to productivity. You will not check anything off your to-do list by praying. This is why a man needs to pray. He needs to know his limits, his creatureliness. Adam could not do everything in the garden. He was not the Creator. He was a creature and was expected to live within limits. Don't eat from this tree; eat from this one. Be fruitful and multiply. Do this; don't do that. Staying within the bounds of a creature places Adam in a submissive relationship with his Creator.

Prayer is the acknowledgment of man's limitations. Prayer for others, then, is especially a man's admission of his inability to do all his calling requires. Before he can commit himself to those entrusted to his care, he must commend them to God.

KING

Finally, Adam is entrusted with the office of king in the Garden of Eden. He is the government, the police force, the schoolhouse, and every form of modern-day political authority all rolled into one man.

Before sin launched creation into a tailspin that could only be corrected by the incarnation and death of God Himself, there was no need for differentiation between any of these roles. The man filled them all. Moreover, before there was sin and disorder, there was no division between church and state. There was only the family, and Adam was intended to be the king of this domain. Because this calling to be king is such an intrinsic part of his identity, the three essential aspects of masculinity—protect, provide, procreate—manifest themselves still today across most cultures. Although urged to repress it by a feminized culture, men have an innate sense of the calling to be kings.

This calling, like the calls to be head and to have dominion, is easily distorted. There are many websites and other media outlets today that pander to man's wounded masculinity, exhorting him to be king again, but doing so with heavy doses of misogyny and pick-up artistry. Having sex with a bunch of women does not make you king of any kingdom. Mistreating women and despising children is the opposite of the reign of a righteous king, as Adam was for a brief moment in the Garden of Eden. Exerting your rule doesn't make you king. Ruling makes you king.

As king of creation, Adam was called to exercise his reign in love. Akin to this headship and dominion, the mark of his reign is not in his ability to exert his control but in his ability to do what is required of him as king.

PROTECTOR, PROVIDER, PROCREATOR

Kings don't exist for their own good. A man's reign is never for his own good. It is always for the good of those placed under his kingdom. He is entrusted with their good. A man is called to employ his strength and prowess for the protection and provision of those committed to his care. His wife and children are his not as status symbols, to somehow confirm his masculinity, but to care for. His to protect. His to shield from the perils in the world. His for whom to provide, for whom to fight for against the chaos and disorder that threaten.

PROTECT

In order to protect, a man needs both courage and strength. In the garden, this task was much easier for Adam than it is for man today. As soon as Adam and his wife rebelled, what was their reaction? The slight sound of God walking in the garden struck fear into their hearts. Sin alienated the man and the woman from the rest of creation. Now even the slightest sound of the wind through the trees sends them fleeing. Things that go bump in the night were not originally frightening. Now, however, they raise alarms and send men groping in the dark for a weapon before heading downstairs to investigate.

Threats abound. Enemies, disasters, deceptions, and worse stand poised to topple a man's kingdom at any moment. For this mission, at times, a man must possess physical strength. That's why this task is given principally to men and not women. In the wake of the 2015 decision to open all military roles to women, even combat roles, there has been much hand-wringing over whether to change physical fitness requirements to allow women to serve on the front lines in combat. This wouldn't even be a conversation if men and women were equally matched in strength. But they're not. And everyone knows that.

So men have a duty to keep themselves strong and healthy, inasmuch as this lies within their power. Not everyone needs to be able to draw attention when he takes off his shirt, and we do well to eschew gaining physical strength simply for vain reasons. But every man will be put to tests of strength. Whether it's employed in warring against the nefarious machines at the pickle production plant that screwed the lids on the jars too tightly or in defending one's family against real, physical enemies, strength is a gift given to men. It's why their bodies produce more testosterone than women's bodies. Their biology equips them, in part, for the task of protecting.

Physical strength, though, is just one aspect of the arsenal of strength a man needs to have at his disposal. And, though his genetics and testosterone naturally equip a man to develop chiseled pecs and impressive lats, to lift heavy objects and endure long bouts of physical exertion, what he needs just as much are the other hallmarks of strength: mental strength, emotional strength, and spiritual strength. He needs a strong, capable mind, which includes not only smarts but also grit, the ability to solve problems and endure more than his mind tells him is possible. He needs emotional strength and resiliency, the ability to remain present and in control of his reactions to situations, cognizant of external stressors and capable of thinking through his response instead of immediately reacting to his own emotions. He needs spiritual strength, the willingness to submit to an authority higher than himself and to commend himself and those entrusted to his protection to God in prayer.

A man is called to protect more than just his family, though. He is called to protect those beyond the walls of his own house as well. In the chaos that has resulted since Adam's fall into sin, the world is constantly ready to inflict violence and harm on man and his community. His tribe needs defenders. His call to exercise his strength for the good of others, to lay his life on the line when the need arises, to see himself as a means by which the lives of others can be shielded from danger and relieved from oppression extends beyond the walls of his house. In order to survive and thrive, a society needs men willing to heed the call to be defenders at the borders.

But any strength by itself is useless without courage. All the strength in the world can't do any good if you don't have the guts to use it. Men must have courage to face challenges and grit to stay until the task is finished. When the Lord was bringing His people into the Promised Land, this was the regular refrain: "Be strong and courageous" (Deuteronomy 31:6, 7, 23; Joshua 1:6, 7, 9, 18; 10:25). Courage is not the denial or the absence of fear. Fearlessness is just naiveté. Courage is acknowledgment of fear and risks, and taking action in spite of fear because someone needs your protection.

The responsibility to protect transcends the domain of king, though. A man must also protect his family as a priest. In a broken world, threats are too great for any man to withstand, and the job of protection far exceeds his ability. Thus he must submit his own protection under the protection of his heavenly Father. Unless God the Father dispatches His angels to defend His people, the work of any man to protect is futile. Storms, disasters, and acts of great evil surpass the ability of a man to ward them off. Thus his work of protection, unless it begins with prayer for those whom he is called to protect, is begun in vain.

His call to be a protector includes his office as prophet as well. This is where Adam failed. As he stood by looking on, he failed to protect his wife against the onslaught of lies from the father of lies. Men are called to use not only their physical strength to protect those under their care, but also their spiritual prowess and strength. Adam knew the Word; he had, after all, preached it to Eve. But at the most critical moment in his and his wife's life, he failed to protect her.

St. Paul calls Christians, men and women alike, to engage in this fight. Men must fight not only for their sakes, but also for the sake of those around them: wife, children, friends, brothers, fellow Christians, and society as a whole.

> Finally, be strong in the Lord and in the strength of His might. Put on the whole armor of God, that you may be able to stand against the schemes of the devil. For we do not wrestle against flesh and blood, but against the rulers, against the authorities, against the cosmic powers over this present darkness, against the spiritual forces of evil in the heavenly places. (Ephesians 6:10–12)

See the nature of this battle? It's cosmic. It's unseen. The final outcome is guaranteed because Christ's death on the cross fully destroyed the power of the devil. The war has been won. The Lord of the Church has triumphed. His Church is unassailable; not even the fiercest powers of hell can harm her (Matthew 16:18). But the battles against individual Christians still rage (Revelation 12:17) like the last flickering lights, the despairing last resorts of a defeated enemy. A man must fight this battle. St. Paul continues,

> Therefore take up the whole armor of God, that you may be able to withstand in the evil day, and having done all, to stand firm. Stand therefore, having fastened on the belt of truth, and having put on the breastplate of righteousness,

> and, as shoes for your feet, having put on the readiness given by the gospel of peace. In all circumstances take up the shield of faith, with which you can extinguish all the flaming darts of the evil one; and take the helmet of salvation, and the sword of the Spirit, which is the word of God, praying at all times in the Spirit, with all prayer and supplication. To that end, keep alert with all perseverance, making supplication for all the saints. (Ephesians 6:13–18)

The world needs men who can fight this spiritual battle. Your wife needs a man who will fight not only for himself but also for her. Your children, likewise, need a father spiritually strong and courageous enough to fight for them against the assaults of the devil with his lies, the world with her allures, and their own sinful selves, selfishly curved in on themselves. The fight is fierce, but the weapons and defenses are just as other-worldly as the forces they must repel. Truth, righteousness, the Gospel, faith, salvation, and the Word of God are instruments forged in the fire of the crucifixion of Christ. And they are given purely as gifts. The call to protect in this concealed conflagration is noble and lofty. Only those under the command of Christ are equipped.

PROVIDE

Closely related to the responsibility to protect is the call to provide. In order to provide, a man needs skills and the ability to take risks. When God created a wife for Adam and presented her to him, after Adam's jubilant "At last," the Lord declared, "Therefore a man shall leave his father and his mother and hold fast to his wife, and they shall become one flesh" (Genesis 2:24). Leaving his father and mother has long been seen as a hallmark of manliness. Once a man can provide for himself, and thereafter, for his bride and children, without reliance on his parents, he has arrived at the precipice of being considered a man.

Many cultures recognize the importance of a man's leaving his parents in order to cleave to his wife. The Masai tribe of southeastern Africa, for instance, initiates a boy into manhood with a lion hunt. When a boy is ready, he will give away all his possessions and embark on a solo lion hunt. Upon returning, he will have his head shaved and his face painted with chalk, before being circumcised. When, months later, his circumcision is fully healed, he will be welcomed back into the tribe as a warrior and a *man*. The ordeal demonstrates his ability both to protect and to provide.

Stories from other cultures—unaffected by Western society's rejection of all things religious or superstitious—of initiating boys into manhood by taking them away from their mothers, either into isolation or into the company of other men, abound. It is for the sake of his wife and future children that a man must leave his father and mother. He must be able to provide.

Nowadays, both sociologists from ivory towers and mom and dad from upstairs bemoan the "boomerang generation," children who return from college to live in their parents' basement while they figure out what they want to do with their lives. In losing rites of initiation that actually separated a boy from his parents and marked his transition into manhood (no, Confirmation doesn't count), we've lost the ability to cultivate the kind of independence required for a man to take full ownership of his family by providing for them. Add to this the fact that many men must (or worse, choose to) also rely on their wife to be cobreadwinner, and the call for a man to provide falls on ears not quite deaf but unfamiliar with such language.

Provision need not imply a man hunting and gathering or raising his own food, though these are certainly manly arts worth relearning and fine ways for a man partly to fulfill this latent drive to be the provider for those who depend on him. To provide is why men go to work (though the notion that work is something we have to go *away* to do is a testament to how we've lost the concept of the family as its own little economy, but that's for a different book). It's why men define themselves by what they do.

PROCREATE

The calling and drive of a man to procreate is inextricably woven into his two other callings of protecting and providing. Procreation gives a man children for whom to provide and whom he is driven to protect. As discussed earlier, even when God withholds the blessing of children from a man's union with his wife, he is by no means relieved of the desire and the necessity to protect and provide for those around him. If a man does not have children who rely on him, others outside his most intimate spheres of influence can be the recipients of his drive to protect and to provide.

But the drive to have children, to procreate, runs deep in a man's psyche. In the same way that gluttony is just disordered hunger, so lust is just a distortion of the God-given drive to father children. In the garden, Adam's drives should have led him to pursue his wife, to woo her, to make her feel safe and secure in his presence. This would allow Eve to open herself up, make herself vulnerable, willing to receive his sexual advances in the shared hope that their union would be fruitful and that together with their children, they would spread their dominion over creation beyond the reach of two people. To have children, for Adam and Eve, was a divinely wrought desire to fill the earth and subdue it.

The very fact that this perfect union had not yet borne any children before the fall into sin is probably an indication of how soon the events of Genesis 3 followed the events of Genesis 2. The serpent sought to interrupt God's plan for creation and thwart the natural procreative desires of the man and woman as soon as possible. If they had children, his evil plan would presumably have been more difficult to carry out.

There's an order to creation. So also there's an order to *pro*creation. Here it is: Man pursues woman. Man catches woman's attention. Man woos woman. Man makes woman feel safe, beautiful, and cherished. Woman allows man inside her. Together, they procreate.

Although sin has fraught this order with chaos, disorder, lust, and selfishness, this is nevertheless the pattern inherent in creation. Men want to pursue. Women want to be pursued. The biological act of procreation testifies to this reality. A woman's reproductive organs are on the inside. The marital union happens inside her. She is a gatekeeper of sorts. He cannot gain access to this union except through her head. She needs to trust that this man is able to protect and provide for her before she will allow him to father her children, whom he will also need to protect and provide for.

If you're not convinced, consider the distortions of this pattern of pursuer and pursued. A man unable to win the affection of a woman, unable to convince her that he is safe for her and committed to the rearing of her children, will seek to procure sex from her by other means. Thus, rape and prostitution are largely perpetuated by men taking advantage of women, taking their pleasure (usually devoid of its procreative function) at her expense, rather than for her mutual benefit. They allow a man to shortcut the ordinary means of pursuit and give him the illusion of having power or being desirable. So also pornography makes innumerable women accessible to a man if he only knows the right words to enter into the search bar. They're all lies, though, perpetrated by the most effeminate of men.

Real procreation, then, like protecting and providing, is not only active, but it's also giving. A man pursues his wife not merely for the goal of orgasm. His procreative goal is to seek the good of his wife, to make her feel loved and protected, and to receive the blessings of children so that he can continue this lifelong work of giving, loving, and serving those who depend on him. The pleasure in the act and the reward for the work is more than just the release.

In order to protect, a man needs physical strength, mental strength, spiritual strength, emotional strength, and a healthy measure of courage to face the fears that he will inevitably confront.

In order to provide, a man needs skills that others are willing to pay for and the ability to take calculated risks.

In order to procreate, a man needs vitality and the risk-taking openness to receive the blessings of children.

In all these traits, Adam was the perfect example of a man until the fall. And now, as men recreated in Holy Baptism, we live our lives toward the future fulfillment of these traits in us. We await a restored Eden, when men will finally and fully be men again. Until then, we live in hope and the practice of disciplines and exercises to cultivate manly traits that no longer come naturally or easily.

THE BATTLE PLAN

A PORTRAIT OF MAN: ADAM

1. What was Adam called to do?

2. Examine your vocations. What are you called to do in order to be a man like Adam was intended to be?

3. How can you improve in these fundamental roles of man? How can you better be of service to others? How can you use your natural strengths and skills for the good of others around you? Set goals for yourself based on you answers.

4. What strategies can you employ to move toward being a good man in pursuit of these goals?

8

A PORTRAIT OF MAN: CHRIST

"Wherefore I beseech you all to become men: since, so long as we are children, how shall we teach them manliness? How shall we restrain them from childish folly? Let us, therefore, become men; that we may arrive at the measure of the stature which hath been marked out for us by Christ, and may obtain the good things to come: through the grace and loving-kindness."

—St. John Chrysostom, Homilies on First Corinthians

Between the creation of man and the day of his re-creation, the picture of man looks pretty bleak. Man is neither what he was created to be nor what he will be in his resurrection. But Christ is the perfect Man. The Second Adam succeeds where the First Adam failed, "For if, because of one man's trespass, death reigned through that one man, much more will those who receive the abundance of grace and the free gift of righteousness reign in life through the one man Jesus Christ" (Romans 5:17). For the time between Adam's sin and the day of our own resurrection, the portrait of man will have to be shaded and colored in by the example of Christ. No other man suffices.

THE PERFECT HUSBAND

We've scratched the surface of Ephesians 5 twice before, but we have not fully plumbed its depths, especially as it describes the role of Christ as the husband of His Bride, the Church. Although guys enjoy reminding their wives of the first verse from Paul's admonitions to husbands and wives, the reality is that Paul's longer exhortation is not for wives; it's for husbands. After writing three verses about the wife's call to submit to her husband as the Church submits to Christ, her Head, Paul writes eight and a half verses describing the husband's call toward his wife.

> Husbands, love your wives, as Christ loved the church and gave Himself up for her, that He might sanctify her, having cleansed her by the washing of water with the word, so that He might present the church to Himself in splendor, without spot or wrinkle or any such thing, that she might be holy and without blemish. In the same way husbands should love their wives as their own bodies. He who loves his wife loves himself. For no one ever hated his own flesh, but nourishes and cherishes it, just as Christ does the church, because we are members of His body. "Therefore a man shall leave his father and mother and hold fast to his wife, and the two shall become one flesh." This mystery is profound, and I am saying that it refers to Christ and the church. However, let each one of you love his wife as himself, and let the wife see that she respects her husband. (Ephesians 5:25–33)

This is what a perfect Man does for His wife, what the perfect Husband, Christ, does for His Bride, the Church.

A MAN LOVES HIS BRIDE

This is more than the emotion of love. That's temporary. Over the course of a marriage, emotions wax and wane. Sometimes a husband has more affection for his bride than other times. That's not love. Not love as Christ loves His Bride, anyway. The love that Christ has for His Church is perfect, sacrificial, and giving. This is the catch-all verb that guides the rest of Paul's description of Christ and exhortation to contemporary husbands. The remaining six verbs describe what this kind of love husbands are called to have is all about. What does Christ do? How does He love? What does this mean a man does for his wife?

A MAN GIVES HIMSELF UP FOR HIS BRIDE

It's little wonder that guys only commit verses 22–24 to memory. It's pretty easy to tell your wife to submit, that this is what the Bible says she ought to do. It's a whole lot harder to live your life for your wife in the way Christ lives for His Church.

Christ gave His life for His Bride, shed His blood for her, died on the cross for her. Everything He did was for her good, not His own. He never had a single selfish motive. He never manipulated her to do what He secretly wanted. He never chose His own needs over hers. He never harmed her in the slightest. So, until you're doing a Christlike job of loving your wife and living your life for her, you might do well to abandon the exhortations for her to submit to you. Let the Word of God command her submission in the same way that it commands your selfless love and perfect sacrifice. You worry about your role; she can worry about her submission. And, truth be told, the better job you do of fulfilling your calling to live your life for the good of your wife, the easier and more natural her submission will be. If she trusts that you have her interests in mind above your own, that you would do anything necessary to provide for her well-being, she'll submit. She won't protest, and you won't notice.

To live your life for the good of your wife, to be Christ to your wife, is one of the highest callings of masculinity, but also the most difficult. Your wife will rarely, if ever, be worthy of this kind of love. Christ's Church is never worthy of the love He shows her. That's the point. He doesn't wait for her to deserve His love. He loves her precisely because she could never deserve it. That's the nature of His love.

A MAN SANCTIFIES HIS BRIDE

If a man is going to be the head of his household, that's a leadership role that comes with a hefty price tag. Leaders of every stripe take ownership of the mistakes and missteps of their teams. Consider Christ. He doesn't hold His Bride responsible for any of her sins or faults. He takes them, claims them as His own, and deals with them. He pays for her sins as though they were His own.

A good husband will never be in the fault-finding business when it comes to his wife. If he lives as Christ toward his wife, in his eyes, she can do no wrong. Imagine how that would completely alter the dynamics of would-be fights in a marriage. The husband sanctifies his wife. He makes her holy. He takes her sins as his own. What, then, is there to fight about? And if she is free from the fear that her mistakes might upset her husband, she is free to live in love and service toward him. She will naturally respect and submit to a man who isn't nitpicking her faults.

A man who lives as Christ does not complain about his wife. Not to the guys. Not to her. Not to himself under his breath.

How you speak about your wife affects how you think about her. Eventually, you'll come to believe your own complaining more than reality. Your wife will become worse in your eyes than she actually is. And you will both suffer.

Fourth-century bishop and preacher John, whose preaching was so highly regarded that he earned the nickname *Chrysostom*, the "golden mouthed," preached on these verses from Ephesians:

> Thou hast seen the measure of obedience, hear also the measure of love. Wouldest thou have thy wife obedient unto thee, as the Church is to Christ? Take then thyself the same provident care for her, as Christ takes for the Church. Yea, even if it shall be needful for thee to give thy life for her, yea, and to be cut into pieces ten thousand times, yea, and to endure and undergo any suffering whatever,—refuse it not. Although thou shouldest undergo all this, yet wilt thou not, no, not even then, have done anything like Christ. For thou indeed art doing it for one to whom thou art already knit; but He for one who turned her back on Him and hated Him. In the same way then as He laid at His feet her who turned her back on Him, who hated, and spurned, and disdained Him, not by menaces, nor by violence, nor by terror, nor by anything else of the kind, but by his unwearied affection; so also do thou behave thyself toward thy wife. Yea, though thou see her looking down upon thee, and disdaining, and scorning thee, yet by thy great thoughtfulness for her, by affection, by kindness, thou wilt be able to lay her at thy feet.[38]

38 John Chrysostom, *Homilies on Ephesians* 20, in *A Select Library of the Christian Church: Nicene and Post-Nicene Fathers: First Series*, ed. Philip Schaff (Reprint, Grand Rapids, MI: Eerdmans, 1952), 13:144.

Take every character fault of your wife, and own them. Take possession of them. You pay for them. Her mistakes are yours. Set her free from blame and accusation. Christ sanctifies His Bride. He does not accuse. He does not blame. He does not make her pay for her mistakes. She is holy—sanctified—because her Groom has made her so. How He sees her is who she becomes to the world.

A MAN CLEANSES HIS BRIDE BY THE WASHING OF WATER AND THE WORD

This is Baptism, of course. Water and the Word converge in only one place in the New Testament and the first centuries of the life of the Church: in Baptism. In the waters of Holy Baptism, Christ takes away the sin of His wife and covers her with His own righteousness: "For as many of you as were baptized into Christ have put on Christ" (Galatians 3:27).

Husbands don't baptize their wives, so what does this description of Christ and His Bride have to do with a man and his wife? Why does St. Paul include this description?

Husbands and wives are together washed by water and the Word, both baptized into the same Baptism, both recipients of the same new life that Christ bestows in Holy Baptism. A husband doesn't cleanse his wife from her sins. Christ does. But a husband must see his wife as a washed, cleansed, forgiven saint in Christ's Church.

And, while he does not cleanse her anew with any water, he does cleanse her regularly with the Word. As the pastor of his family, a man should be the first one to speak words of forgiveness when his wife or children err. He should model the cleansing forgiveness of Christ. His words should always bestow the gifts Christ delivers.

If you're married, you already know that your wife will sin more against you than against anyone else. If you're not married but hoping for this blessing someday, someone should burst your bubble of false fantasies right now. Marriage is not all the euphoric bliss that Disney movies make your future-bride think it will be. It's hard work. And it's the arena in which your wife will hurt you in ways other humans cannot.

In a similar way, you will sin against her more than anyone else. That's simply how it works when God puts you into that kind of intimate relationship. The stakes are higher. You're called to do more to and for your wife than for anyone else. And so you'll screw up in your relationship with her more than in any other relationship you have. So also, she will commit the worst sins of her life against you. You are the one (and also your children, should you be so blessed) toward whom she has the highest calling. And you are the one with whom she will spend the most time. It's only natural that two sinners put in such close, intimate proximity will sin against one another more than against those farther away.

In those times, when your wife sins against you, your words, O man, must be grace-filled, forgiving words. Speak the Gospel to your wife. Assure her of Christ's forgiveness and yours. Absolve her of her offenses, however heinous, against you. This is what Christ does for His Church in Baptism and what you therefore must do for your wife. You needn't wait for her contrition. Forgive her because she needs it, not because she deserves it.

You need to know what forgiveness is, too, if you're going to offer it to your wife. Consider Christ's interaction with His Bride. Forgiveness is not free. It has a tremendous cost. To forgive is not the same as saying "It's okay." To forgive, rather, is to say, "I will pay for that." That's how Jesus forgives, how He has forgiven you and how He has forgiven your wife. So your words, then, as words spoken by a forgiven child of God, as words spoken by a man who represents Christ to his wife, must be words of forgiveness—cleansing words.

A MAN PRESENTS HIS BRIDE TO HIMSELF WITHOUT ANY SPOT, WRINKLE, OR BLEMISH, THAT SHE MIGHT BE HOLY

These three descriptions of a man's relationship with his wife are essentially the same, though they may vary in effects. He sanctifies her, makes her holy, does not hold her sins against her. He cleanses her, forgives her, removes her sin, pays for her transgressions as his own. And he presents her to himself without any blemish.

As Christ presents His Bride to Himself, He covers over her sins with His own righteousness. He thus removes every blemish, every imperfection, every "wrinkle," so that she is beautiful, radiant, peerless. His love for her perfects her so that He desires none other. So also a husband's love for his wife ought to perfect her.

Your wife is probably not the most beautiful woman in the world. But she needs to be the most beautiful woman in *your* world. In fact, St. John Chrysostom, in his same sermon on Ephesians 5, remarked that if your wife is not beautiful, you're probably better off: "Do ye not see how many, after living with beautiful wives, have ended their lives pitiably, and how many, who have lived with those of no great beauty, have run on to extreme old age with great enjoyment."[39]

Regardless of how the rest of the world esteems a woman's beauty, in her husband's eyes, she is to be desired above all others.

39 Chrysostom, *Homilies on Ephesians*, 145.

This is what she wants and needs. Think of the question many a man has been asked by his bride: "Does this dress make me look fat?" The answer is always "No." She doesn't really want to know how anyone else will see her in that dress. She wants to know how her husband sees her. She wants his approval, his acceptance. She wants to know that, no matter how the dress flows around her curves, at the end of the day, she's still *his*.

A man living in a fallen world and in a hypersexualized culture will not always believe this, of course. How he conducts himself will shape his perception of reality. If he is faithful to his wife with his eyes, it increases her attractiveness to him. If his thoughts wander and he lets fantasies play out, he will be less satisfied with what he already has.

Human beings simultaneously want novelty and stability. More than anywhere else, this happens within the lifelong commitment between a husband and wife. Therein, a man and woman have the stability and security that experts say yields better, more fulfilling, and more satisfying sex. And they have one another alongside whom they can experience the novelties of life. Lifelong monogamy is intended to produce great satisfaction. If you learn to love and see your wife the way Christ loves and sees His Church, if you learn to find your greatest earthly delights in her beauty, even the scientists say you'll find deep, abiding satisfaction.[40]

40 For more on the way commitment to your wife can produce both the satisfaction of commitment and the excitement of novelty, see neuroscientist Gregory Berns' *Satisfaction: The Science of Finding True Fulfillment* (New York: Henry Holt, 2005).

A MAN NOURISHES AND CHERISHES HIS BRIDE

St. Paul uses the picture of a head and a body (Ephesians 5:22–24) to illustrate the relationship of a husband to his wife. The apostle then goes on to say, "Husbands love your wives, as Christ loved the church" (v. 25) and, "In the same way husbands should love their wives as their own bodies. . . . For no one ever hated his own flesh, but nourishes and cherishes it" (vv. 28–29). "In the same way" as Christ loves His Bride, the Church, husbands are to love their wives as heads love the bodies to which they're connected.

The relationship between head and body is essential. As of yet, bodies don't survive without heads, nor heads without bodies. Moreover, heads and bodies are not in competition. The head never seeks to abuse the body, nor the body the head. When head and body are at odds, the whole person is about to die. It makes sense that Paul would use this illustration for marriage. In marriage, husbands and wives are placed into a one-flesh relationship that not only is mutually beneficial to heads and bodies but also is critical to the thriving and surviving of each.

Within this model, heads do two things for bodies. Thus, husbands do two things for wives: nourish and cherish. Both of these words are peculiar in the New Testament. The word for nourish is *ektrepho*, which Paul uses just a few verses later to describe how parents should raise their children. "Fathers, do not provoke your children to anger, but *bring them up* (*ektrephete*) in the discipline and instruction of the Lord" (Ephesians 6:4).

This word conveys both the idea of nourishing to maturity and also nurturing or raising, as a parent does a child. A husband does not parent his wife. She is obviously an adult, already mature. But he nevertheless has a responsibility for her ongoing nourishment, not as a parent does for a child, but as a head does for a body. He must see to her physical nourishment and sustenance. He ought to be the primary breadwinner, for her sake as well as his. They both thrive on this order. And he also cares for her spiritual nourishment. He must guard and shepherd her spiritual maturation.

Husbands should spend time in Scripture daily and enable their wives to have the same daily retreat into the Word of God. Pray with your wife. Read Scripture with your wife. Have a devotional book, something doctrinally pure, with which you can agree uncritically and listen and be fed. Study is different from devotion and meditation, the latter being like listening to a sermon. You go to a church that has a confession and preacher with which you are in agreement so that you don't need to filter out false doctrine in the sermon. You want to be fed without having to sort out the poisonous from the profitable. So husbands need to cultivate this daily discipline not only for their own sakes but also for the sake of their wives.

In addition to nourishing, husbands are called to cherish their wives. Although the English translation sounds like it belongs in a Hallmark greeting card, the Greek, *thalpo*, again conveys something deeper. And, again, it's a word used only twice in the New Testament. In the other use, St. Paul describes his work toward the Christians in Thessalonica: "But we were gentle among you, like a nursing mother *taking care of* (*thalpe*) her own children" (1 Thessalonians 2:7).

The sense is once more as a parent raising a child. But this time, it more specifically conveys a mother nursing and rearing her infant children. More broadly, the word also means to care for, to cherish, or to comfort. But the sense that the husband has an almost parental role toward his wife is unmistakable. In the Greek translation of the Old Testament, *thalpo* is used once for a mother bird brooding her eggs or young chicks (Deuteronomy 22:6) and once for an ostrich warming her eggs (Job 39:14). This fits well with Paul's use of *thalpo* in 1 Thessalonians, but it seems quite strange to think of a husband "brooding" his wife.

This maternal sense of the word clearly conveys more than the English "cherish." This kind of cherishing is of a mother toward her newborn child: a cherishing that completely reorients her priorities, inverts her pre-child to-do list, and requires her full-bodied effort. Suddenly, someone else commands her attention, her time, her devotion, and her labor. So it must be with a husband and a wife. A man's wife ought to command his attention, time, devotion, and labor. She needs him to keep her warm, like a broody hen does her chicks. He is to be a safe place for her.

Paul exhorts husbands to provide this kind of metaphorical warmth and safety for their wives because a woman's lusts and fantasies are usually different from a man's. A man is excited by the physical; the sight of flesh titillates him. A woman, too, is excited by the physical, but her fantasies often incline more toward the emotional. She dreams of a man who will hold her and keep her safe. The thought of being touched is as exciting for many women as the thought of having sex is for a man. A man's wife desires this kind of cherishing that is akin to a mother bird keeping her brood safe and warm.

This isn't merely physical, though. Your wife doesn't just need a hug. She needs your life to embrace her in the way her life embraces her children. This is why a marriage is never a competition. It's not a matter of who is more important, more cherished, more loved. No one ought to be concerned about asserting his own self-importance. If you doubt that, consider the icon of the Holy Family. Ask Joseph who is the most important in his family, and his answer will certainly be his (eventual) bride,

Mary. Everything he does is for her, for her good. Even when he resolved to divorce her quietly, it was for her good, not his own. For his own good, he could have had her publicly humiliated. But he didn't. And then once the child Jesus was delivered, Joseph again could have left the whispers and the gossip behind. He could have made a new home for himself apart from the girl who was rumored to have given herself to another man and the boy who was whispered to have been conceived out of wedlock. But he didn't. Joseph's calling was to Mary, to nurture her and to cherish her, in the same way that her calling was to Jesus, to nourish and to cherish Him. Because Joseph fulfilled his calling to Mary, she was free to fulfill her calling to be mother to Jesus.

So a man is called to love his wife selflessly and sacrificially, to give himself up for her, to make her holy by taking away her sins, to cleanse her by his words and the Word of God, and to nurture and cherish her even as he does his own body. What is she called to do? Submit to him and respect him. That's it. Holy smokes. If you're a husband, that's a tall order. From time to time, I try to offer my wife the deal to strike the whole section from Ephesians 5 from our household Bibles. I won't expect her submission and respect, if she will not expect my love, sacrifice, sanctification, cleansing, seeing her as spotless and without blemish, nourishment, and cherishing. She hasn't taken me up on the offer.

Although no man will ever live up to this ideal, it is how Christ loves His Bride the Church. He lives only for her good. He never insists on His own rights. He has ultimate power and authority, yet He will not coerce her. He loves her perfectly and selflessly. And every man who becomes a husband makes vows—promises—to love his wife in exactly the same way.

THE PERFECT MAN

Not only is Christ the perfect husband—the example for men who are called to this holy estate of husband—but He is also the perfect man—the example for all men in whatever their vocations or stations of life. He fulfills what Adam failed to do. Moreover, the way Christ treats His Bride is paradigmatic for how He as a man treats His creation. Even if you are not called into the estate of marriage, if you are a man, Christ's selfless love toward His Bride is the example for you in all your interactions with others.

VIR BONUS EST. A MAN IS GOOD.

Christ is good. Perfectly good. This seems so obvious that it nearly goes without saying. As we discussed in chapter 5, though, good is not the same as *nice*. Nice is often opposed to good. Nice tends toward milquetoast and deferential. Nice compromises. Good does not. A man does not compromise his goodness for any reason. He is always ready to do what's right, what's necessary, what's good. He is always ready to serve others, always ready to defend those in need, always ready to be the instrument for others' good, not his own. His goodness is a tool in his service toward others.

"Good" is a common description of Jesus.

When the rich young ruler went to Jesus (Mark 10:17–22), he asked Him, "Good Teacher, what must I do to inherit eternal life?" Jesus' answer must have caught the man seeking to be "good" completely off guard. "Why do you call Me good? No one is good except God alone." Then Jesus and the young man had a go-round about how faithfully he had kept the commandments, and eventually the young man left disheartened. In the end, he could not be good. He could not be saved. He could not obey the Law perfectly.

This elicited the amazed, "Then who can be saved?" (v. 26) from the disciples. Exactly. No one. No one is good except God alone. Jesus' answer is one of the most misquoted verses in the Bible: "With man it is impossible, but not with God. For all things are possible with God" (v. 27). Certainly you've heard this verse pithily misquoted. When times are tough, when the bill is more than you think you can pay this month, the field goal farther away than you've kicked before, the barbell loaded with more than you've ever cleaned, the sales meeting more nerve-wracking than you can handle, someone quips to you, "All things are possible with God." But bill payments, field goals, Olympic cleans, or successful meetings are not what Jesus promises, of course. God can undertake those, sure. But He doesn't promise to accomplish those impossible things for you. The impossible thing He promises to accomplish for you is saving people who cannot save themselves. This is essential to His *goodness*. No one is good like this except God alone, a description that includes Jesus Himself. He is *good* like this.

Elsewhere, Jesus calls Himself good, in particular, the *Good* Shepherd (John 10:11–18). If you have a real flock of sheep, though, don't take Jesus' example of shepherding as a way to care for your flock. It only works when Jesus does it. What makes this Shepherd good? "The good shepherd lays down His life for the sheep" (v. 11). For ordinary animal husbandry, dying for your flocks and herds is quintessentially terrible husbandry. And yet, the Good Shepherd lays down His life for the sheep. Jesus further explains, "For this reason the Father loves Me, because I lay down my life that I may take it up again. No one takes it from Me, but I lay it down of My own accord. I have authority to lay it down, and I have authority to take it up again" (vv. 17–18).

Only one is good in this way. Only one man is so good that He can lay down His life in love and service for those who are perilously and fatally unable to save themselves and yet who, despite His compassion for them, can never love Him in a way that makes them worthy of His sacrifice. This is good. This is perfect. No other man will be able to do this, but this is the standard, the example *par excellence*.

Jesus is no spineless, easily manipulated, eager-to-please-everybody nice guy. He is good. In the depth of His goodness, He perfectly demonstrates what a man is to be. He is sacrificial. He is self-giving. He is forever focused on the good of others. He is the instrument for their good, for their salvation, for the forgiveness of their sins, for their eternal life and blessedness.

VIR FORTIS EST. A MAN IS STRONG.

Throughout the Old Testament, the triune God is described as the Lord of angelic armies. He is the commander of warrior angels. To understand this, we have to abandon our twofold wrong-headed notions about angels and about God.

First of all, angels are not elegant, beautiful ladies, as they are most often depicted in modern artwork. Nor are they plump, prepubescent, childlike figures as in other popular depictions. They are warriors. They fight. They're not men, but they are muscular and powerful.

In addition to their work of proclaiming the Word of God to the people of God, angels are warriors. They are so powerful and fierce that they always elicit fear when people encounter them. Nearly without exception, the first words angels must say to the people to whom they manifest themselves is "Do not be afraid." It was a single angel who killed a hundred and eighty-five thousand in the camp of the Assyrians (2 Kings 19:35; Isaiah

37:36). It was an angel, Michael the archangel, who defeated Satan by the power of the blood of the Lamb (Revelation 12:7–9). It was an army of angels that gave courage to Elisha's servant and defeated the Syrians (2 Kings 6:15–18).

Second, we need to rid ourselves of the false notion that the triune God is weak or far removed from His creation. Not only are heaven's angelic forces marshaled in impressive power against the enemies of God's people, but also the one commanding them in the battle is God Himself. Throughout the Old Testament, God is identified as the Lord of hosts, *Yahweh Sabaoth*. He is the Commander in Chief of an angelic force that knows no equal, in heaven or on earth. Nothing matches this power.

This description of the Lord is usually rendered "Lord of hosts," though "hosts" doesn't quite capture the power of the army He commands. It sounds more like someone who throws Martha-Stewart-like parties than the Divine Commander of the fiercest force in the universe. When the Old Testament was translated into Greek, about two hundred fifty years before the birth of Christ, this phrase was rendered as *Pantokrator,* literally "all powerful." It was also the translation for the Hebrew *El Shaddai*, or "Lord Almighty."

The icon of Christ as *Pantokrator* has become popular in Eastern Orthodox and Eastern Catholic iconography. Christ is God Almighty, the Lord of angelic armies. And what is the all-powerful Christ doing in the icons? His right hand is held in a posture of blessing, and His left hand is holding a book, usually one of the Gospels. This is how He intends to use all the power at His disposal: to bless and to proclaim His Gospel.

As the Sunday School song teaches, "He's got the whole world in His hands." Every power of the triune God is at His disposal, but what does He do with those hands? He allows them to be nailed to a cross. As we discussed before, Jesus isn't captured and crucified by forces stronger than He is. No one takes His life from Him; He lays it down of His own will.

This power is not manly. It's divine. It's an attribute of Jesus' divinity, not His humanity. But when God became man in the person of Jesus, a human being wielded this supernatural power. At every stage of His life, Jesus possessed this power. Even as a single-celled zygote in the womb of His virgin mother, Christ was the almighty God, the *Pantokrator*.

How He exercises this power is a lesson in true masculinity. Christ is obviously not weak. No matter how often you hit the gym, how many protein shakes you drink, how you cultivate mental toughness or emotional resiliency, you will never possess power that even holds a candle to Jesus'.

So what does He do? He never insists on His rights. He never has to assert His will over others. This is the true, manly exercise of power. Power is in refusing to insist on your own rights, in giving instead of taking. Real power doesn't need to engage in petty squabbles and grappling with others for control. Time and again, Jesus confounds the scribes and the Pharisees. He will not be snared in their traps or bend to their demonic desires. No one takes His life from Him. He lays it down of His own accord.

VIR DAT. A MAN GIVES.

This is the beating heart of masculinity. Jesus is never effeminate, never *malakos*, never self-interested. He exists for the good of others, for mankind, for His creation.

Even when Jesus seems to be at odds with others, when He overturns tables in the temple and drives people out with a homemade whip, when He rebukes His own disciples for their little faith, His goal is never His own good. All He does is for the good of others, even those whom He rebukes with whips or words. His correction is harshest when people have chosen something contrary to their good, when they've erected blockades of sin and rebellion that keep them from receiving His gifts in their fullness. His Law serves to clear away whatever prevents a person from receiving His gifts.

The cross is the perfect demonstration of what a man does. Jesus lives in order to give. This is why the Second Person of the Trinity is incarnate among His creation not as a woman or as a genderless (or gender-confused) person but as a man. He was and remains a man because His mission is to give His life, to give forgiveness, to give eternal life, to give salvation, to give gifts abundantly until the day of His return to His creation. Giving is quintessentially masculine. Jesus is not only perfectly man, but He is also perfectly giving.

Men and women are not the same. In the act of reproduction, men have a one-time function. If a man dies after impregnating his wife, the child will still survive because of the mother's essential role in gestation and nurture. If after the sexual, reproductive union, a woman dies, so does her child. Men are naturally stronger. But they are also naturally more expendable. Even base biology confesses this fact. Men exist to give. Their statistically shorter lives also lend credence to this fact: they spend their lives for the good of others, not for their own self-preservation. In this fundamental core value of masculinity, then, there is no more perfect man than Jesus.

His love and His example set men free to give.

Every boy dreams of being a superhero. He wants to rescue, to save, to be needed, to be essential to the safety of others. He wants to give. It's chiseled into his psyche. As he grows, though, he will be seduced by the opposite, the vice of selfishness. He will be encouraged to think that he exists for his own good before the good of others.

If masculinity were not such a struggle, one that every man since Adam has grappled with, such superhero fantasies would be virtually unheard of. When a boy dons a cape and jumps down a flight of stairs, what he truly wants to be is not a hero from a different planet, but a man on his own. A man gives. A boy needs to be taught how.

VIR AMAT. A MAN LOVES.

Closely related to man's calling to give is his calling to love. Christ perfectly does both, embodies both. The way in which He loves His Bride is the same way in which Christ loves all mankind: sacrificially. He loves by giving. More precisely, He loves by giving of *Himself.*

The way a man loves is not the way of emotional love. He loves with an active love, a love that does, that serves, that gives, that risks. For Christ, and thus for men, love is not a feeling, an emotion. It's an action. Love is something a man is called to do, not something he is supposed to feel.

Consider Christ's love for mankind.

Love is a trendy topic. Especially God's love. God is "love," right? How and whom He loves is of particular interest to people nowadays. The reason for the intense interest is that they want to find a way, an innovation, to excuse things God has eternally forbidden as contrary to His order of creation, replacing love as a call to action with a new, less-concerned-with-holiness, more-lackadaisical love.

In his Gospel, St. John describes Christ's love and then tells of Christ's command to His apostles to love in the same way. "Now before the Feast of the Passover, when Jesus knew that His hour had come to depart out of this world to the Father, having loved His own who were in the world, He loved them to the end" (13:1). Later, after Jesus had taken the posture of the foot-washing servant and washed His disciples' feet, He instructed those whom He called and sent to follow His example in their future work: "A new commandment I give to you, that you love one another: just as I have loved you, you also are to love one another" (v. 34).

Jesus' love sets the paradigm for human love. It defines how those who are identified by His name and His gift of forgiveness are to interact with others. His love is apparent on the cross, where it costs Jesus every ounce of His life and every drop of His blood to love His creation and redeem mankind from the decay of sin and death. For Jesus, love means living His life for the good of those to whom He ministers. So, for man, recreated in Jesus, love must mean likewise living his life for the good of those entrusted to his care.

What does Jesus' love look like? Look out. It's not the stuff of Lifetime movies and conversation hearts. Although it's often used at weddings, the description of love St. Paul gives in 1 Corinthians 13 is less about the love between a man and a woman and principally about the love Christ displays for mankind in His perfect sacrifice:

> Love is patient and kind; love does not envy or boast; it is not arrogant or rude. It does not insist on its own way; it is not irritable or resentful; it does not rejoice at wrong-doing, but rejoices with the truth. Love bears all things, believes all things, hopes all things, endures all things. Love never ends. (vv. 4–8a)

If you want to understand that better, substitute Jesus' name for the word *love*.

> Jesus is patient and kind; Jesus does not envy or boast; He is not arrogant or rude. He does not insist on His own way; He is not irritable or resentful; He does not rejoice at wrongdoing, but rejoices with the truth. Jesus bears all things, believes all things, hopes all things, endures all things. Jesus never ends.

Then, if you want to know what a man is called to do in the world, how he is to conduct himself toward those he is called to care for, read it like this.

> A man is patient and kind; a man does not envy or boast; he is not arrogant or rude. He does not insist on his own way; he is not irritable or resentful; he does not rejoice at wrongdoing, but rejoices with the truth. A man bears all things, believes all things, hopes all things, endures all things. A man never ends.

No man does that. But it's the ideal. It's the example of Christ. So, in Christ, baptized and set free from sin and death, a man lives *toward* the ideal. He knows who he is in Christ, and he endeavors to live that way toward those whom he encounters. This is love.

Christ doesn't love people just because they are good. His love is not a reward.

> For while we were still weak, at the right time Christ died for the ungodly. For one will scarcely die for a righteous person—though perhaps for a good person one would dare even to die—but God shows His love for us in that while we were still sinners, Christ died for us. Since, therefore, we have now been justified by His blood, much more shall

> we be saved by Him from the wrath of God. For if while we were enemies we were reconciled to God by the death of His Son, much more, now that we are reconciled, shall we be saved by His life. (Romans 5:6–10)

Think about these verses. The love Christ has for mankind is not because of any goodness in men. Instead, He gives His life for a bunch of sinners, a band of rebels against Him, a band of jerks, a horde of losers set on nailing the incarnate God to the cross. That's not a commentary about the Jews as "Christ killers." The Jews didn't kill Jesus. Men killed Jesus. Sinners killed Jesus. To whatever group of people, in whatever time God came as man, the result would have been the same. Mankind since Adam was in a state of warfare against God. To give His life for us rebels was His plan—not when we deserved it, but "while we were still sinners." This is unilateral love. Risky love. Love that takes the gamble that it could be unrequited. It's love that doesn't ask anything in return.

Christ's love is unlike selfish depictions of love. It's the opposite. It loves those least lovable. In this way is a man to love others. He loves for the good of the other, not for any selfish reason. He loves in spite of another's flaws. In fact, he loves—in part because of the flaws—the inherent need of another. A man's love is courageous enough to make an unconditional offer to love no matter the response.

A man's love, then, is risky. It's unilateral. It's not a contract. He loves without any promise or guarantee of a return. Love can go unrequited. In that way, it's like mercy and forgiveness. The risk with love is that it can be abused and taken advantage of. The lover naturally exposes himself to the possible caprice of the beloved. As Christ loves, so do men. God's love for sinners exposes Him to the risk of being rejected. His love is not coercive, even though the ability to receive it comes purely as His gift.

Christlike love is the opposite of emotion. It is action without regard for the underlying emotion. It serves, works for the good of the neighbor, in spite of a man's lack of desire to love, in spite of the other's willingness to accept love. A man loves because he has an idealized, or rather, a renewed sense of what is good and righteousness and how the world should be, by virtue of Christ's own redemptive love. He loves toward this ideal, just as Christ loves man toward the sinless ideal.

This is not, of course, unlike the love a man is called to have for his bride, should he be placed into the holy estate of marriage. There is a hierarchy of those whom a man is to love this way. The closer he is placed in relationship to others, the higher and more pressing his call to love. His wife is always foremost. His children are second. No one is closer to a man than his family, so no one needs his self-giving love as much as these people. Next are those in his most immediate spheres of influence: his employer, employees, co-workers, proximate neighbors, and the fellow members of his congregation. Like concentric ripples from a splash in a pond, each circle farther out is bigger and affects more people, but in a less direct way and farther away from the man himself.

To live for other people puts a man in the position of God in His creation. It's an exercise of his dominion, even if it seems to expose man to the risk of rejection.

This sets into context Jesus' call for His disciples to love not only those worthy of love, but also and especially to love those who do not deserve love, to love their enemies.

> But I say to you who hear, Love your enemies, do good to those who hate you, bless those who curse you, pray for

> those who abuse you. To one who strikes you on the cheek, offer the other also, and from one who takes away your cloak do not withhold your tunic either. Give to everyone who begs from you, and from one who takes away your goods do not demand them back. And as you wish that others would do to you, do so to them.
>
> If you love those who love you, what benefit is that to you? For even sinners love those who love them. And if you do good to those who do good to you, what benefit is that to you? For even sinners do the same. And if you lend to those from whom you expect to receive, what credit is that to you? Even sinners lend to sinners, to get back the same amount. But love your enemies, and do good, and lend, expecting nothing in return, and your reward will be great, and you will be sons of the Most High, for He is kind to the ungrateful and the evil. Be merciful, even as your Father is merciful. (Luke 6:27–36)

This is real, robust, masculine love. To love for the sake of the good of another, even another who deserves punishment or wrath, is genuinely manly. A man content with his identity in Christ does not need vengeance against his enemies. He doesn't foolishly expose himself to harm but, instead, heeds the admonishment Jesus made when sending out His apostles: "I am sending you out as sheep in the midst of wolves, so be wise as serpents and innocent as doves" (Matthew 10:16). His confidence in who he is in Christ is so certain that not even threats to his well-being can temper his love for others.

This love is the source of all other virtues. St. Augustine describes love as the foundation for the four cardinal virtues: temperance, fortitude/courage, justice, and prudence/wisdom.

> Temperance is love giving itself entirely to that which is loved; fortitude is love readily bearing all things for the sake of the loved object; justice is love serving only the loved object, and therefore ruling rightly; prudence is love distinguishing with sagacity between what hinders it and what helps it. The object of this love is not anything, but only God, the chief good, the highest wisdom, the perfect harmony. So we may express the definition thus: that temperance is love keeping itself entire and incorrupt for God; fortitude is love bearing everything readily for the sake of God; justice is love serving God only, and therefore ruling well all else, as subject to man; prudence is love making a right distinction between what helps it towards God and what might hinder it.[41]

When a man can love, his world is bigger. Love takes a man outside himself, gives him a bigger purpose, a higher calling. Love enlarges his life to encompass those around him. Love makes a man like Christ to his neighbors. Love is transcendent. It gives a man meaning and purpose. It's not an emotion, to be sure, as emotions are fleeting and temporary. It's an action and a disposition toward the world around him.

VIR CERTAT. A MAN FIGHTS.

It may seem contrary to what was just said about a man's commitment to love, to say that he also fights. Such is the paradox of Jesus Christ, the Prince of Peace, at whose birth the angels announced, "Glory to God in the highest, and on earth

41 Augustine, *On the Morals of the Catholic Church* 15.25, in *A Select Library of the Christian Church: Nicene and Post-Nicene Fathers: First Series*, ed. Philip Schaff (Reprint, Grand Rapids, MI: Eerdmans, 1952), 4:48.

peace among those with whom He is pleased!" (Luke 2:14) and who Himself later proclaimed, "Do not think that I have come to bring peace to the earth. I have not come to bring peace, but a sword" (Matthew 10:34). Peace and not peace. Not peace on earth, per se, but only peace among those with whom He is pleased.

Somewhere between the feminized, nice-guy Jesus with a tender voice and soft hands who walks with you in some ethereal garden and the hypermacho, barroom-brawler Jesus ready to throw down in an instant, there lies the more complex, real God-man. With every power in the universe at His disposal, Jesus is neither weak nor overcome by forces more powerful than He. And yet, He doesn't exert His power and authority to assert His standing within society. Jesus is rather more like a trained and decorated martial artist, who possesses such mastery over His power and skill that He refuses to wield it against others just to pick a fight; He knows His identity without needing to prove it to others with a demonstration of force.

Make no mistake, Christ took on human flesh in the womb of His virgin mother not only to immerse Himself in a longstanding, cosmic struggle, but also to make that cosmic struggle His own. He comes to fight, but He does not fight in the ways expected of Him. Nor does He take on the enemies others might have expected Him to engage. The culmination, the end of the twelfth round, is the death of the incarnate God on the cross. In His crucifixion, Jesus not only fights to the death, but He also triumphs with His death. In sacrifice, He is triumphant.

Therefore, the nature of this fight is unlike any other. Christ comes to suffer and He promises His followers will suffer for their identification with Him.

Blessed are you when others revile you and persecute you and utter all kinds of evil against you falsely on My account. (Matthew 5:11)

Beware of men, for they will deliver you over to courts and flog you in their synagogues, and you will be dragged before governors and kings for My sake, to bear witness before them and the Gentiles. . . . Brother will deliver brother over to death, and the father his child, and children will rise against parents and have them put to death, and you will be hated by all for My name's sake. But the one who endures to the end will be saved. . . . A disciple is not above his teacher, nor a servant above his master. It is enough for the disciple to be like his teacher, and the servant like his master. If they have called the master of the house Beelzebul, how much more will they malign those of his household. (Matthew 10:17–18, 21–22, 24–25)

Before all this they will lay their hands on you and persecute you, delivering you up to the synagogues and prisons, and you will be brought before kings and governors for my name's sake. This will be your opportunity to bear witness. Settle it therefore in your minds not to meditate beforehand how to answer, for I will give you a mouth and wisdom, which none of your adversaries will be able to withstand or contradict. You will be delivered up even by parents and brothers and relatives and friends, and some of you they will put to death. You will be hated by all for My name's sake. But not a hair of your head will perish. By your endurance you will gain your lives. (Luke 21:12–19)

> They will put you out of the synagogues. Indeed, the hour is coming when whoever kills you will think he is offering service to God. (John 16:2)

Yet in all of these as well as in the other warnings Jesus makes, telling His disciples they will face hostility from those who cannot endure the proclamation of His message of forgiveness for sinners, He never exhorts them to oppose this persecution.

The fight is not against persecutors. (Recall His command to love enemies and pray for those who persecute you.) But there is a fight. To be joined into Jesus' death and resurrection through the portal into His Church, Holy Baptism, is to be joined into Jesus' mission as well.

Jesus doesn't fight against any human being. His struggle is not what the first-century Jews in Palestine were hoping for. Their hopes for the Messiah had been reduced from one to deliver them from the cosmic oppressors of their own sin, impending death, and the accusations and afflictions of the adversary, the devil, to hopes for a political messiah to lead them out of oppression by the Roman occupiers. Part of Jesus' fight, then, is against these false hopes. Over and over again, Jesus disappoints His disciples; they wanted to enlist His leadership and might so they could gain the upper hand in their political struggle against the Roman occupiers of Jerusalem. They were ready for a fight, and they wanted Jesus to lead them into battle.

Even when Jesus seems to be engaged in an actual fight against people—for instance, when He overturns the tables of the temple money-changers and drives them and the livestock dealers out with a made-on-the-spot whip—what He's fighting against is not the people (in this case, the money-changers) themselves, but against their false hopes, against idolatry, against their distortion of the worship of God, against sin.

Before He enters Jerusalem in the event that culminated in the table-turning, whip-cracking incident, He's not angry, not preparing for a fight. Instead, as He looks over the Holy City on His way in, He *weeps* over Jerusalem, with this lament: "Would that you, even you, had known on this day the things that make for peace!" (Luke 19:42). Jesus intends peace. He's not bellicose for the sake of fighting. He fights in order to obtain peace. He obtains peace for His people by dying on the cross. He fights by His suffering and death.

And He wins. "[God] disarmed the rulers and authorities and put them to open shame, by triumphing over them in [Christ]" (Colossians 2:15).

As it was for Jesus, so it is for His Christians. They must know what the real fight is and what battles are not worth engaging in. Recall our discussion of a man's fight to protect those entrusted to his care earlier in this chapter. St. Paul makes clear the nature of our fight:

> For we do not wrestle against flesh and blood, but against the rulers, against the authorities, against the cosmic powers over this present darkness, against the spiritual forces of evil in the heavenly places. Therefore take up the whole armor of God, that you may be able to withstand in the evil day, and having done all, to stand firm. (Ephesians 6:12–13)

Your struggle as a man is not against any other person, not against flesh and blood. The fight is bigger. No human being is or can be your real enemy, no matter the persecution he inflicts or the hatred he harbors toward you. Your enemy is Christ's enemy: the devil. Jesus has already won the war. The skirmishes in which you will be engaged are the enemy's last-ditch efforts to do whatever damage he can before he is forced out altogether. There is no peace treaty. This enemy will be utterly destroyed and eternally locked in the hell prepared for him from the foundation of the world (Matthew 25:41).

For the time being, until the return of the Commander in Chief of His armies of angels, Christ's Church is militant. She fights. St. Paul admonishes Timothy, the wet-behind-the-ears pastor, to "fight the good fight of the faith. Take hold of the eternal life to which you were called and about which you made the good confession in the presence of many witnesses" (1 Timothy 6:12). The fight is against the devil and his wiles, against the lure of the world and her seductive vices, against the sinful flesh that continually plots a man's destruction.

How do we fight? In the shadow of the cross. "For the weapons of our warfare are not of the flesh but have divine power to destroy strongholds" (2 Corinthians 10:4). In the certainty of Christ's eternal triumph over our cosmic enemies, we are given clarity about what the real fight is and at the same time enabled to fight.

Our fight is the same as that of the Christian martyrs throughout the history of Christ's Church. The word *martyr* simply means "witness." In the Church's vernacular, though, it quickly came to mean those who bore witness to Jesus Christ not simply with their words, but with their lives. Martyrs died to confess that Jesus is the Lord, the Savior who freely offers forgiveness to sinners. Although both men and women have been martyrs, martyrdom was always considered a masculine calling. The martyrs were soldiers, not in any earthly army, and not against any human adversaries, but in this cosmic warfare between the triumphant Christ and the defeated devil. They fought with their confession of the faith. They triumphed by shedding their blood. Their example gives us courage in the same holy confrontation. As we sing,

> Oh, may Thy soldiers, faithful, true and bold,
> Fight as the saints who nobly fought of old
> And win with them the victor's crown of gold!
> Alleluia! Alleluia!
>
> And when the fight is fierce, the warfare long,
> Steals on the ear the distant triumph song,
> And hearts are brave again, and arms are strong.
> Alleluia! Alleluia! (*LSB* 677:3, 5)

This is a peculiar fight, against adversaries unseen, won not by saving one's life but by spending it in confession of a Savior who triumphed over death by dying and who gives a share in His resurrection from the dead to all who follow Him into death. With this confidence, with Christ as your courage, "Be watchful, stand firm in the faith, act like men, be strong. Let all that you do be done in love" (1 Corinthians 16:13–14).

VIR ORAT. A MAN PRAYS.

Even though Jesus is God in human flesh, the perfect union of divinity and humanity, fully and completely God and Man eternally and at the same time, He nevertheless does something that seems like it ought to be reserved only for the rest of us humans. He prays. The Second Person of the eternal triune God, with human lips and words, takes time regularly to pray to God the Father.

Over and over again, Jesus recuses Himself from the company of His disciples and apostles to be by Himself to pray. After calling some of His first disciples and healing multiple people, Jesus left before sunrise to pray by Himself (Mark 1:35). After feeding five thousand men plus women and children, Jesus sent the disciples off in a boat across the Sea of Galilee and went up on a mountain by Himself to pray (Matthew 14:22–23). Before selecting the twelve disciples whom He would send out as His apostles, Jesus spent the night in prayer (Luke 6:12). He prayed once Lazarus' tomb had been opened, before He raised His friend (John 11:41–42). Jesus prayed in the garden before His crucifixion (Matthew 26:36–44); He prayed for Simon Peter (Luke 22:32) and also for Himself and the fulfillment of His Father's will (vv. 41–44). From the cross, Jesus prayed for forgiveness for those crucifying Him (23:34).

How or why the Second Person of the Trinity would pray to the First Person of the Trinity is a mystery of the unity of the Trinity that human minds are unable to solve. We confess in the Nicene Creed that Jesus is "God of God, Light of Light, very God of very God, begotten, not made, being of one substance with the Father," but still, in His humanity, Jesus prays.

Prayer, submission to the will of God, is an essential part of what it means to be human. As perfect man, Jesus regularly prays. Although in His divinity He is equal to the Father and eternal with Him, in His humanity, He submits to His Father's will.

So must a man, therefore, pray. Unlike the active ways a man lives in service to others, prayer is not active. It's passive. It commits all the other tasks of masculinity—loving, giving, serving, fighting, providing, protecting, procreating—to the will and blessing of God. Unless He grants success, nothing a man endeavors to do will succeed. Thus the way of masculinity begins not with work but with prayer, not on your feet, but on your knees.

THE BATTLE PLAN

A PORTRAIT OF MAN: CHRIST

Use the ideals of masculinity from this chapter to identify your own weaknesses and strategies for growth.

MASCULINE IDEAL	YOUR WEAKNESSES	STRATEGIES FOR GROWTH
A HUSBAND . . .		
loves his bride		
gives himself up for his bride		
sanctifies his bride		
cleanses his bride		
presents his bride to himself without any blemish		
nourishes and cherishes his bride		

MASCULINE IDEAL	YOUR WEAKNESSES	STRATEGIES FOR GROWTH
A MAN . . .		
is good		
is strong		
gives		
loves		
fights		
prays		

THE PORTRAIT OF FATHERHOOD: GOD THE FATHER

"Let us then not consider how to leave our children rich, but how to leave them virtuous."

—St. John Chrysostom, Homilies on the Epistle to the Romans

FATHERHOOD AND THE HEAVENLY FATHER

Before Christ was man, before His incarnation, He existed eternally. This was the conclusion the earliest whole-Church councils reached in the fourth century, which we still confess in the Nicene Creed. The question at hand was whether Christ, the Word of God, was essentially God in the same way that the Father was God. Representing those who answered "No" was a priest from Alexandria, Egypt, named Arius.

What upset Arius was the confession that Christ, like God the Father, was eternal, without beginning, and that He was just as much God as the Father, but that there was nevertheless only one God. Arius thought that saying the Son was one in essence with God the Father disrupted the unity of God and, since Christ eventually had a body, limited the incorporeal God to the body of a man. His concerns were logical. Confessing that three coequal, coeternal persons are one united, divine being is beyond the scope of human reason or mathematics to explain.

In response to Arius and others throughout the Church who refused to confess the full divinity of the Son of God, the Church—over the course of two ecumenical councils, fifty-six years apart, and lots of theological wrangling in between—crafted the Nicene Creed as a way to confess in a clear answer to Arius and his ilk the simple-yet-profound scriptural truth of the Trinity.

Although the controversy centered on a question about the identity of Christ, a confession about God the Father was foundational to the answer. Contending for the true, trinitarian position were influential bishops like Athanasius of Alexandria (who was such a powerful force in defending the doctrine of the Trinity that he lent his name to the third ecumenical creed, the so-called Athanasian Creed, though it was probably composed a hundred or so years after he died) and the theological powerhouse trio of brothers Basil of Caesarea (also called Basil the Great) and Gregory of Nyssa and their friend Gregory of Nazianzus.

In order to make the case that the Son of God is equal to God the Father, Athanasius in particular discussed what it means to call God "Father," as is common in the New Testament. Arius applied a human understanding of fatherhood to God, concluding that just as every human father's son has a beginning, so the Son of God must likewise have a beginning; therefore He must not be eternal or equal to His Father. But Athanasius, instead of seeing God's fatherhood through the lens of human fatherhood, argued for the opposite, saying that human fatherhood can rightly only be understood through the lens of God's fatherhood: "For God does not make man His pattern; but rather we men, for that God is properly, and alone truly, Father of His

Son, are also called fathers of our own children; for of Him 'is every fatherhood in heaven and earth named.'"[42]

It is not our goal to treat all the nuances of this great controversy in a book about masculinity. The point is to examine human fatherhood through the lens of God's fatherhood.

God the Father is eternally Father. The Son of God is eternally Son. Arius was wrong. There was never a time when the Son did not exist. This relationship is older than creation itself. Fatherhood is older than time. And fathers can understand their calling to be fathers only in light of the eternal relation of the Father to His Son. Athanasius made his case that earthly fathers are called "fathers" as a reflection of the identity of God the Father from Ephesians 3, where St. Paul declares, "For this reason I bow my knees before the Father (*pater*), from whom every family (*patria)* in heaven and on earth is named" (vv. 14–15). The apostle's point is not that earthly fatherhood gives us a helpful metaphor by which we can understand the relationship between divine Father and Son. It's that every earthly father derives his identity as father not from the gift of children, but from the nature of God the Father Himself. Every family is named for—created by—God the Father. Men and women, despite their best efforts, can only ever make love; they cannot make babies.

THE FATHER GIVES AND SUSTAINS LIFE

God the Father is man's creator, his source of life. We examined the first three chapters of Genesis already, but noteworthy in this discussion is Eve's exclamation upon the

42 Athanasius, *Against the Arians* 1.7, in *A Select Library of the Christian Church: Nicene and Post-Nicene Fathers: Second Series*, ed. Philip Schaff and Henry Wace (New York, 1890–1900; repr., Peabody, MA: Hendrickson, 1994), 4:320.

birth of her firstborn: "I have gotten a man with the help of the LORD" (Genesis 4:1). Even after His initial work of creation, God nevertheless remains active in His creation. He still creates. As the psalmist confesses, "For You formed my inward parts; You knitted me together in my mother's womb. I praise You, for I am fearfully and wonderfully made. Wonderful are Your works; my soul knows it very well" (Psalm 139:13–14).

Having created man, though, the Father does not thereafter take a hands-off approach. What He has made, He preserves. Consider how Martin Luther treats the First Article of the Apostles' Creed in the Small Catechism:

> I believe that God has made me and all creatures; that He has given me my body and soul, eyes, ears, and all my members, my reason and all my senses, and still takes care of them.
>
> He also gives me clothing and shoes, food and drink, house and home, wife and children, land, animals, and all I have. He richly and daily provides me with all that I need to support this body and life.
>
> He defends me against all danger and guards and protects me from all evil.
>
> *All this He does only out of fatherly, divine goodness and mercy, without any merit or worthiness in me* (emphasis added).

God doesn't provide for His creatures, mankind in particular, because of their inherent goodness. He provides because of who He is, the Creator. He does not dole out what men need because they deserve it. He provides what we need for as many days as He gives us breath. He cares for us more intimately than any earthly father, even knowing the number of hairs on our heads (Matthew 10:30).

And as long as the Creator grants us breath and daily bread, He also protects. He defends against danger, guards and protects from all evil. Evil certainly lingers in the world, a consequence of the brokenness and dysfunction of creation, wrought on the good order by man's original and ongoing sin. But just as good gifts are not a sign of the heavenly Father's extra favor, so disaster is not a sign of His particular wrath against the person it befalls. He gave the full cup of His wrath to His Son to drink in His death on the cross.

This kind of provision and protection—modeled from the fatherhood of the heavenly Father—sets the paradigm for what those who are called "fathers" are to do. The threefold drive within man to procreate, protect, and provide derives from the work of his own Creator. Because God exercises fatherly, divine goodness and mercy, so earthly fathers exercise the same fatherly, divine goodness and mercy, doing good for their children without consideration of their worthiness.

But when comparing the two, no earthly father even holds a candle to the heavenly Father's goodness. The contrast between what men as fathers do and what God the Father does is so stark, that, in teaching on prayer, Jesus says, "Which one of you, if his son asks him for bread, will give him a stone? Or if he asks for a fish, will give him a serpent? If you then, who are evil, know how to give good gifts to your children, how much more will your Father who is in heaven give good things to those who ask Him!" (Matthew 7:9–11). No father, however good he might seem to his children, is close to the goodness or the trustworthiness of God the Father. Even the best earthly fathers fail. And some fathers fail worse than others. The failure of our earthly fathers does not, however, diminish the goodness of the heavenly Father; rather, it highlights it. He alone is the perfect Father (Matthew 5:48).

THE FATHER LOVES

Christ's perfect, endless, selfless love, which defines the way a man is called to love, is not unique to the Second Person of the Trinity. As He is of the same essence of God the Father, so is His love of the same essence as the Father's.

Just as the cross is the perfect demonstration of Christ's self-giving love for all mankind, so also it is an equally perfect depiction of the depths of the heavenly Father's love, that He refused to count any cost too great that He would not pay it to transform rebellious men into His sons. "See what kind of love the Father has given to us, that we should be called children of God; and so we are" (1 John 3:1). God's love is transformative. It makes men different from what they were. It takes rebels and adopts them as sons. It takes sinners and makes them saints. It takes His enemies and makes them equal to His Son.

When people want to distort this fatherly love of God into some kind of great-grandfatherly forgetfulness that simply loves people as they are, they miss the fundamental transformative power of this love, by which God defines Himself. "God is love" (1 John 4:8), right? This is one of the most beloved and misappropriated verses in the Bible (right after "All things are possible with God" [Mark 10:27]). Consider the broader context, though, of how God is described as "love."

> Anyone who does not love does not know God, because God is love. In this the love of God was made manifest among

> us, that God sent His only Son into the world, so that we might live through Him. In this is love, not that we have loved God, but that He loved us and sent His Son to be the propitiation for our sins. (1 John 4:8–10)

Although people often take "God is love" as an invitation to define what God is by what they believe love is, the opposite is actually the case. God isn't defined by love; love is defined by God.

The Father loves like the Son loves. He loves sacrificially. His love is grandiose, extravagant, sparing no expense. The Father sends His Son as the propitiation, the sacrifice that pays for sins, satisfying the eternal justice of God. His love doesn't gloss over sin or diminish its heinousness. Debts are never gone when forgiven. They simply are paid for by another. Sending Christ as the sacrifice for our sins, the Father acknowledges the full evil of our long-standing, inbred rebellion against Him. He fully acknowledges our sins, and He pays for them completely from His own account. This is the very definition of love.

This is the model for a father's love toward his children. No expense is spared, nothing withheld. A father spares no part of himself for the safety, security, well-being, temporal and eternal good of his children. Children need to be able to trust their father to do whatever is in their best interest. They need to know that this man will never choose his own good over the good of his children, that he will always see himself—his strength, his time, his wisdom—as the means by which he can work for their good, by which he can love them. As we say of the heavenly Father, "If God is for us, who can be against us? He who did not spare His own Son but gave Him up for us all, how will He not also with Him graciously give us all things?" (Romans 8:31–32), so children should be able to say of their earthly father, "If dad is for us, who can be against us?" A father's love, modeled after the love of the heavenly Father, is enough to encourage his children in a world of threats and uncertainties.

THE FATHER TEACHES

If you distort the text just right, you can find support in the Bible for just about any agenda you want to push. This is hardly new. Even Jesus dealt with popular misunderstandings of the essence of the Word of God. When the Jews were trying to kill Jesus both for His refusal to keep the man-made Sabbath regulations and also for His teaching that He was equal to the Father (John 5:18), Jesus responded with a lengthy catechesis on His relationship to the Father that includes this poignant correction: "You search the Scriptures because you think that in them you have eternal life; and it is they that bear witness about Me, yet you refuse to come to Me that you may have life" (vv. 39–40).

The Scriptures of Jesus' day were the Hebrew Scriptures, the Old Testament. These testify about Jesus, He says. The Bible is not an instruction book. It's not a rule book. It's not a practical book. It's not a diet book. It's not a collection of secrets waiting to be discovered. It's a book about Jesus. And, also according to Jesus, who is Himself the Word made flesh, it has a very specific twofold purpose. On the evening after He rose from the dead, Jesus appeared to His disciples and said,

> "These are My words that I spoke to you while I was still with you, that everything written about Me in the Law of Moses and the Prophets and the Psalms must be fulfilled." Then He opened their minds to understand the Scriptures, and said to them, "Thus it is written, that the Christ should suffer and on the third day rise from

> the dead, and that repentance for the forgiveness of sins should be proclaimed in His name to all nations, beginning from Jerusalem." (Luke 24:44–47)

This is the function of the Word of God: to proclaim repentance and forgiveness. Any other use of the Word is simply wrong, distorted, false teaching.

With His Word, God the Father aims to give life through faith in Jesus. His Word has two distinct voices: His Law evokes repentance; His Gospel delivers forgiveness. God doesn't teach with His Word in the way we think of classroom instruction. He teaches with His Word to give life and faith.

One of the Church's favorite words to describe this ongoing work of God to teach us is the word *catechesis*, which comes from the Greek word *katecheo*, a word that describes oral, face-to-face instruction. The Father's catechesis is to give life through the Son, to kill sinners and to give them new life. He works through the Word. Faith comes by hearing His Word (Romans 10:17).

Discipline and instruction are the heavenly Father's loving work toward those who are made His sons through the adoption of Holy Baptism.

> It is for discipline that you have to endure. God is treating you as sons. For what son is there whom his father does not discipline? If you are left without discipline, in which all have participated, then you are illegitimate children and not sons. Besides this, we have had earthly fathers who disciplined us and we respected them. Shall we not much more be subject to the Father of spirits and live? For they disciplined us for a short time as it seemed best to them, but He disciplines us for our good, that we may share His holiness. For the moment all discipline seems

> painful rather than pleasant, but later it yields the peaceful fruit of righteousness to those who have been trained by it. (Hebrews 12:7–11)

The heavenly Father catechizes. He instructs His children for life, to draw them to repentance, to deliver to them His gift of forgiveness, to discipline us toward the fruit of righteousness.

So fathers are called into this work of catechizing their children. Their goals are the same: life and faith. Life through repentance and forgiveness and faith that continually draws them to the source of forgiveness.

Those to whom a father has given earthly life, whose temporal well-being he strives to protect and to provide for, are also entrusted to him for good beyond this earthly life. If he cares about the task of being a protector and provider for his children for this life, how much more ought a man be concerned about the eternal welfare of his children? Simply put, there is nothing better a man can do for his children that has the potential to yield eternal profit for them (and therefore for him) than to see that they are well catechized.

Just as Adam did in the garden for his wife and men have endeavored to do since, a man ought to preside over his household as a priest. Fathers are the chief catechists of their children. St. Paul exhorts, "Fathers, do not provoke your children to anger, but bring them up in the discipline and instruction of the Lord" (Ephesians 6:4). In the same way the Lord disciplines and instructs with His Word, fathers are likewise to do.

How do fathers catechize their children? First and foremost, they must lead by example. Children, especially boys, will emulate their fathers. Girls will too, of course, especially in traits that are not gender specific, like piety, devotion to the Word, and dedication to prayer. In all things, but especially in catechizing and instructing his children in the Word of God, a father leads from the front. That is, his catechesis is always "Follow me," never "Go and do." He doesn't send his kids to church; he takes them with him. He blazes the trail. He catechizes his family first by his example.

His leadership says "Follow me." A man brings his children into the heavenly Father's care, into the family of God, as he carries them to the font to be made children of God in the Sacrament of Baptism. A man says "Follow me" when he shows his children the value of prayer by regularly and visibly praying. A man leads the way in repentance and forgiveness when he makes regular use of God's gift of confession and absolution. He teaches his children to own their mistakes and confess their sins when he is capable of doing so himself. And he shows them that the solution for sin is never found within himself, but always in the Lord's gift of forgiveness, which comes from the outside in. A man says "Follow me" to his wife and children as he leads them to the Lord's altar to receive Holy Communion. Although "women and children first" is a chivalrous way for a man to conduct himself in most aspects of his life, it's not how a man conducts himself in church. "Follow me," he says. Do what I do, his actions confess. This is the way. Let's go.

Second, a man is active in teaching the fundamentals of the faith to his children. He leads them into the Word in the same way the heavenly Father uses the Word to gently and patiently shape His children into a cross-shaped way of living. So fathers, then, deliberately teach the Word to their children. They ought to have regular, weekly time devoted to learning the Word. Toward this end, for the purpose of catechesis, the church has always relied on catechisms. The catechism's style of question and answer is like a scripted conversation. It is a father's best resource for catechizing his children. This is how it is intended to be used, as each of the six sections of the catechism begins, "As the head of the family should teach it in a simple way to his household." In his preface to the Large Catechism, Luther describes a father's work: "It is the duty of every father of a family to question and examine his children and servants at least once a week and see what they know or are learning from the catechism. And if they do not know the catechism, he should keep them learning it faithfully" (Short Preface, 4). When a father uses the catechism as his primary catechetical tool, the words and phrases of the catechism will become the language of his family's confession of the faith. They will learn to speak the same way, united as a family, which is what the word *confess* means, to say the same thing.

Further, a father must teach the rest of the Scriptures to his children. The catechism contains the fundamentals, the Word distilled down to the six most fundamental parts. But catechesis in the rest of the Scriptures will support his work of teaching these fundamentals. As he teaches the Scriptures, letting the history, the poetry, the prophecy unfold, a father will teach correctly, bearing in mind that the whole content of the Scriptures is Jesus, and the message is always repentance and forgiveness in His name.

It is impossible to overstate the importance of this task of catechesis given to a father. It is his highest calling as a father, more important than temporal provision, making money, providing experiences, cultivating growth, or any other aspect of fatherhood. On the value of catechesis, Luther writes,

> All live on as though God gave us children for our pleasure or amusement. . . . No one is willing to see that this is the command of the Supreme Majesty. . . . Nor does anyone see that there is so much need to be seriously concerned about

> the young. For if we wish to have excellent and able persons both for civil and Church leadership, we must spare no diligence, time, or cost in teaching and educating our children, so that they may serve God and the world. We must not think only about how we may amass money and possessions for them. God can indeed support and make them rich without us, as He daily does. But for this purpose He has given us children and issued this command: we should train and govern them according to His will. Otherwise, He would have no purpose for a father and a mother. Therefore, let everyone know that it is his duty, on peril of losing the divine favor, to bring up his children in the fear and knowledge of God above all things. (Large Catechism, I, 170–74)

It does not take a village to catechize a child. It takes a father and a mother. It takes the leadership of the child's father. It takes the example of the one he calls "Dad" to show him what it means to be a Christian. God can use a variety of means to support children, but He uniquely uses parents to teach His Word. He gives us earthly fathers to stand in His stead. He calls them "fathers" because of His own nature as the eternal Father. In His example, fathers will know what they are to do. In His mercy, they will find forgiveness when they fail to live up to this impossible standard. Together with their children, they will live in repentance and forgiveness.

THE BATTLE PLAN

THE PORTRAIT OF FATHERHOOD: GOD THE FATHER

In your callings as a father, what can you do to sharpen your focus on your children and their good? How can you hone your skills as a father? Use these questions to help you brainstorm.

To better give and sustain life

What are you not providing for your children that they need?

Is your drive to provide for your children keeping you from giving them your time?

To love

If love implies sacrifice, what can you do to better love your children?

How can you balance the sacrifice of parenting with the authority of being a father?

To teach

What are the greatest obstacles to your faithful catechesis of your children?

How can you set a better example of one taught by the Word of God so that your children will follow in your steps?

A PARADOXICAL PORTRAIT

> *"Masculinity is paradoxical: It is the privilege of dying that others may live, which is, in the highest philosophical and religious sense, a privilege."*
>
> —*Leon Podles, The Church Impotent*

The portrait of a man we've set forth here, as perfect man, perfect husband, perfect father, is not one-dimensional. As tempting as it is to reduce the quest for masculinity to easy-to-do maxims, the nature of what it means to be a man is not so tidy. This is perhaps why our society is quick to embrace the flattened-out caricatures of masculinity, resulting in the rejection of masculinity by the egalitarians or the hypermacho distortion of masculinity by the self-centered, immature men insisting on their "rights." Masculinity is not that easy. Instead of the easy, one-dimensional definitions of masculinity, these portraits of Adam, Christ, and God the Father provide a picture of masculinity that embraces rather than flattens out the inherent paradoxes of masculinity.

Being a man is learning to live with these paradoxes, to live between the extremes, to refuse to give in to either the emasculating forces of feminism or the emasculating forces of hypermachismo.

THE PARADOX OF HEADSHIP AND SUBMISSION

Although a man is called to be the head of his wife, the head of his family, he is not his own head. In a rightly ordered creation, he is not in charge of himself. "But I want you to understand that the head of every man is Christ, the head of a wife is her husband, and the head of Christ is God" (1 Corinthians 11:3). A man is a head under the Head, Christ. Before he can expect submission from his wife, he must learn to be submissive to Christ. Before he can take the lead, he must be led. Before he can love his wife as Christ loves His Church, he must be loved by Christ within His Church.

Moreover, a father has his own fathers. The Fourth Commandment remains in force throughout a man's life: Honor your father and your mother. As long as they live, a man's parents are his parents, to whom he owes love, honor, service, and obedience. If he knows how to be a son, a man can know how to be a good father. He also owes love, honor, service, and obedience to his other fathers, as well, those who derive their authority from the office of father: princes and pastors. Those in positions of authority derive their authority from God: "Let every person be subject to the governing authorities. For there is no authority except from God, and those that exist have been instituted by God" (Romans 13:1). And those who serve in the office of pastor exercise a spiritual authority as well: "Obey your leaders and submit to them, for they are keeping watch over your souls, as those who will have to give an account. Let them do this with joy and not with groaning, for that would be of no advantage to you" (Hebrews 13:17).

No man can be his own boss, or his leadership will devolve into authoritarian selfishness. But if his headship is governed by the headship of Christ, he will lead and rule in the same way as Christ leads and rules His Church and the world: lovingly, sacrificially, patiently, gently.

THE PARADOX OF POWER AND KINDNESS

A man is to be strong, but his strength is never chiefly for his own good. The stronger a man is, the more he is able to assert his will over others or bend their wills to his own, by force of body or mind.

A man must be both powerful and kind. He must be both fierce and sensitive. Strength must not be used against others selfishly. That's weakness. That's cowardice. Strength must serve a man's calling. It must be used for the protection of others and to provide for those in a man's charge. Christ spent all His strength on the cross. A man spends his in sacrificial love and service toward those entrusted to his care. He ought to cultivate and increase his strength, but not merely for the purpose of strutting shirtless around the pool. His strength is a tool in his arsenal for the good of others. His body is his gift to give, not a means of self-indulgence.

Yet a man must have not only physical but also mental and spiritual strength. A man's strength begins in faith: "In the fear of the LORD one has strong confidence, and his children will have a refuge" (Proverbs 14:26). Before he can provide physical safety for his family, he must provide spiritual safety, entrusting himself and his family to the Lord, disciplining and instructing them in faith, even as he himself is disciplined and instructed in the faith. Moreover, wisdom is strength. Knowledge is strength. Knowing your own limits and seeking the counsel of those wiser than you is strength: "A wise man is full of strength, and a man of knowledge enhances his might, for by wise guidance you can wage your war, and in abundance of counselors there is victory" (Proverbs 24:5–6).

Christ, finally, is the stronger man, from whose strength a man can draw strength, and from whose example a man can learn to exercise strength. He fights a battle against powers stronger than any man, but He exercises strength for the good of all mankind:

> If it is by the finger of God that I cast out demons, then the kingdom of God has come upon you. When a strong man, fully armed, guards his own palace, his goods are safe; but when one stronger than he attacks him and overcomes him, he takes away his armor in which he trusted and divides his spoil. Whoever is not with Me is against Me, and whoever does not gather with Me scatters. (Luke 11:20–23)

THE PARADOX OF ASSERTIVENESS AND HUMILITY

Christ is no milquetoast man. He is confident and composed. He embodies the perfectly assertive man. He is never wrong, but He certainly doesn't need to win every argument. His interactions with His adversaries are not exercises in demonstrating His superior competence or even His correct grasp of the truth about God. He is never pushed around or bullied by those who eventually seek to kill Him. In every interaction with the Pharisees or scribes who went to Jesus with a question to put Him to the test (Matthew 16:1; 19:3; 22:35; Mark 8:11; Luke 10:25; 11:16; John 8:5–6), Jesus remains perfectly in control of the situation. Sometimes He answers. Sometimes He refuses. Sometimes He asks a question of His own.

Assertiveness navigates the narrow course between pushed-around passivity on one side and forcing-your-will-on-others aggression on the other. Jesus never forces His will on anyone. And He will never allow others to force their will on Him. He came to give His life, but He will lay it down on His own terms, of His own accord. And yet, Jesus is perfectly God. The extent of His power, circumscribed as it may be in the limits of His humanity, makes His putting up with tests, accusations, false charges, lies, and more seemingly ridiculous—or foolish, which is the essence of the cross to our human understanding (1 Corinthians 1:25).

And yet, despite His assertiveness, Christ is perfectly humble. Recall our discussion in chapter 6 of the Christ hymn in Philippians 2. Although Christ is equal with God the Father, He did not count equality a thing to be grasped, but made Himself nothing, took the posture of a slave, and died the humiliating death of a criminal on a cross. As is often quipped, humility is not thinking less of yourself; it's thinking of yourself less. And, with every ounce of strength He had, with every fire of a synapse, Christ never thought of Himself or His own good once. His singular focus, which makes Him perfectly humble, is the good of others, particularly mankind.

So must a man also maintain this paradox, being both assertive and humble. If his identity and self-worth is not found in himself, but in who he is in Christ and who he is called to be for others, he is free from the dangers of both aggressiveness and passivity. He knows who he is and who he is called to be, so he can be confident and assertive, not for his own rights, but for the good and the rights of others.

And if a man's identity comes from outside himself, in his vocations—his *callings,* as the word means—to be a father, son, worker, hearer of the Word, brother, friend, or leader, he is also set free from the encumbrance of his own ego. He may be humble, may think of others, may see himself as a means for the good of others, because he knows his identity as a man in Christ is secure, given purely as a gift, and his callings to be a man for the good of others are likewise given to him as a gift. His faltering self-confidence is replaced with confidence in Christ. With this confidence, a man doesn't need anyone else's affirmation to know who he is.

In being assertive, a man is firm and stalwart. He is not easily taken advantage of. In being humble, he is compassionate and selfless. He is quick to be merciful.

Nowhere is this humble assertiveness better displayed than in repentance. Acknowledging his faults without needing to justify them or make excuses makes a man both assertive in his honesty and humble in admitting his faults. Repentance keeps a man's ego at bay. It is not a once-and-done item on the to-do list. Rather, repentance is how a man should always see himself. He is always sorry for his shortcomings and ready to confess them for the good of those he is called to serve. Likewise, his willingness to receive forgiveness simultaneously shows his humbleness and assertiveness. And it's how a man can live each day confidently focused on the good of others around him.

THE PARADOX OF COURAGE AND SACRIFICE

Courage is not the opposite of fear. Without fear, there can be no courage. Courage forces a man to acknowledge the risks and to act in spite of them, whereas cowardice shies away from danger.

The wicked flee when no one pursues,

but the righteous are bold as a lion. (Proverbs 28:1)

St. John Chrysostom relates this verse to Adam's flight from God when he heard Him walking in the garden and observes that such fleeing is a mark of cowardice, brought on by his sin:

> Such [fleeing in fear] is the habitual custom of those who have committed sin. They are suspicious of all things; they tremble at shadows; they are in terror at every sound, and they imagine that every one is approaching them in a hostile manner. . . . For such is the nature of sin, that it betrays whilst no one finds fault; it condemns whilst no one accuses; it makes the sinner a timid being; one that trembles at a sound; even as righteousness has the contrary effect. Hear, at least, how the Scripture describes this cowardice of the former, and this boldness of the latter. "The wicked flee when no man pursueth." How doth he flee when no man pursueth? He hath that within which drives him on—an accuser in his conscience; and this he carries about everywhere; and just as it would be impossible to flee from himself, so neither can he escape the persecutor within; but wherever he goeth, he is scourged, and hath an incurable wound! But not such is the righteous man. Of what nature then is he? Hear: "The righteous is bold as a lion!"[43]

Guilt and shame make a man timid and afraid, not just of God, though. Of everything. Adam tucks his tail and runs for cover at the sound of wind rustling the leaves in the garden.

43 John Chrysostom, *Homilies on the Statues to the People of Antioch* 8, in *A Select Library of the Christian Church: Nicene and Post-Nicene Fathers: First Series*, ed. Philip Schaff (Reprint, Grand Rapids, MI: Eerdmans, 1952), 9:396.

Every person is potentially an adversary. Cowardice is inwardly focused. Repentance is courageous. It commits a man to the mercy of Another, which is inherently risky. He has to step outside of himself. He has to own his errors. He has to confess his failures.

The courage to confess sins is always met with the gift of forgiveness. "If we confess our sins, He is faithful and just to forgive us our sins and to cleanse us from all unrighteousness" (1 John 1:9). With God's gift of righteousness, then, with the forgiveness He imparts, a man is set free from guilt and shame, and—ultimately—from cowardice. With this righteousness, he is as bold as a lion. He can face any person, any situation, with a confidence that comes from outside himself.

With this courage, a man can look fear in the eye and not flinch. If he is delivered from the worst of himself and the just, eternal consequences of his sins, what would he ever need to fear? But instead of making a man confident and courageous for himself, this external Christ-confidence orients his gaze outward. Unlike a self-centered boldness or fearlessness, courage enables a man to sacrifice himself for the good of others.

Masculinity is a calculated risk. A man need not pursue danger simply for the sake of proving himself. This is selfish. But he can endure danger for the sake of others. This is sacrifice.

THE PARADOX OF GIVING AND RECEIVING

If there is one thing you take away from this manifesto, it should be this: the essence of masculinity is to give.

Since the fall, giving doesn't come naturally to anyone, least of all to us men. Ever since Adam's downward gaze that revealed to him his nakedness and shame, men have had to struggle against the gravity of the flesh. Every force in the world is working against a man to keep him focused on himself. If his eyes are drawn away from himself, if he can fix his eyes on others and see their good as superior to his own, there is virtually no limit to the good he can accomplish. Heroes don't navel-gaze. Heroes serve others. Heroes give of themselves.

Here, then, is the final and greatest paradox of masculinity: a man must be receptive in order to be giving.

But before a man is free to give of himself, he must be given to.

Before he can give, he must receive.

Before he can be a man, he must be a boy.

Before he can be a father, he must be a son.

Before he can be of service to others, he must be served by the One who came not to be served but to serve (Matthew 20:28).

Before a man can give life, he must receive life.

Before a man can provide, he must be provided for.

Before a man can protect, he must be protected.

Before a man can fight, he must be fought for.

Before a man can pray, he must be prayed for.

Before a man can love, he must be loved.

Before a man can be the instrument of good for others, he needs Someone to be an instrument of good for him.

Before a man can truly be a man, Christ had to be Man.

THE BATTLE PLAN

A PARADOXICAL PORTRAIT

The Paradox of Headship and Submission

To whom must you submit? Under whose headship are you?

The Paradox of Power and Kindness

How can you cultivate power and strength for the good of others?

The Paradox of Assertiveness and Humility

How is your ego dangerous to your expression of masculinity?

The Paradox of Courage and Sacrifice

Where can you find courage to confront your sins and failings?

The Paradox of Giving and Receiving

What challenges or prevents you from receiving the gifts God intends to give you in the Divine Service?

WHAT DOES A MAN DO?

"Be strong, Polycarp, and play the man!"

—The Martyrdom of Polycarp

These last two chapters are probably why you bought this book. Or why your wife bought it for you. Or your mom. Or your kids. Or why you picked it up for free from the pile of discarded books outside your pastor's study. These are the what-to-do chapters. You didn't really want a history of humanity since Adam's fall. You weren't acutely interested in the effects of feminism on modern-day masculinity. You probably weren't even ready for all the talk about Jesus. You wanted to know what to do. You wanted another tool in your self-improvement arsenal. I didn't set out to frustrate you at every turn, but I'm a little glad I did.

You want to know what to do, and rightly so. Men take action. They don't talk too much. Unless they're already frustrated in their own quest to be men, they probably don't put up with ten chapters of some blowhard pontificating about the state of masculinity in our society. They don't overthink things. They just *do*.

So, this is it. The quick and dirty list of one guy's advice for how to be a better man. I hesitated to include this kind of advice because it makes me seem like an expert on the subject. Well, I'm not. I can say a heck of a lot more about the struggle to be a good man than about what good men do. And though a list like this is what a man will latch on to and make part of his daily routine, masculinity is not reducible to a to-do list. It's not some things you do. It's who you are. Masculinity is a practice, a habit. It's not a list; it's a lifestyle. You can't just do some things and be a man. You have to be a man. And then you do these things.

So, you are (and so am I) caught in a Catch-22. You can't act like a man unless you are one. And you can't really be a man unless you act like one. This list of things to do is bound to frustrate you (much like the rest of the book). You simply can't do it well. If you could, if it were easy for those of us who aren't the enfleshment of God, the perfect Man, no one would write or sell books on masculinity. But a quick search on Amazon or a browse through the new releases at your local library will result in a list of many books on the subject. Those who aren't struggling with what it means to be a man or how to be a better man simply haven't taken the time to evaluate their own masculinity.

All that is to say that this is not a comprehensive list of what to do to be a man. Really, living as a man means nothing more than living your life for the good of others. But since that's a bit elusive, here are some practical suggestions. If they don't pertain to you or your situation, forget 'em. If they don't equip you to better serve those whom it is your vocation to serve, don't worry about 'em.

But if they challenge you, if they draw you outside yourself, good. And if they force you to realize the magnitude of what it means to live as a good man, confess your inability to do so, and rely ever more on the goodness of the one good man, Jesus, better. So, here we go, Dante. I'll be your Virgil. You know by now that the Man I would hold up to you as the example is not me but Christ. With Him in mind as both the ideal and the solution for those of us who cannot match the ideal, let's embark.

THE DAILY TO-DO LIST: *ORA, AMA, DA, CERTA*

Put these on your calendar, though you can write them in English, if you want. Pray, love, give, fight. These are your everyday tasks. But unlike "mow the lawn" or "soccer practice," they don't get checked off. They're never done. And you must commit to them anew each day. They are the core tasks of masculinity. They direct your mind-set for the day and orient your gaze up from your navel to the lives of others. You can't do them well or poorly. You simply do them or don't do them. You live for yourself or live for others. You're effeminate or masculine.

ORA. PRAY LIKE A MAN.

Even secular writers have come to realize the value of beginning the day with prayer and meditation. For a man, this is essential. Before he takes up the things he has to do, he needs to acknowledge what he cannot do. He needs to entrust his own doing, his calling to be a man, to the constant provision and protection of his own heavenly Father.

Manly prayer paradoxically requires courage and submission. A man submits to the Father's will, praying, as Jesus did, "Not as I will, but as You will" (Matthew 26:39). Before he endeavors each day to love, give, and fight for the good of those entrusted to his care, a man entrusts them to the care of God. This prayer also requires courage. He must trust that he and his loved ones are able to weather storms and trials bigger than his and their own endurance because of the protection and provision of God.

A man learns to dare and risk greatly by trusting and believing that his identity in Christ is safe and secure, come what may.

A man can and should pray boldly. St. Paul gives this counsel, "For you did not receive the spirit of slavery to fall back into fear, but you have received the Spirit of adoption as sons, by whom we cry, 'Abba! Father!'" (Romans 8:15). So a man may approach the throne of the Creator of all things impetuously, courageously, in the confidence that he has been made a son of God through the adoption of Holy Baptism.

Although prayer intends to make a man receptive, it does not make him weak. It is like a soldier deferring to the authority of his commanders or a worker submitting to the leadership of his bosses.

Want a manly way to pray? Want a pattern to use or to emulate? Consider the Litany. The Litany (*LSB*, p. 288) is an expansion of one of the oldest prayers in the history of Christianity, the Kyrie. The Kyrie (Greek for "Lord") is simply the prayer, "Lord, have mercy." This is what beggars in the first century would cry out to those passing by.

> Streets in the ancient world were filled with beggars that accosted those who passed by. These beggars had no assured livelihood; most of them had no family network of support and could not work due to a disability. Those who were disadvantaged, such as the crippled or the blind, infirm or aged, widowed or orphaned, had no social security system to provide for them. They depended on the mercy of the well-to-do for their livelihood.
>
> There was an art to begging. From bitter experience beggars knew that they were far more likely to receive a handout if they approached people nicely and appealed to their bet-

ter nature with a little discreet flattery rather than if they were aggressive and demanding. So they usually appealed for help by saying, "*Kyrie, eleison!*," "Lord, have mercy!" This cry was heard almost every day in every street. The Gospels tells us that needy people used the same cry when they appealed to Jesus for His help.[44]

Because this was the petition of many who approached Jesus in humility, seeking redress for their concerns (the Canaanite woman in Matthew 15:22, a man with an epileptic son in 17:15, two blind men in 20:30, blind Bartimaeus in Mark 10:47, ten lepers in Luke 17:13, and others), the Church appropriated this petition and made it one of the oldest parts of her Sunday morning liturgy. It's not just a prayer; it's also a confession. Before God, we are all beggars, in need of the Lord's mercy just to make it through each day.

The simple "Lord, have mercy," grew into the longer back-and-forth prayer of the Litany as a prayer to be prayed in times of persecution or oppression, or in particular times of devotion. In the sixth century, when a wave of sickness broke out from the overflow of the Tiber River in Rome, Gregory the Great commanded a litany be prayed in procession around the city. Luther removed prayers to the saints from the Litany and suggested its weekly use on Sunday mornings to pray against the looming Turkish invasion. It's hard to find a more robustly masculine prayer than the Litany.

Among other petitions, the Litany prays,

From all sin, from all error, from all evil; From the crafts and assaults of the devil; from sudden and evil death;

44 John W. Kleinig, *Grace Upon Grace: Spirituality for Today* (St. Louis: Concordia, 2008), 27–28.

> From pestilence and famine; from war and bloodshed; from sedition and from rebellion; From lightning and tempest; from all calamity by fire and water; and from everlasting death: Good Lord, deliver us. . . .
>
> To put an end to all schisms and causes of offense; to bring into the way of truth all who have erred and are deceived; To beat down Satan under our feet . . . : We implore You to hear us, good Lord.
>
> To raise those who fall and to strengthen those who stand; and to comfort and help the weakhearted and the distressed: We implore You to hear us, good Lord. (*LSB*, pp. 288–89)

These are robust prayers, prayers that acknowledge the scope and significance of the spiritual warfare that surrounds us, prayers that are neither presumptuous to think these concerns can be handled by any person nor too cowardly to petition for needed assistance, prayers that are courageous and submissive. These are masculine prayers.

The Litany is a great prayer for a man to lead his family in praying, though it can also be prayed by a man alone. It, like every other prayer handed down by millennia of Christians, joins his prayers with the cacophony of voices that have preceded him in this quest and this struggle. Let this model of prayer give structure and shape to your own prayers. There's no need to reinvent the wheel every time you pray; this will leave you intimidated and hesitant to begin. Use resources. Rely on the wisdom and experience of others who have gone before you. Pray the Lord's Prayer. Pray the Church's historic collects for each Sunday in the Church Year. Get a resource for prayer like the *Lutheran Book of Prayer* (Concordia, 2005) or *Treasury of Daily Prayer* (Concordia, 2008), or ask your pastor what he uses.

Let the petitions of those who were courageous enough to yield their lives rather than surrender their confession of the faith give both words and encouragement to your life of prayer. And then pray with and for others. "I desire then that in every place the men should pray, lifting holy hands without anger or quarreling" (1 Timothy 2:8).

Sing like a man.

If you want to learn to pray like a man, you also need to learn to sing like a man. Although singing isn't today regarded as very manly, and people today don't sing very much, singing together was once an ordinary manly endeavor.

Men working together often sang together. From the sea shanties of sailors to the call-and-response songs of field hands, men have regularly used song to unite themselves to one another, to teach stories (and tall tales), to entertain, to synchronize their work, or to pass time. In other cultures, men sing in pubs, to celebrate their soccer teams, to indoctrinate their children in cultural rituals, and more.

So also in the Church, men have regularly sung together. The Reformation restored singing to the role of the congregation so that singing became again the means by which Christians confessed the faith to one another. And hymns have always had a masculine vigor to them. Yet as early as 1903, Episcopal priest Rev. Ernest F. Smith lamented the rise of unmanly hymns:

> It is an insult to ask a *man* to sing some hymns which are found in a good many of the best collections, and which were written by women or invalids for persons of a certain

> effeminate temperament. There is nothing effeminate or invertebrate about the old hymns of the pre-Reformation Church; they were written by men and sung by men, and will last as long as the Church lasts. The permanence of a hymn depends more on its vigor and virility than on almost any other quality.[45]

So, check your love songs to Jesus at the door, confirm that your testes still secrete testosterone, and join in the more robust, more vigorous marching cadences of Christian men. These hymns are certainly vigorous. You might grow chest hair just by singing them.

Any hymn that describes the battle between Michael the Archangel and the devil is bound to inspire a fighting spirit in men.

> Christ, the Lord of hosts, unshaken
> By the devil's seething rage,
> Thwarts the plan of Satan's minions;
> Wins the strife from age to age;
> Conquers sin and death forever;
> Slams them in their steely cage.
>
> Michael fought the heav'nly battle,
> Godly angels by his side;
> Warred against the ancient serpent,
> Foiled the beast, so full of pride,
> Cast him earthbound with his angels;
> Now he prowls, unsatisfied.

45 Ernest F. Smith, "Hymns and Their Tunes: A Review and a Criticism," *The Church Eclectic*, vol. 33, no. 2 (November 1903): 110.

Long on earth the battle rages,
Since the serpent's first deceit;
Twisted God's command to Adam,
Made forbidden fruit look sweet.
Then the curse of God was spoken:
"You'll lie crushed beneath His feet!"

Jesus came, this word fulfilling,
Trampled Satan, death defied;
Bore the brunt of our temptation,
On the wretched tree He died.
Yet to life was raised victorious;
By His life our life supplied.

Swift as lightning falls the tyrant
From his heav'nly perch on high,
As the word of Jesus' vict'ry
Floods the earth and fills the sky.
Wounded by a wound eternal
Now his judgment has drawn nigh!

Jesus, send Your angel legions
When the foe would us enslave.
Hold us fast when sin assaults us;
Come, then, Lord, Your people save.
Overthrow at last the dragon;
Send him to his fiery grave. (*LSB* 521)

Fighting, crushing, conquering, setting free, and more compose a vigorously masculine story of courage, sacrifice, giving, and fighting that puts to shame the "Do you love me Jesus, check ❑ yes or ❑ no" shtick of pop Christianity. Or consider the way the work of the martyrs is praised in a hymn that's rarely sung but is as fightin' a hymn as there is.

> The Son of God goes forth to war A kingly crown to gain.
> His blood-red banner streams afar; Who follows in His train?
> Who best can drink His cup of woe, Triumphant over pain,
> Who patient bears his cross below—He follows in His train.
>
> The martyr first, whose eagle eye Could pierce beyond the grave,
> Who saw his master in the sky And called on Him to save.
> Like Him, with pardon on His tongue In midst of mortal pain,
> He prayed for those who did the wrong—Who follows in his train?
>
> A glorious band, the chosen few, On whom the Spirit came,
> Twelve valiant saints—their hope they knew And mocked the cross and flame.
> They met the tyrant's brandished steel, The lion's gory mane;
> They bowed their necks their death to feel—Who follows in their train?
>
> A noble army, men and boys, The matron and the maid,
> Around the Savior's throne rejoice, In robes of light arrayed.
> They climbed the steep ascent of heav'n Through peril, toil, and pain.
> O God, to us may grace be giv'n To follow in their train!
> (*LSB* 661)

If singing this hymn doesn't cause you to leap from your pew with a loud "Hooyah!" and charge off into battle against the powers of darkness that threaten your family and your friends, you should check your pulse. And then maybe go check yourself into the hospital.

Any hymn or song that deals with the core events of the Christ narrative—His incarnation, crucifixion, resurrection, and ascension—is bound to have the robustly masculine themes of sacrificial love, perfect sacrifice, triumph and conquest, resilient hope, and determined giving.

Age certainly isn't a guarantee of the virility of any song, though having weathered the scrutiny and implacability of time is a good indicator of a hymn's robustness. A hymn doesn't have to be old to be manly. It has to be gritty, more narrative than emotive. It has to be singable, even unaccompanied by instruments. And it has to courageously confess the crazy truths of Christianity.

The relatively new Easter hymn "All the Earth with Joy Is Sounding" confesses serious truths in a bold way. Consider the first two verses.

> All the earth with joy is sounding:
> Christ has risen from the dead!
> He, the greater Jonah, bounding
> From the grave, His three-day bed,
> Wins the prize:
> Death's demise—
> Songs of triumph fill the skies.
>
> Christ, the devil's might unwinding,
> Leaves behind His borrowed tomb.
> Stronger He, the strong man binding,

Takes, disarms his house of doom;
In the rout
Casting out
Pow'rs of darkness, sin, and doubt. (*LSB* 462)

However, just because a song is accompanied by an organ or included in a hardback hymnal does not necessarily make it worthy of being sung. Take "Beautiful Savior" for instance. Yes, truth is beautiful. Creation is beautiful. So also the Creator is beautiful. But Jesus' most praiseworthy characteristic is not His dashing good looks. The words do not praise Christ for the beauty of His perfect sacrifice, merely for His beauty, and His fairness, especially compared to flowers. Not only does the prophet Isaiah disagree with the statements in this hymn (see Isaiah 53:2), but it's also pretty hard to understand why any guy would want to sing along with this romance-novel-like homage to Jesus.

Nor are all so-called praise songs akin to "Jesus is my boyfriend" smarminess. Many hit the theological nail squarely on the head, confessing a robustly incarnate, masculine Christ who conquered sin and death with His vicarious suffering and death and rescued mankind from bondage to death and decay. Whatever the age of the words or the instruments used to accompany the singing, sing the manly songs of Christ's perfect sacrifice and victorious triumph over sin, the grave, and Satan.

Sing like a man in order to pray like a man. Let the richness of the Church's song shape your confession. Let her songs give words to your prayers. Let the call and response of the Liturgy keep you planted in the field the Lord is harvesting. Let the tales of her saints and martyrs encourage you in your vocation. Let the story of salvation be your marching cadence as you train yourself for godliness, as you venture forward in this quest to live as a man for the good of others. Sing to train yourself and to encourage your brothers under the cross. We need to hear your voice in this great cacophony of tenors, baritones, and basses. And you need to hear ours.

AMA. LOVE LIKE A MAN.

A man's love is selfless. It does not look for a reward for the effort it exerts or a response from those to whom it's shown. It simply does.

Consider the four different types of love C. S. Lewis articulated as an outline for the way a man loves others. Above all, a man's love is Christlike, *agape* love. He is called to model the love Christ has for His creation, for all mankind in particular, in all his relationships. It's not the stuff of Hallmark sentiment, but of cruciform sacrifice. He is not self-interested or selfish.

St. Paul's description of Christ's love in 1 Corinthians 13 sets the model for how a man should love. Patience and kindness ought to be his disposition toward those around him. He does not need to assert his rights or insist on fairness. He knows his identity in Christ is secure, no matter how anyone treats him or responds to his love. He needn't envy or boast, as these transform love into self-love, which is not love at all. He is not arrogant or rude. He does not insist on his own way. He is not irritable or resentful. After all, how much selfish action is borne out of a resentful spirit or excessive irritability? Only when a man's own needs hold his rapt attention does he descend into resentment or irritation. If, however, the needs of others are the compass by which he charts the course of his day, he needn't resent anyone who keeps him from getting his way. Thus, with the greater good of others as a man's priority, he is free to bear all things, believe all things, hope all things, and endure all things.

Agape sets the paradigm for love. In his love for his wife, the romantic love of *eros,* a man is not self-seeking. Intimacy is not a selfish aim. A man holds fast to his wife in the naked embrace of two lovers; he does not use her as merely a means for his own sexual gratification. Thus *eros*, like *agape*, is giving. A man seeks not chiefly his own pleasure, but the pleasure of his wife. He seeks to allure her, to win her, to make her feel desired and pursued as a whole person, not as a collection of body parts that he desires or needs.

As you endeavor to love your bride as Christ loves His Church, you'll be set free from the usual conflicts that plague a marriage. If you are more interested in covering over your wife's sins than pointing them out and correcting her, you'll never have the kinds of petty fights that emerge when a husband nitpicks his wife. Don't love who she is in your eyes, as you'll always see and focus on her faults. Love who she is in Christ. This love is courageous and risky. Instead of shaping her into the person you think she should be, love who Christ declares her to be: sinless, beautiful, holy. Then you'll set her free to live up to the ideal. It's not the Law that makes us good by coercion. It's the Gospel, it's forgiveness, that changes us into good people by grace.

So also, *storge*, a man's love for his family, is carried out under the umbrella of *agape*, selflessness. A man's children are not status symbols. His tribe does not exist to confirm his worth as a man. His worth as a man exists in his ability to shepherd and nurture his children chiefly for their own good.

Irritability with your children is a sign of selfishness. Even when they are rebellious or disobedient, your children do not change who you are as a man. How you love them and remain committed to them despite their tendency to test the bounds of your authority is an exercise in selfless *storge*, love that seeks their good above your own.

You don't need to make your children good to be a good father. If you focus instead on yourself as an instrument, if you work on being a good father, they will become good; they will follow your lead. *Storge* concerns a man more with what he can do for his children than with what he can get his children to do. There is a time and a place for the latter, and we'll return to the manly call of fatherhood in just a bit. For now, though, love focuses a man on his work for others, not their response.

Finally, a man needs to love other men. He needs *philia*. He needs the friendship, the camaraderie, of a man or a group of men for whom he can give of himself, spend himself, for their good, to sharpen them. This kind of love needs an arena in which to be exercised. *Philia* needs a common goal, a shared task, from a sport to a hobby, men as friends must work side-by-side. As we discussed earlier, this is what distinguishes *eros* from *philia*. *Eros* orients two complementary lovers toward each other. They *make love* face-to-face. Men do not. *Philia* asks of a man that he be trustworthy enough that his brothers in love can trust him without looking at him. He gives of himself without ever being noticed. *Philia* joins men shoulder to shoulder in a common endeavor. They risk together, fight together, venture together. Your friend needs you to be courageous, bold, productive, sacrificial, and selfless. This is how you love him.

Each of these four kinds of love requires commitment. As such, none of these active forms of love depends on any emotion. Emotions wax and wane. Sometimes you will be more emotionally interested in this calling to love than other times. As a man, though, you must be eternally, zealously, and selflessly committed to these four kinds of love.

DA. GIVE LIKE A MAN.

A man needs to see himself as a means to an end, not as the end himself. He exists for the good of those he has been entrusted with serving. You must learn to see yourself as a gift to be given to others. Then you will be a man.

Insisting that men take back what is rightfully theirs is not courageous. It's cowardly. Your rights as a man are not external to you. They're not *out there* for you to *take back*. Only when a man selfishly feels entitled to be the recipient of the work of others does he get his panties in a twist about not getting what he thinks is rightly his. This is the thinking of a boy, not a man. Children receive. Men give.

By now, you should be sufficiently disabused of the notion that this book will help you put your foot down and claim your place in the world as a man. Instead of your foot, you can put your life down. You can give your strength, your courage, your grit, your prowess, your skill, your knowledge, your goodness, your honor, your rights, and your life for the good of others around you.

But there is only one of you. You only have one life to give. A man must prioritize his love, his sacrifice, his relationships. Imagine a target with three rings. *Agape* is the umbrella for all of your life, the call to be selfless, but *eros* and *storge* are the particulars. These callings are in the center. They are the bull's-eye. They must take priority over lesser loves, lower callings, outer rings. If you have been given a wife and children, they command your highest attention and your greatest sacrifice. The second ring of the target, which encompasses more people but requires less precision, less one-on-one interaction, is your community, your immediate neighbors. This includes those in your church community, co-workers, people who live near you, those you interact with on a regular basis. They also need your sacrifice, your giving. Third are the people you don't typically interact with, people on a broader scale: your nation, the whole Church, mankind. The farther from the center of the target, the less impact your gift of your self will make. And yet, they also need your sacrifice. Your country needs men to give their lives in order to thrive and endure. The Church grows when watered with the blood of the martyrs. Mankind profits from the gift of selfless men offering their lives for noble causes.

As you can see, it's impossible to faithfully serve everyone who needs your service. You cannot give your strength to everyone who demands it. A man's self-giving must be calculated. There is no clear decision calculus. But once you stop seeing yourself as the end and everyone else as the means to your own good, when you can look at yourself as a gift and opportunities to serve as chances to exercise your masculinity, you're on the right path. Don't worry about mistakes. If your goal is to give, your work is already successful. Making mature decisions about when and to whom to give of yourself comes from the practice of living as a man. Learning how to give is part of this quest.

CERTA. FIGHT LIKE A MAN.

Jesus was a fighter. He never knocked out the Pharisees when they sought to trap Him with their questions. He did not take up arms against those who arrested Him by force in the Garden of Gethsemane. He refused to defend Himself to the high priest against the trumped-up charges. He didn't pick fights. And He never let any peripheral concerns distract Him from the battle He came to endure. He was a fighter, sure, and a man, perfectly. But He only fought the fights that mattered.

And when He fought, He held nothing back. It's hard to imagine a story better suited for a comic book or a superhero movie. To defeat a powerful nemesis and rescue mankind from their captivity to this ancient foe, the Creator sent His own Son to be one with those who needed to be saved. He withstood temptations to quit, to join forces with the adversary, and He was never even momentarily deterred from His mission. Along the way, He helped those He encountered, freeing them from momentary and lesser afflictions of the enemy. He repeatedly taught His followers that He would free all mankind from their bondage, but they continuously misunderstood Him. Finally, as the events of His great, cosmic battle unfolded, even one of His closest friends turned into a traitor. When a horde of those who should have been first to trust in this Hero became the unwitting accomplices of the enemy, even those who were closest to this Man fled. In great distress, the Hero faced His battle alone.

He was beaten and abused by those who were vastly His inferiors. He who could have displayed colossal power to free Himself from His captors, but who in so doing would have missed out on His perfect aim, was mocked for His seeming powerlessness. Finally, with the fate of the entire world hanging in the balance, He stared His foe in the face, ready to endure whatever it took, pay whatever price was necessary, or suffer any consequence except His loss of this fight. With cool, steely resolve, He bent His will to the One who sent Him. The Hero endured the fate that the captives deserved, and, in giving His life in exchange for theirs, won them a lasting freedom that nothing can hinder. The good Guy defeated the bad guy through His death. And then, in a miraculous show of strength, He even defeated death. He rose from the dead.

This is the plot summary of every good versus evil story that has ever been told.

Do you like action movies? Do you like tales of come-from-behind victory? Do you like stories of those willing to make the ultimate sacrifice? Do you get a little bit teary-eyed when the good guy triumphs, gets the girl, saves the day, wins the prize, gives himself completely? Does it make you cringe when something unfair happens, when evil seems to triumph, when the villain seems to have vanquished the forces of light? This is why. The story of Jesus' conquest of sin and death, His rout of the devil's assault against humanity, His rescuing His creation from death and decay by dying and rising triumphant from the grave is the story that lends its plot to every other story that's worth telling.

But do not mistake this story for a comedy or a romance. It is purely a fight story. It's the story of the showdown between life and death, light and darkness, good and evil, righteousness and sin. What Jesus endured on His way to the cross—on His way to fulfill His mission of redeeming mankind by defeating the captors sin, death, and the devil with His own innocent suffering and death—is as pure and gritty as a fight story could be. And He won.

Fight like Jesus. Learn how to be steadfast in your mission and how to have grit in the face of distractions. Know what you're fighting for. Jesus picked His battles; He never lost focus when peripheral annoyances could have drawn His energy to less important concerns. Had Jesus been concerned with defending Himself or His own reputation, then His mission to obliterate the stronghold of the axis of evil—sin, death, and the devil—would not have succeeded. His fight had to be for another. So must yours. He had to fight to the bitter end in order to succeed. And so must you.

Primary Target: Against Yourself

The first fight is unseen. Before you can fight for another, you must learn to fight against yourself. Your selfish tendencies, normal in all men since the fall, imperil your ability to fight for the good of others. Your sinful flesh hates to give. It hates to love selflessly. It hates manning up.

Repentance helps you fight against your sinful flesh. Constant sorrow over your sin is a gift from God that keeps you acutely aware of the power of your sinful inclinations and evermore reliant on Him for mercy and forgiveness. This is good. You cannot rely on yourself in this fight. Faith is in Christ, not in yourself. You must rely entirely on Him. And then fight. Practice spiritual disciplines. These are like hitting the gym to strengthen your spiritual muscles. St. Paul exhorted Timothy, "Train yourself for godliness; for while bodily training is of some value, godliness is of value in every way, as it holds promise for the present life and also for the life to come" (1 Timothy 4:7–8). Training for godliness. That's what spiritual disciplines do. They help a man fight against his own flesh.

The fundamental disciplines Jesus encourages are prayer, fasting, and almsgiving. In the Sermon on the Mount, Jesus catechizes on these three disciplines, saying, "When you give to the needy, . . . when you pray, . . . when you fast, . . ." (see Matthew 6:1–18). He doesn't say "If you give, if you pray, if you fast." He simply assumes His disciples do these things. All three guard against the power of the flesh. Prayer, as we've said earlier, is the opposite of productivity. It commends the success of everything a man does, as well as the things he is unable to do, to the care of his heavenly Father.

Giving, likewise, is a discipline that protects against love of money and possessions. There's no set figure for how much

Christians should give to the Church and to the needy. In the Old Testament, a *tithe*, a tenth, was the norm. In the New Testament, St. Paul, well catechized in the Law, simply commands generosity (2 Corinthians 8:1–15). A tenth is a good place to start. But if you give away a tenth of your income and still love money, still trust in money or possessions more than you trust in your heavenly Father, give more. Giving disciplines your flesh against this idolatry, against love of money and Mammon. If you're anxious about how much you give, this is a sure sign that you're still trusting in money. Give more. And if you praise yourself for your generosity when you give, this likewise is a sign that your focus is on yourself and not on your neighbor. So give more. Give until you do not trust in money or possessions to make you happy or secure.

Fasting, too, though a largely neglected Christian discipline, is a healthy way to teach your flesh that your desires do not control you. Properly speaking, true fasting involves hunger. Gorging yourself on fish and beer every Friday in Lent is the opposite of fasting. There's nothing sinful about eating, of course. But abstaining from eating for a time teaches you that your belly is not your god. Fasting puts hunger back into its proper place. Originally a desire intended to lead Adam and Eve to the tree of life in the Garden of Eden and teach them to rely daily on their Creator, in the fall, hunger is instantly disordered. Instead of teaching gratitude and dependence, hunger inclines toward gluttony.

How do you fast? There are several ways Christians have historically fasted. Wednesdays and Fridays are traditional fast days, as is Saturday night in preparation for receiving Communion on Sunday morning. The forty days of Lent are also a time for fasting, as Christians may choose to restrict their daily intake of food to a meal and a half each day. However you fast, be hungry.

Replace the time you would spend eating with time in prayer. Take money saved by skipping a meal or avoiding finer delicacies and give it away. Prayer, fasting, and almsgiving go together.

The belly is relatively easy to discipline, but it's a gateway to the body's other desires. Especially for men, learning that the belly is not your god through fasting is a stepping stone on the path to learning that neither are your reproductive organs in control of you. In many ways, disordered hunger is no different from lust, disordered sexual desire. Start by learning to discipline your belly and say no to hunger, just for a time. This will also help you develop the ability to say no to your gonads and sexual desire.

In addition to these three disciplines, the daily practice of reading, studying, meditating on, and memorizing the Word is helpful in training the flesh for godliness. Reading is what it sounds like. Simply reading the Word. Study is reading intensified. It involves exploring themes, common words and phrases, and digging into the richness of the text. To study well, you'll have to rely on external resources, notes in *The Lutheran Study Bible*, commentaries, sermons from Church Fathers on the text, dictionaries, and more. Meditation is different. If study is broad, meditation is narrow. Christian meditation is not like the mind-emptying meditation of Eastern religions. In Christian meditation, the goal is to focus on one small part of the Word, a word or phrase, and to fixate your mind on that. It can happen in quiet minutes spent simply contemplating that nugget of Scripture and praying on it. Think of how cows digest grass by bringing it up from the different chambers of their stomachs to chew on it some more before passing it to the next stomach. Meditation is chewing, slowly processing and digesting a small piece of the Word to savor its richness. Finally, memorization helps you internalize the words and patterns of Scripture and learn them by heart so that you can readily recall and recite them. The goal is to shape your words and thoughts with the words of Holy Writ. It's a discipline against your flesh, against the unnaturally disordered ways of thinking that result from man's fall into sin.

These are the tactics of the warfare against your sinful flesh. Use them daily. This fight against your selfishness is essential to your ability to live as a man for the good of others.

> Therefore, since we are surrounded by so great a cloud of witnesses, let us also lay aside every weight, and sin which clings so closely, and let us run with endurance the race that is set before us, looking to Jesus, the founder and perfecter of our faith, who for the joy that was set before Him endured the cross, despising the shame, and is seated at the right hand of the throne of God.
>
> Consider Him who endured from sinners such hostility against Himself, so that you may not grow weary or fainthearted. In your struggle against sin you have not yet resisted to the point of shedding your blood. (Hebrews 12:1–4)

The first fight you face every day is against sin. Use these disciplines to equip you for this fight.

Secondary Target: For Others

With each day begun fighting against your sinful flesh, you'll be better prepared to live in love, service, and giving toward others around you. As you get up from your knees, as you emerge from study and meditation on the Word of God, you'll be armed to fight for the good of those you serve in your daily vocations. When you can fight against your selfish inclinations, you are enabled to fight for the good of others.

A good, godly man should have this fighting spirit. He should care passionately about what's good and right, and he should be willing to pursue those ends at great personal expense. He should never fight merely for himself, though he should be capable and competent to defend himself so that he can continue to fight, to serve, and to lead his wife and children. Fighting for what's right is good and a sign of strong, masculine character. Picking a fight is not and shows an effeminate weakness of character. Not every threatening situation needs to escalate to actual violence. But a man equipped with strength, courage, and a sense of purpose to defend the good of others will wisely know that, in a broken world, sometimes you might have to throw a punch to keep your loved ones safe.

Jesus fought for His Bride. He delivered her from captivity to sin and the devil; and He guards her from the constant assault of the devil and the world. He also fights for His brothers and sisters, those made sons of God in the adoption of Holy Baptism. But He doesn't need to fight to defend His own honor.

Most of a man's fight for the good of others is not about fisticuffs or violence. It's usually a battle of wits and words. He should be able to defend his family not just from physical assaults but also from verbal ones. The world will assault with lies that can inflict as much damage as any physical blow. Consider the lies that besiege a man's family.

1. God rewards you for being good.

2. A woman is only as valuable as her beauty, or worse, her sex appeal.

3. If you work hard, you can do anything you want.

4. The child growing inside your wife's womb is not a living person worthy of protection.

5. God wants you to be happy.

6. Sex is a commodity that can be traded or sold.

7. Marriage isn't forever.

8. Children are a burden.

9. There is no absolute truth.

10. Boys and girls should be treated the same.

And more. It will take courage and conviction to oppose these tenets of a society that is tolerant of everything except biblical Christianity. You will need to fight with words, with prayer, and with the truth of God's Word.

When you take up the armor of God to be a warrior for the good of your wife, your children, your friends, your neighbors, your countrymen, the defenseless or helpless, those bullied or oppressed, consider the resolve of Christ. He fought for what was good. He did not retreat even momentarily. And He did not consider any cost too great that He would not endure it for the good of those for whom He was fighting.

In order to be a warrior, a fighter for those who depend on you, you've got to stop being nice. Be good instead. Take the lead. Be courageous. Fight for something. Spend yourself in the pursuit of the good of another. Take risks for the good of someone else. Know what you're fighting for. And know whom you're fighting against. Although you may have to stand up to another person, know that no person is ever truly your enemy. The enemy is more powerful than any person. But he is also already defeated by the One who joins you into His own fighting stance.

THE BATTLE PLAN

WHAT DOES A MAN DO?

Get tactical about your day. Make a daily planner that helps you identify goals and targets, sets your mind on track at the beginning of each day, and helps you reflect at the end of the day on how you have succeeded or failed in these objectives. This may be a helpful pattern to follow. Adjust according to your needs. Begin by reading and meditating on Scripture.

What is a man? Who are you by virtue of your Baptism into the Christ?

Then ask

What am I called by God to do as a man?

WHAT A MAN DOES—TODAY

GOALS FOR TODAY:

Short term:

Long term:

	WHOM DOES THIS SERVE?	SPECIFIC ACTIONS	HOW DID IT GO? PROGRESS? SUCCESS? SETBACKS?
Pray			
Love			
Give			
Fight			

Take the chart and use it to visualize yourself serving others, making decisions for their good, using yourself as an instrument for the greatest good. Then, pray for courage, endurance, guidance, and forgiveness. Finally, greet the day.

GROW AS A MAN

> *"Let us train boys from earliest childhood to be patient when they suffer wrongs themselves, but, if they see another being wronged, to sally forth courageously and aid the sufferer in fitting measure."*
>
> —*St. Chrysostom, An Address on Vainglory and the Right Way for Parents to Bring Up Their Children*

> *"The glory of God is a living man; and the life of man consists in beholding God."*
>
> —*St. Irenaeus, Against Heresies*

To accomplish your to-do list of praying, loving, giving, and fighting every day; of being an instrument for the good of others around you; and of leaving effeminate selfishness behind; you've got to grow as a man. You've got to mature beyond boyish fascinations and immaturity. Although the following is not a comprehensive list, as such a list would be impossible to compile, it can help you in this endeavor. Consider these good ideas, ideas you can add to the growing list of practices, disciplines, mind-set shifts, and techniques you've gained throughout this book. Masculinity is not a single character trait. It's a lifestyle. It's a collection of attributes. It's a better way of living in the world that has the potential not merely to make you a better man, but, more importantly, to enable you to make those around you better. It's not a destination. It's a way to travel. It's a quest.

FIND MENTORS

Manhood doesn't just happen. There's no magic threshold that will transform you from a boy into a man when you cross it. You need the advice and the examples of those who have traveled this path before you.

Ideally, this task falls first on the father. A boy needs a man to show him how to be a man. He needs someone to model the everyday, ordinary kind of masculinity that's sorely lacking in western societies. But sometimes the father is absent. Or he doesn't know himself what it means to be a man. Even if your father was a shining example of selfless masculinity, you need other mentors.

Where can you find them? Start in church. But before you cozy up to the guy in the Affliction T-shirt and bedazzled blue jeans, think older. Find the oldest men in your congregation and get to know them. They may attend a men's Bible study together or simply show up early for church and sit by themselves. Maybe they go out for coffee once a week. Get to know them. Listen to their stories. Chances are high that they've lived through things you will never experience. They may be war heroes or widowers or both. If they grew up before the era when being a man was the punch line for sitcoms and commercials, all the better.

In this, the Church is a unique institution. In other arenas of life, men tend to gather with others of similar ages. But the Church with her timeless liturgy, ageless hymns, and eternal truths draws men from every stage of life. Unless all you aspire to be is just one of the bros, don't squander your Sundays paling around only with others in your age bracket. If the men around you on Sunday mornings don't include the white-haired octogenarians that society tends to marginalize and discard, you're stunting your growth in genuine masculinity.

There are no perfect mentors. There are just men at different stages of this journey. Your role model is Christ. But these fellow travelers who are farther along than you know the way better. They've learned by trial and error. They've wooed wives, raised children, fought wars, plowed soil, built cities, and kept the lights on and the pipes from leaking at church. They've also failed in these and numerous other endeavors. You'll probably learn more—and they'll have more to teach—from their lessons gleaned in the classrooms of experience and errors than from the academies of their achievements. If you gain their confidence, you may learn these stories.

And then, when you're just a few steps farther down the road than you are now, turn around and help the rest of us. Find young men and boys in your congregation and befriend them. Volunteer to teach Sunday School. Train the acolytes. Bring them along to the men's gatherings. Set an example of prayer, piety, patience, and persistence. Eventually, be vulnerable enough to share the lessons learned from mistakes in your life. Model repentance and fervent dependence on forgiveness. Be a man enough to give of yourself to those who aren't even far enough into this quest to know they're on a journey. We're all in this together. As the saying goes, a rising tide lifts all boats. The better other men know how to be men, the healthier and safer their society will be. Genuine masculinity benefits us all.

HEAR THE MARTYRS

If there are any stories that bear retelling to encourage you in your quest for masculinity, it is the stories of the Christian martyrs, those who died to give a faithful confession of Jesus as their Savior. Martyrdom has always been a particularly masculine end to one's life. It is the highest calling of a Christian and one of the most masculine things possible to do. To confess Christ, not just with words or deeds but with blood and your last breath, is to have no regard for those who can merely kill the body but cannot harm the soul (Matthew 10:28). Learn these stories. Tell them to others. Teach them to your children.

Sure, many of the stories of martyrdom have probably been embellished with time. They're not all in Scripture. They don't need to be perfectly accurate. They must simply inspire your courage, your steadfastness, and your endurance in the threat of persecution. They certainly have their basis in truth. Jesus' warnings that His disciples would endure fierce persecution have all come true. The Church has never cowered in a climate of persecution nor bent her knee to worldly authorities who called for her to give up preaching the Savior of sinners.

Consider one of the oldest stories of persecution, the account of the martyrdom of St. Polycarp. According to the earliest histories, Polycarp was instructed by St. John (the evangelist, the "disciple whom Jesus loved," brother of James, one of the *Boanerges*—the sons of thunder). As the bishop of the church in Smyrna, Polycarp, like other leaders in the Church, was pressured to curtail his preaching and proselytizing and to pledge his allegiance to the emperor and offer incense in worship to him. He refused. So he was arrested and brought into the arena to be burned at the stake.

According to the account of his martyrdom, when the soldiers came to arrest Polycarp,

> he went downstairs and talked with them, while those who looked on marveled at his age and constancy, and at how there should be such zeal over the arrest of so old a man. Straightway he ordered food and drink, as much as they wished, to be set before them at that hour, and he asked them to give him an hour so that he might pray undisturbed.[46]

Finally, having fed the men who came to arrest him and having been strengthened in courage by his hour of praying, Polycarp was arrested, bound, and finally brought into the arena where he would be given the opportunity to renounce Christ and save his own life. "As Polycarp was entering the arena, a voice from heaven came to him, saying, 'Be strong, Polycarp, and play the man.' No one saw the one speaking, but those of our people who were present heard the voice."[47] Encouraged, Polycarp continued to refuse to praise Caesar. "But the proconsul was insistent and said: 'Take the oath, and I shall release you. Curse Christ.' Polycarp said: 'Eighty-six years I have served him, and he never did me any wrong. How can I blaspheme my King who saved me?' "[48]

Refusing ample opportunities to save himself, telling his captors that nailing him to the stake would be unnecessary, as he would stay put in the fire, Polycarp is finally bound to the stake to be burned.

---

46 "The Martyrdom of Polycarp," in *Early Christian Fathers*, ed. Cyril C. Richardson (Philadelphia: Westminster Press, 1953), 151.

47 "The Martyrdom of Polycarp," 152.

48 "The Martyrdom of Polycarp," 152.

> And with his hands put behind him and tied, like a noble ram out of a great flock ready for sacrifice, a burnt offering ready and acceptable to God, he looked up to heaven and said: "Lord God Almighty, Father of thy beloved and blessed Servant Jesus Christ, through whom we have received full knowledge of thee, 'the God of angels and powers and all creation' and of the whole race of the righteous who live in thy presence: I bless thee, because thou hast deemed me worthy of this day and hour, to take my part in the number of the martyrs, in the cup of thy Christ, for 'resurrection to eternal life' of soul and body in the immortality of the Holy Spirit; among whom may I be received in thy presence this day as a rich and acceptable sacrifice, just as thou hast prepared and revealed beforehand and fulfilled, thou that art the true God without any falsehood. For this and for everything I praise thee, I bless thee, I glorify thee, through the eternal and heavenly High Priest, Jesus Christ, thy beloved Servant, through whom be glory to thee with him and Holy Spirit both now and unto the ages to come. Amen."[49]

After this intrepid confession of Christ, the soldiers attending to him attempted to light the fire under Polycarp. But the flames surrounded him without harming him. So they commanded an executioner to stab him to death. So he did. And for being a Christian, and a bishop, and a bold confessor of Christ as his Savior, Polycarp, like so many other Christians in the first generations of the Church, died. As a martyr.

49 "The Martyrdom of Polycarp," 154.

"Play the man, Polycarp." So he did. He prayed, he loved, he gave himself completely, he fought against the tyranny of the godless, and he died.

Tell these stories. Tell them to your sons, your friends, the men in your congregation. Tell them about the ten apostles who likewise died for confessing Christ to be the Son of God who died and who rose from the dead. Tell about James whom Herod decapitated. Tell about Peter crucified upside down or Andrew crucified on an X-shaped cross. Tell about Bartholomew, skinned alive.

Tell about the company of forty Roman soldiers who, after converting to Christianity, were forced to stand naked overnight on a frozen lake outside the city of Sebaste, and so froze to death. Tell about Lucy with her eyes gouged out. Tell about John Hus who was burned at the stake for preaching the Gospel in its purity one hundred years before Luther posted his Ninety-Five Theses. Tell about Jim Elliot, Nate Saint, Ed McCully, Pete Fleming, and Roger Youderian—missionaries killed by the notoriously violent Auca tribe in Ecuador. Tell about the twenty-one young Christian Egyptian men led out onto a beach and beheaded by Islamic extremists. Tell them about Father Jacques Hamel, the eighty-five-year-old priest whose throat was slit by enemies of Christ while he was celebrating the Mass on a Tuesday morning.

Tell these stories. The accounts of the martyrs are tales of perfect giving, perfect selflessness, perfect masculinity. Stories of a Church that not only survives persecution but also thrives and grows under the threat of bloodshed can do nothing but inspire courage in the young men who are called to be Christlike to their neighbors.

The lack of martyr stories in contemporary Christianity may not be the cause of the sissification of Christians, but it certainly doesn't help them recover. Within these stories—stories of those so transformed by the good news of full and complete forgiveness because of the perfect sacrifice of Jesus on the cross that they would endure anything, even torture and death, rather than give up their belief in this beautiful truth or their confession of it—there is courage for the rest of us to be changed by this transforming, selfless love, of Christ. When we stop telling the stories of the martyrs, we soften the message of the Church and emasculate men.

PRACTICE SACRIFICE

Sacrifice doesn't come naturally to anyone. Self-denial is no longer part of our DNA. Since, as a man, you're called to live sacrificially for others, and because this sacrifice encompasses the whole of your life, not just the occasional act, you've got to practice it. You're called to live your life for your wife, your children, your neighbors, your countrymen, your friends, and sometimes to lay your life down for them.

Sacrifice is as much a mind-set as it is a lifestyle. Sacrifice imbues a man's daily routine with meaning. It gives his life purpose. In order to be capable of making big sacrifices, you need to be able to make small sacrifices. If you can't practice self-denial in minutiae, you won't be able to practice it in more important matters. Just as fasting teaches the ability to deny basic urges of the body and the other spiritual disciplines enable you to mature in godliness, so discipline in small, daily self-denial sharpens your focus on the things that matter.

St. Paul uses the illustration of training for an athletic contest.

> Do you not know that in a race all the runners run, but only one receives the prize? So run that you may obtain it. Every athlete exercises self-control in all things. They

> do it to receive a perishable wreath, but we an imperishable. So I do not run aimlessly; I do not box as one beating the air. But I discipline my body and keep it under control, lest after preaching to others I myself should be disqualified. (1 Corinthians 9:24–27)

The more elite the athlete, the more the small decisions matter. They must carefully monitor what they eat, how much they sleep, and how intensely they train. Even a donut, a beer, or snoozing the alarm is a distraction and potentially a setback when the goal is a world record, a gold medal, a championship, or an elusive victory.

In Christ, you have purpose. You have both daily as well as lifelong callings. You are a man on a mission. Keep track of your goals and your responsibilities. Write them down. Include them in your prayers. Know why you wake up. Wake up early and take ownership of the day for the good of others. Know whom you serve and who benefits from your daily endeavors. Make exercise a part of your daily schedule, not just so you look good or feel good, though these are fine secondary and tertiary benefits, but chiefly so you can be of maximum service to your friends, your wife, or your children. Take time every morning for prayer and meditation. Devote time every evening to name things for which you are grateful through the day. All these little sacrifices enable you to give the best version of yourself for the benefit of others. Each good decision is the cultivation of a new habit of giving, preparing you for the proving ground of masculinity, the big sacrifices that await.

CULTIVATE SATISFACTION

In addition to their accusatory, condemning function, God's Commandments are also something of a blueprint for the original design of creation. They show the way things are supposed to work. And, when they're adhered to, things generally do work better. Although this is not the primary function of God's Law, each of the Commandments, in a way, is intended to protect a gift God intends for His creatures to receive.

Therefore, when I teach the Commandments, I often invite catechumens to attempt to identify the gift God intends to deliver with each one. Once they get the hang of it, they can identify the first eight pretty easily. In order to give the gift of Himself, God forbids you to have any other gods. In order to give the gift of His name, God prohibits misuse or disuse of His name. In order to give the gift of His Word, God commands you to hold it sacred, to hear it gladly, not to despise preaching. On it goes through the rest of the Commandments (Fourth: parents and other authorities; Fifth: life; Sixth: marriage; Seventh: possessions; Eighth: reputation) until we come to the Ninth and Tenth Commandments. In both of these, God prohibits coveting. Coveting isn't really any outward action. It's internal. It's desire. More precisely, it's desire for things that you don't have. So what gift does He intend to give and to protect with a prohibition against inward desire for things He has not given? Contentment.

At the end of two of his letters, the apostle Paul takes up the topic of contentment and satisfaction.

> But godliness with contentment is great gain, for we brought nothing into the world, and we cannot take

> anything out of the world. But if we have food and clothing, with these we will be content. (1 Timothy 6:6–8)

> I have learned in whatever situation I am to be content. I know how to be brought low, and I know how to abound. In any and every circumstance, I have learned the secret of facing plenty and hunger, abundance and need. (Philippians 4:11–12)

In a world filled with ever-increasing distractions, more creature comforts than any time in history, and greater affluence and more stuff than previous generations could have imagined were available, the one thing that is in scarce supply anymore is satisfaction.

God intends for us to be satisfied with what He gives. He wants us to believe that His provision of daily bread, which according to the catechism includes everything from food and clothing to good friends and good weather, is enough.

For a man, for whom drive and ambition are necessary to be the best protector and provider he can be, this sets up another paradox. On one hand, a man must zealously pursue the good of those he is given to serve and love. He must be driven. He must be ambitious. He must work hard. He must possess a sense of hustle and grit. And yet, he must acknowledge that without provision from his heavenly Father, not even the most tireless work would provide any of his daily bread. He must work as if everything depends on him and simultaneously trust that nothing depends on him.

Covetousness is an unhealthy pursuit of more and more that prevents a man from living for the good of others. Workaholism has kept many a man from the greater good of spending time with his wife or children. The desire to provide can quickly devolve into mere love of more and more money or possessions. Satisfaction is learning to live in this paradox. A healthy step toward satisfaction is learning to pray for daily bread, which teaches a man that what God provides is always enough.

SEX AND SATISFACTION

Can a man and a woman live together in a lifelong monogamous relationship and be truly satisfied with one another? If you want to answer that question in the negative, you can easily find allies both in the scientific community and in the pickup artist community. The lab scene is not unlike the bar scene in giving license to infidelity. Even if the arguments are true that humans aren't naturally monogamous, who cares? Those who believe original sin has distorted human nature and men's desires to the point that they simply don't function like they were intended won't be surprised to discover that science confirms man's inability to live as he ought. The question is not whether lifelong monogamy is natural. It is. Or it was. It's the original union between the man and woman, and it is a reflection of the eternal union between Christ and His Bride. But being *natural* doesn't make it *easy*. The question, then, is how a husband and wife can cultivate satisfaction within their marriage.

This is not as difficult as it might seem. Here's the quick and dirty way to cultivate satisfaction: have sex. With each other. And only each other.

That's it, really.

Sure, you can go to marriage retreats, couples' counseling, read books on marriage together, schedule date nights, and lots more. Those are meet, right, and salutary. But nothing can replace the bond cultivated in the embrace of two naked people, vulnerable and exposed, giving themselves to each other completely.

We won't descend too far down the rabbit hole of neurobiology and endocrinology, though it's pretty fascinating. The hormone oxytocin, released by the pituitary gland at the base of the brain, is remarkable. We don't yet understand all of what it does, but we're slowly learning its role in human happiness and satisfaction as well as in the ability of a man and woman to find contentment and a sense of safety in a lifelong bond with each other. Oxytocin causes two people to trust one another and feel safe with each other. In both males and females, oxytocin is released throughout the act of sex. The man also benefits from the hormone vasopressin, released in his brain during an erection, which intensifies his emotional bond with his partner and makes him want to protect her. In the female brain, oxytocin is also released in conjunction with childbirth and nursing. Oxytocin causes contraction of a woman's uterus in order to give birth, triggers the letdown of her milk in order to nurse, and fosters the mother's lifelong maternal bond with her baby. Even nonsexual physical contact releases oxytocin.

But oxytocin and vasopressin are not the only pleasure hormones. There's also dopamine, which is the most intense pleasure hormone, as well as serotonin, which contributes to longer feelings of happiness and well-being. Because dopamine thrives on novelty, it might seem to contradict the bonding role of oxytocin, which helps to bond couples more closely the longer they are together, monogamous, and intimate. But pure pleasure is not satisfaction. The rush of dopamine is easy to obtain. The thrill of novelty easily excites. The endurance of long-term satisfaction is more elusive.

What in the world does all this have to do with being a man? Quite a bit.

Too many guys are stuck in a search for the thrill of novelty that leaves them without enduring satisfaction. Whether you're chasing every skirt that passes by, spinning the hedonistic hamster wheel of pornography, or simply meandering in the labyrinth of lust, you'll never find the satisfaction you want and need.

Pornography is an industry that thrives on dissatisfaction. It provides a fantasy with just enough reality to dupe you into believing that those girls are real or really interested in you. But each new, naked girl is never enough. There is always the possibility of a newer one, a better one, with just one more click of the mouse. Whether you're married or not, this barrage of flesh is intended to leave you dissatisfied. Porn producers need you to keep coming back. It's time to check out of Pornotopia.

Masturbation, too, is by its very nature dissatisfying. It provides a release of oxytocin with the frustration of self-stimulation. Pair-bonding with your hand and your own world of fantasy can do nothing but further entrench you in this plague of selfishness and dissatisfaction.

If you want to be a good man, heck, if you want to be a man at all and not merely a boy, you've got to quit porn and/or masturbation. If you've tried unsuccessfully before to quit, you'll probably need help. First of all, as with any sin, and especially with habitual sins that are difficult to give up, go to your pastor. Confess to him in order to receive a clear and certain word of freedom, complete forgiveness from Christ. Consider him a resource. You may find it helpful to find a professional counselor, probably someone who specializes in cognitive behavioral therapy, whose specialty is helping people change difficult, destructive behaviors. There are also twelve-step groups that apply the program from Alcoholics Anonymous to other behavioral addictions, including addictions to sex or porn.

Get help and get out of this pattern of destructive, selfish behavior. Not only does it cultivate a mind-set of dissatisfaction, but it also makes it impossible to be committed to loving and giving yourself to others in a genuinely masculine way. Instead, it leaves you fixated on yourself—your own needs and desires—and ultimately effeminate.

Genuine satisfaction will be found in the lifelong, monogamous union of a husband and wife who fulfill their need for novelty with each other. This doesn't mean that their sex life will always be novel but that their lives together, in the bedroom and out of it, will be filled with novelty as two different people continue to grow together and experience new things together.

BE PRESENT. QUIT ESCAPING.

Men work. It's what they do. When two men greet one another, "What do you do?" is one of the first things they ask. And yet, the great temptation of modern man is to check out, to disengage, to hide and escape. Porn is one easy escape. It's far easier to cultivate a relationship with a girl made of pixels who responds positively to your mouse clicks. But there are many other options for a guy to rely on to disengage.

There are video games, sure. Or there's sports. Or more work. Or Facebook. Or a smartphone. Or the computer. Or hobbies. Or friends. Or anything. Escaping is less a matter of what a man is doing than it is about what he's neglecting.

That's the problem. None of these things is wrong for a man to do or to engage in. The problem arises when they're chronic, when they regularly take a man away from his callings. Even good things, healthy diversions, working to provide, enjoying an occasional mindless distraction, can be misused. There's a difference between the escapism of running away from difficult situations, people, or responsibilities and the Sabbath-keeping restfulness of retreating from the world for a time in order to refresh and refocus.

Masculinity is hard work. Loving, giving, serving, fighting, and praying require both your promise and your presence. It requires you to be intensely and purposefully present for the good of those you're called to serve. Sometimes, for their good, you've got to retreat and regroup. But when retreat is the normal posture, when escape is the default, then selfishness is inhibiting your ability to be a man who is fully present for the good of others. If you can be honest with yourself, and if you genuinely desire to grow as a man, you'll know the difference, and you'll want to remain present where and when you're needed. You'll also seek the companionship and camaraderie of other men in real life, not just their video game avatars or their Twitter handles.

KEEP GOING

Sometimes the phrase "Man up!" is simply a way of saying "Keep going." It's what men do. A man needs to be undeterred by adversity or hardship. He needs grit and endurance. He needs courage to take the next step, do the next thing, keep putting one foot in front of the other. This can only happen if a man knows what he's doing. His purpose gives him passion. His passion for those he is called to serve gives him the strength to press on.

Know what you're doing and why you're doing it. Practice visualization. In your mind, create a picture of what a good man would do. See a good husband loving his wife, denying his selfish inclinations in order to serve his wife, to give her what's in her best interests, to see himself as an instrument for her good. See in your mind's eye a good father—carefully, consistently, and patiently catechizing his children; investing his time and his energy into these young people entrusted to him; warding off dangers from within or without. Picture a good man who, everywhere he goes, in every interaction he has, sees himself as an instrument of God for the good of those he encounters and thus continuously asks himself, "How can I serve?"

In short, imagine Christ in your shoes. This is the inverse of how we usually think about Christ's work, right? It's not that Christ is in your shoes. It's that you are in His. That's Baptism, where you were joined into His death and His resurrection.

Yet, "If anyone is in Christ, he is a new creation. The old has passed away; behold, the new has come" (2 Corinthians 5:17). And as St. Paul says, "I have been crucified with Christ. It is no longer I who live, but Christ who lives in me. And the life I now live in the flesh I live by faith in the Son of God, who loved me and gave Himself for me" (Galatians 2:20).

What can give greater measure of grit and determination to keep going than this? Christ lives in you. You live in Christ. The perfect Man. His strength is yours. His goodness is yours. His virtue is yours. His service is yours. In your quest to be masculine, to live for the good of others, even when the world would assault you on this journey and deter you from fulfilling this simple mission, "Consider Him who endured from sinners such hostility against Himself, so that you may not grow weary or fainthearted" (Hebrews 12:3). In Jesus, the perfect Man, who endured until proclaiming, "It is finished," you have endurance. Grit. Determination. You can keep going because He went all the way. Hang in there. Your mission is worth it.

AIM FOR SIGNIFICANCE

There's a difference between being successful and being significant. In the eyes of the world, you attain success when you amass enough stuff. Enough money, enough things, enough notoriety, enough friends, whatever. Success always aims at the self, though.

Significance reverses the inflow of success into the outflow of giving, investing in others. Significance is found in the masculine traits of giving to and serving others. Success risks being merely self-centered, *malakia*, effeminate (see chapter 1). Success can start and end with you. When you're dead, so is your success. Significance, the benefit you have on others, endures beyond your own lifetime.

Every man desires to leave a legacy. He wants to be remembered. He wants to be known for something. The easiest place to be the most significant is in your own family. There are no lives you can influence as much as those of your wife and children. Then there are those in outer spheres of influence, in your church community or your neighborhood. If you have a wife and children, spend the bulk of your time, effort, and resources there. If you don't, get involved with others, especially with those marginalized by society. Teach Sunday School. Coach a kids' sports team. Be a Boy Scout leader. Become an advocate for the unborn. Volunteer in a women's shelter or a homeless shelter (or both). Teach classes to others interested in a skill or hobby of yours. Invest in noble causes, both with your time and your money. Look around you. You'll find ways you can utilize the best of yourself for the betterment of others. Whatever you have is meant to be given away. In getting, there may be success, but in giving, there is significance.

MAKE THINGS

One mark of the maturation from boyhood to manhood is the transition from consuming to producing. To make something is to begin to assume an active role of giving and doing instead of the passivity of simply being given to.

Made in the image of a God who creates, who gives life, who gives Himself, this is what men are driven to do. To produce more than you consume is to begin to take ownership of your life. What can you make? Start by thinking of the things you buy. Food is an easy place to start. Although you probably won't produce all of your own food, you can begin to produce some if you simply plant a garden or have a few chickens in your backyard. Music is another easy option. Although nowadays most people's idea of music is what you download from iTunes, in days past, music was what you sat down with your friends and *played.* Another accessible option is to begin to perform your own car repairs. People gripe about the technological complexity of modern automobiles, but the same technology has yielded crowd-sourced how-to guides. If you can figure out what's wrong, there is certainly a YouTube video or a write-up on an owners' forum for you particular car that walks you through each step. In the same vein, if you're a homeowner, you can begin tackling your own repairs instead of calling in a professional. Again, the Internet is an invaluable resource for a would-be do-it-yourselfer. Or, better than the Internet is the collective wisdom of other men who have grappled with these skills before. Learning to make things can pretty easily be coupled with learning the ropes of masculinity if you find an older man willing to teach you.

Have you already mastered one or all of these more basic endeavors? Move on to some kind of productive hobby. There is nothing quite so fulfilling as taking a raw piece of wood, metal, or leather and transforming it into something someone else will give you money for. Or take up electronics. Or computer programming. Or blacksmithing. Or anything.

In a hyperconsumerist culture, where we buy what we need and lots more that we don't, and simply discard what breaks or collects dust, men may never move beyond consuming more than they produce. But simply producing *something* will begin to liberate you from boyish consumerism. It will start to change your perspective. Simply possessing the skills to make something will help to shift your focus outward. You'll begin to see yourself as a producer of something valuable and helpful to someone else. You'll begin to see yourself as capable of being of service to someone else. And you'll cultivate skills that you can share with other men or boys, enriching your own masculine quest by passing on manly knowledge and skills and fostering relationships with other men.

The temptation, of course, will be to escape into these creative endeavors and duck out on more immediate responsibilities. That serves no one but yourself. Keep your priorities in check. Let your production mind-set draw you into service of others. Through producing something, cultivate the manlier virtues of giving, sharing, and serving.

FOR FATHERS

There's not really anything unique to being a father that's not common to the rest of the masculine endeavor. The better you are at being a man, the better you are at being a father, with a couple nuances. If you're a father or hope to be, even if your "children" are surrogates, boys or girls you mentor or care for in the absence or dereliction of their own fathers, take heed to these subtleties.

Perhaps one of the most delightful depictions of fatherhood is Vincent Van Gogh's painting *First Steps*. Although his painting is simply a recreation of an earlier work by Jean-Francois

Millet, Van Gogh's painting is better known. Put the book down for a second and go look it up. Go ahead. I know it's been a real page-turner. But I'll be here when you get back.

In Van Gogh's take, as in Millet's original, there is a family of three: father, mother, and child. The mother has brought the child out of the house to the field where the father has been working in the garden with a shovel and wheelbarrow. But now he's set his shovel down, interrupted his work, to squat down and stretch his arms out, beckoning his child to walk out to him. This single-frame, frozen depiction of a family pretty acutely captures the distinct roles of mothers and fathers.

The mother has presumably carried the child out to the field. Her role is nurturing, protecting, sheltering. The father has been sweating and shoveling to provide food for his family, but now he gives that secondary task a break while he turns his attention to his child. Although he is certainly responsible for protecting the child, his kind of protection differs from a mother's nurturing. He calls his child out of the safety of his mother's embrace. He beckons him to come out into the world. To take the first few risky steps of his life, to venture into the unknown with only the promise that, if his father says it's safe and good, it must be both.

So a man who has been blessed to become a father does exactly this. He calls his child out of the safety of the home into the wilderness of work, into the danger of the unknown, into the risk of new adventures. He ventures out ahead of his family and then turns around to beckon them to follow. He secures the way ahead of his children, venturing on the path to manliness and sacrifice, and then coaxes them to follow his footsteps. He does not ask them to go anywhere he has not gone or has been unwilling to go. Having learned from his own mistakes, he is better equipped to show his children a better way.

This is how a father leads his family: from the front, beckoning them out into the world with him. His leadership of his children ought never be reduced to "go and do" but must always be "come and try." Men, you should live a life worthy of emulation. You should want your children to do what you do because they invariably will. This doesn't mean that you always have to get it right. The greatest model you can be for your children is not of a guy who always does what's right or necessary, but of a guy who is capable and courageous enough to admit his mistakes when he fails, confess those failings to his children, and model a life of repentance and dependence on Christ's abundant forgiveness. He should never expect his children to do something he is unwilling to do himself. He leads more by doing than by telling.

RAISE YOUR SONS TO BE GOOD MEN AND YOUR DAUGHTERS TO DESIRE GOOD MEN

Just as men and women, husbands and wives, mothers and fathers are not the same, so a man's sons are different from his daughters. There are some things that both genders require. From a broader perspective, sons and daughters require the same protection and provision. They need a good man to be their father. They need him to take up the three-way mantle of prophet, priest, and king of his family. They need him to catechize them, to pray for them, and to rule over them with the heavenly Father's loving dominion.

But in order for a boy to grow into a man and a girl to mature into a woman, they require different things from their fathers. Boys need a father to teach them how to *be* a man. Girls need a father to teach them how to *identify* a man. He will need to be one. She will need to marry one.

A boy needs a father who is strong and compassionate, courageous and encouraging. He needs a man to model manhood. A father needs to be able to draw his son out of his mother's embrace, to foster this break with the security and safety of the feminine in order to venture out into the riskiness and adventure of sacrificial masculinity. A boy doesn't need more things from his father; he needs more time with his father. He needs to learn virtue from you. He needs to learn to see himself as an instrument for the good of others. He needs to learn to pray from you. He needs to learn how to face his fears and embark with courage on what needs to be done. He needs to spend time alongside you, learning big skills as well as little ones. He needs to be disciplined when he does wrong; and he needs to be forgiven. He needs to be taught—by example as well as with rules—the way of self-control and self-denial. He needs you to have high expectations for him and he needs your undiminished love and unwavering forgiveness when he does not live up to those standards. If he is going to become a good man, he needs a father who is one.[50]

A girl needs a father who is strong and tender, loving and protecting. She needs you to cherish her and to make her feel treasured. The way you feel about her will be the way she expects her future husband to feel about her. She will evaluate every other man in her life by comparing him to you. Model courage and humility. Teach her resilience and grit by your example. Help her feel pretty without succumbing to the debasing drive of the culture to make her *sexy*. Teach her modesty. Shield her from the rampant sexualization of young girls by taking an

50 Two excellent books fathers of sons should read are Dr. Meg Meeker's *Boys Should Be Boys* (Ballantine, 2009) and Eric Davis's *Raising Men* (St. Martin's, 2016). Meeker is a doctor and bases her advice on clinical and personal experience. Davis is a Navy SEAL and draws his lessons from his experience training SEALs. A word of caution: Davis's book includes some profanity that is common among men training together and fighting alongside one another in combat.

interest in what she wears. Show her she is a person, not an object. Be attentive to the cultural pressures around her; your naïveté is not a virtue. Protect her. Teach her to be strong, to stand up for herself and for what's right. If she is going to be a strong woman who is cherished by a good man, she needs a father who cherishes her and her mother.[51]

The most important thing a father must do is raise his sons to be good men and his daughters to desire good men.

LOVE THE MOTHER OF YOUR CHILDREN

The second most important thing a father can do for his children is to love their mother. She needs to be his priority even above his children. He will set the example for them of what a good man is to do for his wife. His sons will aspire to be like him. And his daughters will aspire to marry a guy like him. Love your wife. Fight for your marriage. Discipline yourself against selfishness. Do it not just for your wife but also for your children. The success and strength of your marriage will equip your children for their own successful and strong marriage as well as give them lifelong strength and success as individuals. The task of being a good father is inseparable from the task of being a good husband. To do one necessitates the other.

CULTIVATE A GROWTH MIND-SET

Carol Dweck, Professor of Psychology at Stanford University, has reconfigured how people think about character traits, skills, abilities, talents, and more. Her 2007 book *Mindset*[52] highlights

---

51 The best book I've read on fathers raising daughters is Dr. Meeker's *Strong Fathers, Strong Daughters* (Ballantine, 2007). If you are a man with a daughter, you simply must read this book.

52 Sorry to max out your library card, but this is another book that you should read if you are in

the difference between what she sees as the two different kinds of people in the world: those who have a fixed mind-set and those who have a growth mind-set. A person with a fixed mind-set believes his talents and abilities (and those of others) are generally fixed and unchangeable. A person with a growth mind-set believes abilities and aptitudes are changeable and that a person can grow in any area in which he decides to apply himself and excel.

Dweck's work dovetails with all the emerging data on the malleability of the human brain, or neuroplasticity. Science is slowly coming to understand that the human brain is not a fixed feature. Its abilities grow or diminish with variations of diet, exercise, and learning. Dweck's suggestion is that not only external factors contribute to the capacity of the human mind, but so do internal variables. What you think affects what you can do, Dweck says. And the best way of thinking is to believe that your traits and characteristics are not set in stone but rather flexible, adaptable, improvable, and changeable over time.

Parents with a fixed mind-set will praise the accomplishments of their children, the end results instead of the efforts. Although this seems logically to encourage kids to try harder, Dweck counters,

> Parents think they can hand children permanent confidence—like a gift—by praising their brains and talent. It doesn't work, and in fact has the opposite effect. It makes children doubt themselves as soon as anything is hard or anything goes wrong. If parents want to give their children a gift, the best thing they can do is to teach their children

---

the practice of reading books, which, we know you are, because not only are you in the last chapter of a book, but you're also reading footnotes. Get Carol Dweck's *Mindset* (Ballantine, 2007) and read it.

> to love challenges, be intrigued by mistakes, enjoy effort, and keep on learning. That way, their children don't have to be slaves of praise. They will have a lifelong way to build and repair their own confidence.[53]

When children believe their skills and aptitudes are fixed assets, they will have greater fear of failure. When they believe that their talents and abilities are something they can improve with hard work, and when they are praised for hard work and endurance in the face of adversity, they will view adversity as a challenge to be overcome and failures as opportunities for growth.

So praise your children's hard work, their effort, their determination, and the process by which they approach difficult tasks. Don't praise their achievements, unless you want the fear of failure to keep them from taking on new and more difficult tasks.

Fathers play a particular role in this endeavor to cultivate a growth mind-set in their children. Praise from a father is different from praise from a mother. Because men are not naturally nurturing like mothers are, their praise is received uniquely because it's rarer. So children crave praise from their father, sometimes more than praise from their mother. At the least, they need a father's affirmation in a very unique way. It tells a son that he's acceptable as a man, and it tells a daughter that someday she will be attractive to a man.

So men, when you praise your children or give them affirmation (which you should do regularly so that they are confident of their father's affection and affirmation despite the other uncertainties of life), simply praise them for their effort and hard work. Praise them for hard work and risk, even when—especially when—they fail. This is the essence of Van Gogh's painting. The

53 Carol S. Dweck, *Mindset: The New Psychology of Success* (New York: Ballantine, 2007), 176–77.

father wants his child to take the first step. More important to him than whether he successfully navigates the gap between father and mother is that he is willing to try. And, should he fall, the father will praise him for the effort and encourage him to try again, to rethink his approach, to use a different strategy, but never to stop trying until the elusive goal is either obtained or deemed not worth pursuing.

Cultivating this growth mind-set is not all that different from a man's calling to encourage his children to be capable and courageous enough to take risks. It's what he has to learn to do to be a good man, so it's what he will be equipped to call his children to do. Take risks. Be courageous. Embrace failure. Try again. Keep going. Learn. Grow. Expect and encourage your children toward the same.

HAVE A FAMILY ALTAR

This is the most important part of a father's role: be your family's spiritual leader. Nothing else matters as much as this. If you do everything else perfectly but fail to catechize your children in the faith you possess, you have left them ill-equipped for whatever years and challenges await them.

What does this look like in practice?

We already dealt with a man's practice of the faith for himself. For his own sake, he needs to be prayerful and faithful. He needs to see himself as a son of God before he can be competent for the task of being anyone else's spiritual leader. He needs to know his sin, his failures, his utter inability to live, do, and believe as he ought. He needs to know repentance. He needs to learn complete dependence on his Savior with nothing held back for self-reliance or do-it-yourself salvation. He needs to have his own life of faith and prayer before he can bequeath prayer to his children. He needs to be completely dependent on the work of God to save him apart from any effort or response on his part, in order to inculcate a similar kind of dependence on the Lord in his children.

So, . . . how? First of all, just man up and do it. Do something. Try and fail and then try something else. Take your kids with you to church. And then bring the things of church home with you. Learn to be the pastor of your household from your own pastor.

Although largely absent from the curricula of contemporary interior design schools, every home needs a family altar. You need a dedicated space where you can gather as a family at least once a day, light candles, crack open hymnals, and pray as a family one of the Church's prayer offices. You can have a real altar or a shelf with a cross and candles. Hang up a crucifix, so you can meditate on the sacrifice of Christ for you and for your family. You can use icons or pictures of the life and work of Christ. Or you can use a common space, like the table after dinner's been cleared, and bring the sacred into the everyday gathering place of the family, putting a standing cross and a pair of candles in the center of the table from which you've just been fed with the Lord's gift of daily bread. Use ritual to make the time and the space set apart from the ordinary.

If you gather your family for prayer and worship in the morning, which is a nice way to set the mood for the rest of the day, use the office of Matins or Morning Prayer. If you do it in the evening, which is a great way to wrap up the day's activities and return everyone to a receptive, prayerful state of mind, use Vespers or Evening Prayer. If you do it as the last thing before lights out and bed time, use Compline. Or use the Litany. Or use one of the shorter orders of daily prayer in the hymnal. Whatever you do, do something. And don't make it up off-the-cuff. Use something that has survived the test of time. Use something that joins your prayers and worship to the prayers of the Lord's Church throughout time and space.

Teach your children the catechism. By heart. And if you don't know it by heart, learn it with them. Recite it together. Pray it together.

Use a hymnal. Sing the Church's Hymn of the Day from Sunday throughout the following week. Sing the manliest, fightin'est, grittiest, boldest, most sacramental, bloodiest, fiercest, most-Christ-confessing hymns you can find. Let the richness of their proclamation of Christ's sacrifice encourage you in your manly call to be a sacrifice for these people you've gathered to lead in prayer and in the hearing of the Word.

Make this a daily practice. Read the Word to your wife and children. Take up the mantle of leadership in this most important arena, the spiritual health and eternal well-being of your family. Don't let the perfect be the enemy of the good. Don't wait until your own piety is correct. Simply start. Do something.

If you attend to it each day, if this time in your schedule is inviolable, your children will learn the incalculable value of prayer. They will watch your folded hands and bowed head and mimic you from the earliest ages. And from their father's example, they will come to trust in their heavenly Father who has called them in Holy Baptism to an eternal inheritance. The weight of this task is tremendous. If you neglect the spiritual health of your family, you do so at risk of their spiritual peril. But there's a lightness to the work. It's not really up to you to make it *work*, to make it successful. The Lord works through His Word. You simply have to be faithful. He will accomplish what He intends to accomplish. Simply by being faithful to the task of catechizing your children, you will have done something so significant that the legacy of faith may endure for generations to come.

This to-do list is not comprehensive. Anything that falls under the umbrella of sacrificial giving is part of a man's to-do list. That will vary from one man's life to the next. This is simply intended to get you thinking as a man about how you can love and serve those to whom God has given you in order that you might spend your life in service toward them.

Pray. Love. Give. Fight. Then man up and do it again.

THE BATTLE PLAN

GROW AS A MAN

Here are the strategies that were discussed in this chapter. Circle the ones that will help you on your manly quest to learn to give to others. To the right, identify strategies that will help you implement these tactics.

Find mentors.

Hear the martyrs.

Practice sacrifice.

Cultivate satisfaction.

Be present. Quit escaping.

Keep going.

Aim for significance.

Make things.

For Fathers

Raise your sons to be good men.

Raise your daughters to desire good men.

Love the mother of your children.

Cultivate a growth mind-set.

Have a family altar.

THE PERFECT MAN

I hope this book has frustrated you. It might make me a jerk, but that has been partly my intent. I want the ideal of masculinity to call you to higher aims and more noble pursuits. I want you to have the same experience in your quest that I regularly have in mine. It should be frustrating. It's hard work. It's constant self-denial. It's a regular gut-check against your normal inclination toward self-preservation.

I want you to have moments in this quest where the ideal of masculinity and your practice are so far apart that you chuck this book, throw up your hands, and want to quit. I want you to have that reaction because it's my struggle too. I want you to come to the point where you are comfortable admitting your failures. I want the impossibility of simply being a good man to keep you ready at any moment to fall to your knees and pray for strength, courage, and forgiveness.

This frustration with yourself is intended to level the playing field a bit. There is only one good Man. There is only one Guy who gets this right all the time. He is, of course, the Second Person of the eternal Trinity who, knowing the impossible predicament of all men, became Man. Jesus, the incarnate, enfleshed God, is the only perfect Man.

That means that the rest of us, who are so far from this divine ideal, are all in it together. There may be some of us who do better than others when comparing mortal men to their peers.

But when any of us are held to the standard of Jesus, we are all equally failures. To say that this levels the playing field, though, might give the impression that masculinity is some kind of contest. It's not. Rather, the fact that we are all roughly the same distance from the ideal enables us to help one another as peers and partners to be better men.

More than your example for how to be a good man, you need Jesus to be your Savior. Then, with His perfect righteousness, His genuine masculinity, His sacrificial love credited to you, you finally are what you set out at the beginning of this book to be—a good man. The gift of perfection that Jesus gives both completes and enables your quest for masculinity. His forgiveness makes you a good man. And it enables you to venture out and work on being of service to those you're called to love and serve.

Although you were won by the promise of a book about masculinity and how to attain genuine manliness, I hope you don't feel hoodwinked to have discovered that, inside the cover, it's simply a book about Jesus. No one else has embodied or ever will perfectly embody the spirit of sacrificial love and self-giving that is the essence of masculinity. Nowhere else do manly strength and godly virtue perfectly intersect than at the bisection of the wooden timbers on which the Son of God gave Himself as the Man to redeem men.

His love is perfect. And it is for you. There is perhaps no more fitting way to close a book on masculinity than with this love song. Hopefully by now, you'll understand why. Sing along. There's a chorus of men singing with you. We'll see you out there, on the road, on this quest.

> O love, how deep, how broad, how high,
> Beyond all thought and fantasy,

That God, the Son of God, should take
Our mortal form for mortals' sake!

He sent no angel to our race,
Of higher or of lower place,
But wore the robe of human frame,
And to this world Himself He came.

For us baptized, for us He bore
His holy fast and hungered sore;
For us temptation sharp He knew;
For us the tempter overthrew.

For us He prayed; for us He taught;
For us His daily works He wrought,
By words and signs and actions thus
Still seeking not Himself but us.

For us by wickedness betrayed,
For us, in crown of thorns arrayed,
He bore the shameful cross and death;
For us He gave His dying breath.

For us He rose from death again;
For us He went on high to reign;
For us He sent His Spirit here
To guide, to strengthen, and to cheer.

All glory to our Lord and God
For love so deep, so high, so broad;
The Trinity whom we adore
Forever and forevermore. (*LSB* 544)

Carry on, man. The quest is worth the effort. People are depending on you.